THE WORKS OF
WILLIAM
SHAKESPEARE

VOLUME ONE

WILLIAM SHAKESPEARE

THE WORKS OF WILLIAM SHAKESPEARE

VOLUME ONE

All's Well that Ends Well
Antony and Cleopatra
As You Like It
The Comedy of Errors

THE PEEBLES CLASSIC LIBRARY
SANDY LESBERG, *Editor*

ISBN 0-85690-039-7

Published by Peebles Press International
U.S.A.: 10 Columbus Circle, New York, NY 10019
U.K.: 12 Thayer Street, London W1M 5LD

Distributed by WHS Distributors

PRINTED AND BOUND IN THE U.S.A.

CONTENTS

ALL'S WELL THAT ENDS WELL

DRAMATIS PERSONÆ

KING OF FRANCE
DUKE OF FLORENCE
BERTRAM, *Count of Rousillon*
LAFEU, *an old lord*
PAROLLES, *a follower of Bertram*
Steward⎫
Clown ⎬ *Servants to the Countess of Rousillon*
A Page⎭

COUNTESS OF ROUSILLON, *mother to Bertram*
HELENA, *a gentlewoman protected by the Countess*
A Widow *of Florence*
DIANA, *daughter to the Widow*
VIOLENTA⎫ *neighbours and friends to the Widow*
MARIANA ⎭

Lords, Officers, Soldiers, etc., French and Florentine

SCENE—*Partly in France, and partly in Tuscany*

ALL'S WELL THAT ENDS WELL

ACT ONE

SCENE I.—Rousillon. A Room in the COUNTESS's Palace

Enter BERTRAM, *the* COUNTESS OF ROUSILLON, HELENA, *and* LAFEU, *all in black*

Count. In delivering my son from me, I bury a second husband.

Ber. And I, in going, madam, weep o'er my father's death anew; but I must attend his majesty's command, to whom I am now in ward, evermore in subjection.

Laf. You shall find of the king a husband, madam; —you, sir, a father. He that so generally is at all times good, must of necessity hold his virtue to you, whose worthiness would stir it up where it wanted, rather than lack it where there is such abundance.

Count. What hope is there of his majesty's amendment?

Laf. He hath abandoned his physicians, madam; under whose practices he hath persecuted time with hope, and finds no other advantage in the process but only the losing of hope by time.

Count. This young gentlewoman had a father,—O, that 'had!' how sad a passage 't is!—whose skill was almost as great as his honesty; had it stretched so far 'twould have made nature immortal, and death should have play for lack of work. Would, for the king's sake, he were living! I think it would be the death of the king's disease.

Laf. How called you the man you speak of, madam?

Count. He was famous, sir, in his profession, and it was his great right to be so:—Gerard de Narbonne.

Laf. He was excellent, indeed, madam: the king very lately spoke of him, admiringly and mourningly. ·He was skilful enough to have lived still, if knowledge could be set up against mortality.

Ber. What is it, my good lord, the king languishes of?

Laf. A fistula, my lord.

Ber. I heard not of it before.

Laf. I would it were not notorious.—Was this gentle-woman the daughter of Gerard de Narbonne?

Count. His sole child, my lord; and bequeathed to my overlooking. I have those hopes of her good that her education promises: her dispositions she inherits, which make fair gifts fairer; for where an unclean mind carries virtuous qualities, there commendations go with pity; they are virtues and traitors too; in her they are the better for their simpleness; she derives her honesty, and achieves her goodness.

Laf. Your commendations, madam, get from her tears.

Count. 'Tis the best brine a maiden can season her praise in. The remembrance of her father never approaches her heart, but the tyranny of her sorrows takes all livelihood from her cheek.—No more of this, Helena,—go to, no more; lest it be rather thought you affect a sorrow, than to have.

Hel. I do affect a sorrow, indeed; but I have it too.

Laf. Moderate lamentation is the right of the dead, excessive grief the enemy to the living.

Count. If the living be enemy to the grief, the excess makes it soon mortal.

Ber. Madam, I desire your holy wishes.

Laf. How understand we that?

Count. Be thou blest, Bertram; and succeed thy
          father
In manners, as in shape! thy blood and virtue,
Contend for empire in thee, and thy goodness
Share with thy birthright! Love all, trust a few,
Do wrong to none; be able for thine enemy
Rather in power than use, and keep thy friend
Under thy own life's key; be checked for silence,
But never taxed for speech. What Heaven more will,
That thee may furnish and my prayers pluck down,
Fall on thy head! Farewell.—My lord,
'Tis an unseasoned courtier: good my lord,
Advise him.

Laf.   He cannot want the best
That shall attend his love.

Count. Heaven bless him!—Farewell, Bertram.

                                        [*Exit*

Ber. [*To Helena*] The best wishes that can be forged in your thoughts be servants to you. Be comfortable to my mother, your mistress, and make much of her.

Laf. Farewell, pretty lady: you must hold the credit of your father.   [*Exeunt Bertram and Lafeu*

Hel. O, were that all!—I think not on my father;
And these great tears grace his remembrance more
Than those I shed for him. What was he like?

12

I have forgot him: my imagination
Carries no favour in 't but Bertram's.
I am undone: there is no living, none,
If Bertram be away.   It were all one
That I should love a bright particular star,
And think to wed it, he is so above me:
In his bright radiance and collateral light
Must I be comforted, not in his sphere.
The ambition in my love thus plagues itself:
The hind that would be mated by the lion
Must die for love.   'T was pretty, though a plague,
To see him every hour; to sit and draw
His archéd brows, his hawking eye, his curls,
In our heart's table; heart too capable
Of every line and trick of his sweet favour:
But now he's gone, and my idolatrous fancy
Must sanctify his relics.—Who comes here?
One that goes with him: I love him for his sake,
And yet I know him a notorious liar,
Think him a great way fool, solely a coward;
Yet these fixed evils sit so fit in him,
That they take place, when virtue's steely bones
Look bleak in the cold wind: withal, full oft we see
Cold wisdom waiting on superfluous folly.

Enter PAROLLES

Par.   Save you, fair queen!
Hel.   And you, monarch!
Par.   No.
Hel.   And no.
Par.   Are you meditating on virginity?
Hel.   Ay.   You have some stain of soldier in you; let
me ask you a question.   Man is enemy to virginity; how
may we barricado it against him?
Par.   Keep him out.
Hel.   But he assails; and our virginity, though valiant
in the defence, yet is weak.   Unfold to us some warlike
resistance.
Par.   There is none: man, sitting down before you, will
undermine you, and blow you up.
Hel.   Bless our poor virginity from underminers and
blowers up!—Is there no military policy, how virgins
might blow up men?
Par.   Virginity being blown down, man will quicklier
be blown up: marry, in blowing him down again, with
the breach yourselves made, you lose your city.   It is not
politic in the common wealth of nature to preserve virginity.
Loss of virginity is rational increase; and there was never
virgin got, till virginity was first lost.   That you were

13

made of, is metal to make virgins. Virginity, by being
once lost, may be ten times found: by being ever kept, it
is ever lost. 'T is too cold a companion: away with 't.

Hel. I will stand for 't a little, though therefore I die a
virgin.

Par. There 's little can be said in 't; 't is against the
rule of nature. To speak on the part of virginity is to
accuse your mothers, which is most infallible disobedience.
He that hangs himself is a virgin; virginity murders itself,
and should be buried in highways, out of all sanctified
limit, as a desperate offendress against nature. Virginity
breeds mites, much like a cheese, consumes itself to the
very paring, and so dies with feeding his own stomach.
Besides, virginity is peevish, proud, idle, made of self-love,
which is the most inhibited sin in the canon. Keep it not:
you cannot choose but lose by 't. Out with 't: within the
year it will make itself two, which is a goodly increase, and
the principal itself not much the worse. Away with 't.

Hel. How might one do, sir, to lose it to her own liking?

Par. Let me see: marry, ill, to like him that ne'er it
likes. 'T is a commodity will lose the gloss with lying; the
longer kept, the less worth: off with 't, while 't is vendible:
answer the time of request. Virginity, like an old courtier,
wears her cap out of fashion; richly suited, but unsuitable:
just like the brooch and the toothpick, which wear not
now. Your date is better in your pie and your porridge
than in your cheek: and your virginity, your old virginity,
is like one of our French withered pears: it looks ill, it
eats dryly; marry, 't is a withered pear; it was formerly
better; marry, yet, 't is a withered pear. Will you anything with it?

Hel. Not my virginity yet.—
There shall your master have a thousand loves,
A mother, and a mistress, and a friend,
A phœnix, captain, and an enemy,
A guide, a goddess, and a sovereign,
A counsellor, a traitress, and a dear;
His humble ambition, proud humility,
His jarring concord, and his discord dulcet.
His faith, his sweet disaster; with a world
Of pretty, fond, adoptious christendoms,
That blinking Cupid gossips. Now shall he—
I know not what he shall:—God send him well!—
The court's a learning-place;—and he is one—

Par. What one i' faith?

Hel. That I wish well.—'T is pity—

Par. What's pity?

Hel. That wishing well had not a body in 't,
Which might be felt; that we, the poorer born,
Whose baser stars do shut us up in wishes,

Might with effects of them follow our friends,
And show what we alone must think: which never
Returns us thanks.

Enter a Page

Page. Monsieur Parolles, my lord calls for you.   [*Exit*
Par. Little Helen, farewell: if I can remember thee, I
will think of thee at court.
Hel. Monsieur Parolles, you were born under a charit-
able star.
Par. Under Mars, I.
Hel. I especially think, under Mars.
Par. Why under Mars?
Hel. The wars have so kept you under, that you must
needs be born under Mars.
Par. When he was predominant.
Hel. When he was retrograde, I think, rather.
Par. Why think you so?
Hel. You go so much backward when you fight.
Par. That's for advantage.
Hel. So is running away, when fear proposes the safety
But the composition that your valour and fear makes in
you is a virtue of a good wing, and I like the wear well.
Par. I am so full of businesses, I cannot answer thee
acutely. I will return perfect courtier; in the which my
instruction shall serve to naturalise thee, so thou wilt be
capable of a courtier's counsel, and understand what advice
shall thrust upon thee; else thou diest in thine unthank-
fulness, and thine ignorance makes thee away: farewell.
When thou hast leisure, say thy prayers; when thou hast
none, remember thy friends. Get thee a good husband,
and use him as he uses thee: so farewell.   [*Exit*
Hel. Our remedies oft in ourselves do lie,
Which we ascribe to heaven: the fated sky
Gives us free scope; only doth backward pull
Our slow designs when we ourselves are dull.
What power is it which mounts my love so high,
That makes me see, and cannot feed mine eye?
The mightiest space in fortune Nature brings
To join like likes, and kiss like native things.
Impossible be strange attempts to those
That weight their pains in sense, and do suppose
What hath been cannot be. Who ever strove
To show her merit that did miss her love?
The king's disease—my project may deceive me,
But my intents are fixed, and will not leave me.   [*Exit*

15

SCENE II.—Paris. A Room in the King's Palace

Flourish of cornets. Enter the KING OF FRANCE *with
letters ; Lords and others attending*

King. The Florentines and Senoys are by the ears;
Have fought with equal fortune, and continue
A braving war.
    First Lord. So 't is reported, sir.
    King. Nay, 't is most credible: we here receive it
A certainty, vouched from our cousin Austria,
With caution, that the Florentine will move us
For speedy aid; wherein our dearest friend
Prejudicates the business, and would seem
To have us make denial.
    First Lord.   His love and wisdom,
Approved so to your majesty, may plead
For amplest credence.
    King.   He hath armed our answer,
And Florence is denied before he comes:
Yet, for our gentlemen, that mean to see
The Tuscan service, freely have they leave
To stand on either part.
    Sec. Lord.   It may well serve
A nursery to our gentry, who are sick
For breathing and exploit.
    King.   What 's he comes here?

Enter BERTRAM, LAFEU, *and* PAROLLES

First Lord. It is the Count Rousillon, my good lord,
Young Bertram.
    King.   Youth, thou bear'st thy father's face:
Frank nature, rather curious than in haste,
Hath well composed thee. Thy father's moral parts
May'st thou inherit too! Welcome to Paris.
    Ber. My thanks and duty are your majesty's.
    King. I would I had that corporal soundness now,
As when thy father and myself in friendship
First tried our soldiership. He did look far
Into the service of the time, and was
Discipled of the bravest: he lasted long;
But on us both did haggish age steal on,
And wore us out of act. It much repairs me
To talk of your good father. In his youth
He had the wit which I can well observe
To-day in our young lords; but they may jest
Till their own scorn return to them unnoted,
Ere they can hide their levity in honour.

So, like a courtier, contempt nor bitterness
Were in his pride or sharpness; if they were,
His equal had awaked them, and his honour,
Clock to itself, knew the true minute when
Exception bid him speak, and at this time
His tongue obeyed his hand: who were below him
He used as creatures of another place,
And bowed his eminent top to their low ranks,
Making them proud of his humility;
In their poor praise he humbled.　Such a man
Might be a copy to these younger times
Which, followed well, would demonstrate them now
But goers backward.
    Ber.   His good remembrance, sir,
Lies richer in your thoughts than on his tomb:
So in approof lives not his epitaph,
As in your royal speech.
    King.   Would I were with him!　He would always say,—
Methinks, I hear him now: his plausive words
He scattered not in ears, but grafted them
To grow there and to bear,——'Let me not live,'—
Thus his good melancholy oft began,
On the catastrophe and heel of pastime,
When it was out, 'Let me not live,' quoth he,
'After my flame lacks oil, to be the snuff
Of younger spirits, whose apprehensive senses
All but new things disdain; whose judgments are
Mere fathers of their garbs; whose constancies
Expire before their fashions.'—This he wished:—
I, after him, do after him wish too,
Since I nor wax nor honey can bring home,
I quickly were dissolvéd from my hive,
To give some labourers room.
    Sec. Lord.   You are loved, sir;
They that least lend it you shall lack the first.
    King.   I fill a place, I know't.—How long is 't, count,
Since the physician at your father's died?
He was much famed.
    Ber.   Some six months since, my lord.
    King.   If he were living, I would try him yet:—
Lend me an arm:—the rest have worn me out
With several applications: nature and sickness
Debate it at their leisure.　Welcome, count;
My son 's no dearer.
    Ber.   Thank your majesty.   [*Exeunt*

17

SCENE III.—Rousillon.   A Room in the COUNTESS'S Palace

Enter COUNTESS, *Steward, and Clown*

Count.   I will now hear: what say you of this gentlewoman?

Stew.   Madam, the care I have had to even your content,
I wish might be found in the calendar of my past endeavours;
for then we wound our modesty, and make foul the clear-
ness of our deservings, when of ourselves we publish them.

Count.   What does this knave here?   Get you gone,
sirrah: the complaints I have heard of you, I do not all
believe: 't is my slowness, that I do not; for I know you
lack not folly to commit them, and have ability enough to
make such knaveries yours.

Clo.   'T is not unknown to you, madam, I am a poor
fellow.

Count.   Well, sir.

Clo.   No, madam; 't is not so well, that I am poor,
though many of the rich are damned.   But, if I may have
your ladyship's good will to go to the world, Isbel your
woman and I will do as we may.

Count.   Wilt thou needs be a beggar?

Clo.   I do beg your good will in this case.

Count.   In what case?

Clo.   In Isbel's case, and mine own.   Service is no
heritage, and, I think, I shall never have the blessing of
God, till I have issue of my body, for they say, barnes are
blessings.

Count.   Tell me thy reason why thou wilt marry.

Clo.   My poor body, madam, requires it: I am driven on
by the flesh, and he must needs go that the devil drives.

Count.   Is this all your worship's reason?

Clo.   Faith, madam, I have other holy reasons, such
as they are.

Count.   May the world know them?

Clo.   I have been, madam, a wicked creature, as you
and all flesh and blood are; and, indeed, I do marry that
I may repent.

Count.   Thy marriage, sooner than thy wickedness.

Clo.   I am out o' friends, madam; and I hope to have
friends for my wife's sake.

Count.   Such friends are thine enemies, knave.

Clo.   You are shallow, madam; e'en great friends;
for the knaves come to do that for me, which I am aweary
of.   He that ears my land spares my team, and gives me
leave to inn the crop: if I be his cuckold, he's my drudge.
He that comforts my wife is the cherisher of my flesh and
blood; he that cherishes my flesh and blood loves my flesh

and blood; he that loves my flesh and blood is my friend: *ergo*
he that kisses my wife is my friend. If men could be con-
tended to be what they are, there were no fear in marriage;
for young Charbon the Puritan and old Poysam the Papist,
howsome'er their hearts are severed in religion, their heads
are both one; they may joll horns together, like any deer
i' the herd.

Count. Wilt thou ever be a foul-mouthed and caluminous
knave?

Clo. A prophet I, madam; and I speak the truth the
next way.

> For I the ballad will repeat,
>   Which men full true shall find ;
> Your marriage comes by destiny,
>   Your cuckoo sings by kind.

Count. Get you gone, sir: I'll talk with you more anon.

Stew. May it please you, madam, that he bid Helen
come to you; of her I am to speak.

Count. Sirrah, tell my gentlewoman, I would speak with
her; Helen I mean.

Clo. Was this fair face the cause, quoth she,
>   Why the Grecians sacked Troy ?
> Fond done, done fond,
>   Was this King Priam's joy ?
> With that she sighéd as she stood,
> With that she sighéd as she stood,
>   And gave this sentence then ;
> Among nine bad if one be good,
> Among nine bad if one be good,
>   There 's yet one good in ten.

Count. What! one good in ten? you corrupt the song
sirrah.

Clo. One good woman in ten, madam, which is a
purifying o' the song. Would God would serve the world
so all the year! we 'd find no fault with the tithe-woman,
if I were the parson. One in ten, quoth 'a! an we might
have a good woman born but for every blazing star, or
at an earthquake, 't would mend the lottery well: a man
may draw his heart out, ere he pluck one.

Count. You 'll be gone, sir knave, and do as I command
you!

Clo. That man should be at woman's command, and
yet no hurt done!—Though honesty be no Puritan, yet
it will do no hurt; it will wear the surplice of humility
over the black gown of a big heart.—I am going, forsooth:
the business is, for Helen to come hither.   [*Exit*

Count. Well, now.

Stew. I know, madam, you love your gentlewoman
entirely.

Count. Faith, I do: her father bequeathed her to
me; and she herself, without other advantage, may law-
fully make title to as much love as she finds: there is more
owing her than is paid, and more shall be paid her than
she'll demand.

Stew. Madam, I was very late more near her than,
I think, she wished me: alone she was, and did communicate
to herself, her own words to her own ears; she thought,
I dare vow for her, they touched not any stranger sense.
Her matter was, she loved your son. Fortune, she said, was
no goddess, that had put such difference betwixt their two
estates; Love, no god, that would not extend his might,
only where qualities were level; Diana, no queen of
virgins, that would suffer her poor knight surprised,
without rescue in the first assault or ransom afterwards.
This she delivered in the most bitter touch of sorrow that
e'er I heard virgin exclaim in; which I held my duty
speedily to acquaint you withal, sithence in the loss that
may happen, it concerns you something to know it.

Count. You have discharged this honestly: keep it
to yourself. Many likelihoods informed me of this before,
which hung so tottering in the balance that I could neither
believe nor misdoubt. Pray you, leave me: stall this
in your bosom, and I thank you for your honest care. I
will speak with you further anon.   *[Exit Steward*
Even so it was with me when I was young.
  If we are nature's, these are ours; this thorn
Doth to our rose of youth rightly belong;
  Our blood to us, this to our blood is born:
It is the show and seal of nature's truth,
Where love's strong passion is impressed in youth:
  By our remembrances of days foregone,
Such were our faults,—or then we thought them none.

Enter HELENA

Her eye is sick on 't: I observe her now.
  Hel. What is your pleasure, madam?
  Count.   You know, Helen,
I am a mother to you.
  Hel. Mine honourable mistress.
  Count.   Nay, a mother.
Why not a mother? When I said, a mother,
Methought you saw a serpent: what 's in mother,
That you start at it? I say, I am your mother,
And put you in the catalogue of those
That were enwombéd mine. 'T is often seen,
Adoption strives with nature; and choice breeds
A native slip to us from foreign seeds;
You ne'er oppressed me with a mother's groan,

Yet I express to you a mother's care.—
God's mercy, maiden! does it curd thy blood,
To say, I am thy mother?   What's the matter,
That this distempered messenger of wet,
The many-coloured Iris, rounds thine eye?—
Why? that you are my daughter?
    Hel.   That I am not.
    Count.   I say, I am your mother.
    Hel.   Pardon, madam;
The Count Rousillon cannot be my brother:
I am from humble, he from honoured name;
No note upon my parents, his all noble:
My master, my dear lord, he is; and I
His servant live, and will his vassal die.
He must not be my brother.
    Count.   Nor I your mother?
    Hel.   You are my mother, madam: would you were—
So that my lord, your son, were not my brother—
Indeed my mother!—or were you both our mothers,
I care no more for than I do for heaven,
So I were not his sister.   Can no other,
But, I your daughter, he must be my brother?
    Count.   Yes, Helen, you might be my daughter-in-law.
God shield you mean it not! daughter and mother
So strive upon your pulse.   What, pale again?
My fear hath catched your fondness: now I see
The mystery of your loneliness, and find
Your salt tears' head.   Now to all sense 't is gross,
You love my son: invention is ashamed,
Against the proclamation of thy passion,
To say, thou dost not: therefore tell me true;
But tell me then, 't is so:—for, look, thy cheeks
Confess it, the one to the other; and thine eyes
See it so grossly shown in thy behaviours,
That in their kind they speak it: only sin
And hellish obstinacy tie thy tongue,
That truth should be suspected.   Speak, is 't so?
If it be so, you have wound a goodly clue;
If it be not, forswear 't: howe'er, I charge thee,
As Heaven shall work in me for thine avail,
To tell me truly.
    Hel.   Good madam, pardon me.
    Count.   Do you love my son?
    Hel.   Your pardon, noble mistress.
    Count.   Love you my son?
    Hel.   Do not you love him, madam?
    Count.   Go not about: my love hath in 't a bond,
Whereof the world takes note.   Come, come, disclose
The state of your affection, for your passions
Have to the full appeached.

Hel.   Then, I confess,
Here on my knee, before high Heaven and you,
That before you, and next unto high Heaven,
I love your son.—
My friends were poor, but honest; so 's my love:
Be not offended, for it hurts not him
That he is loved of me.   I follow him not
By any token of presumptuous suit;
Nor would I have him till I do deserve him,
Yet never know how that desert should be.
I know I love in vain, strive against hope;
Yet, in this captious and intenible sieve
I still pour in the waters of my love,
And lack not to lose still.   Thus, Indian-like,
Religious in mine error, I adore
The sun, that looks upon his worshipper
But knows of him no more.   My dearest madam
Let not your hate encounter with my love
For loving where you do: but, if yourself,
Whose agéd honour cites a virtuous youth,
Did ever in so true a flame of liking
Wish chastely and love dearly, that your Dian
Was both herself and Love: O, then, give pity
To her, whose state is such that cannot choose
But lend and give where she is sure to lose;
That seeks not to find that her search implies,
But riddle-like, lives sweetly where she dies.
      Count.   Had you not lately an intent—speak truly,—
To go to Paris?
      Hel.   Madam, I had.
      Count.   Wherefore?—tell true.
      Hel.   I will tell truth; by grace itself I swear.
You know, my father left me some prescriptions
Of rare and proved effects, such as his reading
And manifest experience had collected
For general sovereignty; and that he willed me
In heedful'st reservation to bestow them,
As notes, whose faculties inclusive were,
More than they were in note.   Amongst the rest,
There is a remedy approved set down
To cure the desperate languishings whereof
The king is rendered lost.
      Count.   This was your motive
For Paris, was it? speak.
      Hel.   My lord, your son, made me to think of this;
Else Paris, and the medicine, and the king,
Had, from the conversation of my thoughts
Haply been absent then.
      Count.   But think you, Helen,
If you should tender your supposéd aid,

22

He would receive it?   He and his physicians
Are of a mind; he, that they cannot help him,
They, that they cannot help.   How shall they credit
A poor unlearnéd virgin, when the schools,
Embowelled of their doctrine, have left off
The danger to itself?
    Hel.   There's something in 't
More than my father's skill, which was the greatest
Of his profession, that his good receipt
Shall, for my legacy, be sanctified
By the luckiest stars in heaven: and, would your honour
But give me leave to try success I 'd venture
The well-lost life of mine on 's grace's cure
By such a day and hour.
    Count.   Dost thou believe 't?
    Hel.   Ay, madam, knowingly.
    Count.   Why, Helen, thou shalt have my leave, and love,
Means, and attendants, and my loving greetings
To those of mine in court.   I'll stay at home,
And pray God's blessing into thy attempt.
Be gone to-morrow; and be sure of this,
What I can help thee to, thou shalt not miss.   [*Exeunt*

ACT TWO

Scene I.—Paris.   A Room in the King's Palace

Flourish.   Enter King, *with divers young Lords taking
    leave for the Florentine war ;* Bertram, Parolles,
    and Attendants

    King.   Farewell, young lords: these warlike principles
Do not throw from you:—and you, my lords, farewell.—
Share the advice betwixt you; if both gain all,
The gift doth stretch itself as 't is received,
And is enough for both.
    First Lord.   'T is our hope, sir,
After well-entered soldiers, to return
And find your grace in health.
    King.   No, no, it cannot be; and yet my heart
Will not confess he owes the malady
That doth my life besiege.   Farewell, young lords;
Whether I live or die, be you the sons
Of worthy Frenchmen: let higher Italy—
Those bated, that inherit but the fall
Of the last monarchy—see, that you come
Not to woo honour, but to wed it: when
The bravest questant shrinks, find what you seek,

That fame may cry you loud.   I say, farewell.
 Sec. Lord. Health, at your bidding, serve your majesty!
 King. Those girls of Italy, take heed of them:
They say, our French lack language to deny,
If they demand: beware of being captives,
Before you serve.
 Both.   Our hearts receive your warnings.
 King. Farewell.—Come hither to me.
        [Exit, led out by Attendants
 First Lord. O my sweet lord, that you will stay behind us!
 Par. 'T is not his fault, the spark.
 Sec. Lord.   O, 't is brave wars!
 Par. Most admirable: I have seen those wars.
 Ber. I am commanded here, and kept a coil with,—
'Too young,' and 'the next year,' and ''t is too early.'
 Par. An thy mind stand to 't, boy, steal away bravely.
 Ber. I shall stay here the forehorse to a smock,
Creaking my shoes on the plain masonry
Till honour be bought up, and no sword worn
But one to dance with.   By Heaven! I'll steal away.
 First Lord. There's honour in the theft.
 Par.   Commit it, count.
 Sec. Lord. I am your accessary; and so farewell.
 Ber. I grow to you, and our parting is a tortured body.
 First Lord. Farewell, captain.
 Sec. Lord. Sweet Monsieur Parolles!
 Par. Noble heroes, my sword and yours are kin.   Good
sparks and lustrous, a word, good metals:—you shall
find in the regiment of the Spinii, one Captain Spurio,
with his cicatrice, an emblem of war, here on his sinister
cheek: it was this very sword entrenched it: say to him,
I live, and observe his reports for me.
 Sec. Lord. We shall, noble captain. *[Exeunt Lords*
 Par. Mars dote on you for his novices!—What will
you do?
 Ber. Stay; the king—

Re-enter the KING, *led back to his chair by
Attendants*

 Par. Use a more spacious ceremony to the noble lords:
you have restrained yourself within the list of too cold
an adieu: be more expressive to them; for they wear
themselves in the cap of the time, there do muster true
gait, eat, speak, and move under the influence of the
most received star; and though the devil lead the measure,
such are to be followed.   After them, and take a more
dilated farewell.
 Ber. And I will do so.
 Par. Worthy fellows, and like to prove most sinewy
swordsmen.   *[Exeunt Bertram and Parolles*

Enter LAFEU

Laf. [*Kneeling*] Pardon, my lord, for me and for
    my tidings.
King. I'll fee thee to stand up.
Laf. Then here's a man stands, that has bought his
    pardon.
I would, you had kneeled, my lord, to ask me mercy,
And that, at my bidding, you could so stand up.
    King. I would I had; so I had broke thy pate,
And asked thee mercy for 't.
    Laf. Good faith, across. But, my good lord, 't is thus:
Will you be cured of your infirmity?
    King. No.
    Laf. O, will you eat no grapes, my royal fox?
Yes, but you will, my noble grapes, an if
My royal fox could reach them. I have seen
A medicine that 's able to breathe life
Into a stone,
Quicken a rock, and make you dance canary
With spritely fire and motion; whose simple touch
Is powerful to araise King Pepin; nay,
To give great Charlemain a pen in 's hand,
And write to her a love-line.
    King.   What 'her' is this?
    Laf. Why, Doctor She. My lord, there's one arrived,
If you will see her:—now, by my faith and honour,
If seriously I may convey my thoughts
In this my light deliverance, I have spoke
With one, that in her sex, her years, profession,
Wisdom, and constancy, hath amazed me more
Than I dare blame my weakness. Will you see her—
For that is her demand—and know her business?
That done, laugh well at me.
    King.   Now, good Lafeu,
Bring in the admiration, that we with thee
May spend our wonder too, or take off thine
By wondering how thou took'st it.
    Laf.   Nay, I'll fit you,
And not be all day neither.   [*Exit*
    King. Thus be his special nothing ever prologues.

Re-enter LAFEU *with* HELENA

Laf. Nay, come your ways.
    King.   This haste hath wings, indeed.
    Laf. Nay, come your ways.
This is his majesty, say your mind to him:
A traitor you do look like; but such traitors
His majesty seldom fears. I am Cressid's uncle,
That dare leave two together. Fare you well.   [*Exit*

King. Now, fair one, does your business follow us?
Hel. Ay, my good lord.
Gerard de Narbonne was my father,
In what he did profess, well found.
   King.   I knew him.
   Hel. The rather will I spare my praises towards him;
Knowing him, is enough.   On 's bed of death
Many receipts he gave me; chiefly one,
Which, as the dearest issue of his practice,
And of his old experience the only darling,
He bade me store up as a triple eye,
Safer than mine own two, more dear. I have so;
And, hearing your high majesty is touched
With that malignant cause wherein the honour
Of my dear father's gift stands chief in power,
I come to tender it and my appliance,
With all bound humbleness.
   King.   We thank you, maiden;
But may not be so credulous of cure,
When our most learned doctors leave us, and
The congregated college have concluded
That labouring art can never ransom Nature
From her inaidable estate; I say, we must not
So stain our judgment, or corrupt our hope,
To prostitute our past-cure malady
To émpirics, or to dissever so
Our great self and our credit, to esteem
A senseless help, when help past sense we deem.
   Hel. My duty then shall pay me for my pains:
I will no more enforce mine office on you;
Humbly entreating from your royal thoughts
A modest one, to bear me back again.
   King. I cannot give thee less, to be called grateful.
Thou thought'st to help me, and such thanks I give
As one near death to those that wish him live;
But what at full I know, thou know'st no part,
I know all my peril, thou no art.
   Hel. What I can do, can do no hurt to try,
Since you set up your rest gainst remedy.
He that of greatest works is finisher,
Oft does them by the weakest minister:
So holy writ in babes hath judgment shown,
When judges have been babes; great floods have flown
From simple sources; and great seas have dried,
When miracles have by the greatest been denied.
Oft expectation fails, and most oft there
Where most it promises; and oft it hits
Where hope is coldest and despair most fits.
   King. I must not hear thee: fare thee well, kind maid.
Thy pains, not used, must by thyself be paid:

Proffers, not took, reap thanks for their reward.
    Hel. Inspiréd merit so by breath is barred.
It is not so with Him that all things knows
As 't is with us that square our guess by shows;
But most of it is presumption in us when
The help of Heaven we count the act of men.
Dear sir, to my endeavours give consent;
Of Heaven, not me, make an experiment.
I am not an impostor, that proclaim
Myself against the level of mine aim;
But know I think, and think I know most sure,
My art is not past power, nor you past cure.
    King. Art thou so confident? Within what space
Hop'st thou my cure?
    Hel.   The great'st grace lending grace
Ere twice the horses of the sun shall bring
Their fiery torcher his diurnal ring,
Ere twice in murk and occidental damp
Moist Hesperus hath quenched his sleepy lamp;
Or four-and-twenty times the pilot's glass
Hath told the thievish minutes how they pass,
What is infirm from your sound parts shall fly,
Health shall live free, and sickness freely die.
    King. Upon thy certainty and confidence,
What dar'st thou venture?
    Hel.   Tax of impudence,
A strumpet's boldness, a divulgéd shame,
Traduced by odious ballads; my maiden's name
Seared otherwise; ne worse of worst extended,
With vilest torture let my life be ended.
    King. Methinks, in thee some blessed spirit doth speak
His powerful sound, within an organ weak;
And what impossibility would slay
In common sense, sense saves another way.
Thy life is dear; for all, that life can rate
Worth name of life, in thee hath estimate;
Youth, beauty, wisdom, courage, all
That happiness and prime can happy call:
Thou this to hazard, needs must intimate
Skill infinite, or monstrous desperate.
Sweet practiser, thy physic I will try,
That ministers thine own death, if I die.
    Hel. If I break time, or flinch in property
Of what I spoke, unpitied let me die,
And well deserved. Not helping, death 's my fee:
But, if I help, what do you promise me?
    King. Make thy demand.
    Hel.   But will you make it even?
    King. Ay, by my sceptre, and my hopes of heaven.
    Hel. Then shalt thou give me with thy kingly hand

What husband in thy power I will command:
Exempted be from me the arrogance
To choose from forth the royal blood of France,
My low and humble name to propagate
With any branch or image of thy state;
But such a one, thy vassal, whom I know
Is free for me to ask, thee to bestow.
    King. Here is my hand; the premises observed,
Thy will by my performance shall be served:
So make the choice of thy own time; for I,
Thy resolved patient, on thee still rely.
More should I question thee, and more I must,—
Though more to know could not be more to trust,—
From whence thou cam'st, how tended on; but rest
Unquestioned welcome, and undoubted blest.—
Give me some help here, ho!—If thou proceed
As high as word, my deed shall match thy deed.
                            [*Flourish. Exeunt*

SCENE II.—Rousillon. A Room in the COUNTESS's
Palace

Enter COUNTESS *and Clown*

    Count. Come on, sir: I shall now put you to the height
of your breeding.
    Clo. I will show myself highly fed, and lowly taught.
I know, my business is but to the court.
    Count. To the court? why, what place make you
special, when you put off that with such contempt?—'But
to the court?'
    Clo. Truly, madam, if God have lent a man any
manners, he may easily put it off at court: he that cannot
make a leg, put off 's cap, kiss his hand, and say nothing,
has neither leg, hands, lip, nor cap; and, indeed, such a
fellow, to say precisely, were not for the court. But, for
me, I have an answer will serve all men.
    Count. Marry, that's a bountiful answer, that fits all
questions.
    Clo. It is like a barber's chair, that fits all buttocks;
the pin-buttock, the quatch-buttock, the brawn-buttock,
or any buttock.
    Count. Will you answer serve fit to all questions?
    Clo. As fit as ten groats is for the hand of an attorney,
as your French crown for your taffeta punk, as Tib's rush
for Tom's forefinger, as a pancake for Shrove Tuesday,
a morris for Mayday, as the nail to his hole, the cuckold
to his horn, as a scolding quean to a wrangling knave, as
the nun's lip to the friar's mouth; nay, as the pudding
to his skin.

Count. Have you, I say, an answer of such fitness for all questions?

Clo. From below your duke to beneath your constable, it will fit any question.

Count. It must be an answer of most monstrous size, that must fit all demands.

Clo. But a trifle neither, in good faith, if the learned should speak truth of it. Here it is, and all that belongs to 't: ask me, if I am a courtier; it shall do you no harm to learn.

Count. To be young again, if we could. I will be a fool in question, hoping to be the wiser by your answer. I pray you, sir, are you a courtier?

Clo. O Lord, sir!—there's a simple putting off.—More, more, a hundred of them.

Count. Sir, I am a poor friend of yours, that loves you.

Clo. O Lord, sir!—Thick, thick, spare not me.

Count. I think, sir, you can eat none of this homely meat.

Clo. O Lord, sir!—Nay, put me to 't, I warrant you.

Count. You were lately whipped, sir, as I think.

Clo. O Lord, sir!—Spare not me.

Count. Do you cry, 'O Lord, sir!' at your whipping and 'Spare not me?' Indeed, your 'O Lord, sir!' is very sequent to your whipping: you would answer very well to a whipping, if you were but bound to 't.

Clo. I ne'er had worse luck in my life, in my 'O Lord, sir!' I see, things may serve long, but not serve ever.

Count. I play the noble housewife with the time. To entertain it so merrily with a fool.

Clo. O Lord, sir!—why there 't serves well again.

Count. An end, sir: to your business. Give Helen this, And urge her to a present answer back: Commend me to my kinsmen, and my son. This is not much.

Clo. Not much commendation to them?

Count. Not much employment for you: you understand me?

Clo. Most fruitfully: I am there before my legs.

Count. Haste you again.   [*Exeunt severally*

SCENE III.—Paris. A Room in the KING's Palace

Enter BERTRAM, LAFEU, *and* PAROLLES

Laf. They say, miracles are past; and we have our philosophical persons, to make modern and familiar, things supernatural and causeless. Hence is it that we make trifles of terrors, ensconcing ourselves into seeming know-

ledge when we should submit ourselves to an unknown
fear.

Par.   Why, 't is the arrest argument of wonder that
hath shot out in our later times.

Ber.   And so 't is.

Laf.   To be relinquished of the artists,—

Par.   So I say: both of Galen and Paracelsus.

Laf.   Of all the learned and authentic fellows,—

Par.   Right; so I say.

Laf.   That gave him out incurable,—

Par.   Why, there 't is; so say I too.

Laf.   Not to be helped,—

Par.   Right; as 't were a man assured of a—

Laf.   Uncertain life, and sure death.

Par.   Just, you say well; so would I have said.

Laf.   I may truly say, it is a novelty to the world.

Par.   It is, indeed: if you will have it in showing, you
shall read it in—what do you call there?—

Laf.   A showing of a heavenly effect in an earthly
actor.

Par.   That 's it I would have said; the very same.

Laf.   Why, your dolphin is not lustier: 'fore me, I
speak in respect—

Par.   Nay, 't is strange, 't is very strange, that is the
brief and the tedious of it; and he is of a most facinorous
spirit, that will not acknowledge it to be the—

Laf.   Very hand of Heaven.

Par.   Ay, so I say.

Laf.   In a most weak—

Par.   And debile minister, great power, great transcend-
ence: which should, indeed, give us a further use to be made,
than alone the recovery of the king, as to be—

Laf.   Generally thankful.

Par.   I would have said it; you say well.   Here comes
the king.

Enter KING, HELENA, *and Attendants*

Laf.   Lustick, as the Dutchman says: I'll like a maid
the better, whilst I have a tooth in my head.   Why, he's
able to lead her a coranto.

Par.   *Mort du vinaigre !*   Is not this Helen?

Laf.   For God, I think so.

King.   Go, call before me all the lords in court—

[*Exit an Attendant*

Sit, my preserver, by thy patient's side:
And with this healthful hand, whose banished sense
Thou has repealed, a second time receive
The confirmation of my promised gift,
Which but attends thy naming.

Enter several Lords

Fair maid, send forth thine eye: this youthful parcel
Of noble bachelors stand at my bestowing,
O'er whom both sovereign power and father's voice
I have to use: thy frank election make.
Thou hast power to choose, and they none to forsake.
   Hel.   To each of you one fair and virtuous mistress
Fall, when Love please!—marry, to each, but one.
   Laf.   I'd give bay curtal and his furniture,
My mouth no more were broken than these boys',
And writ as little beard.
   King.   Peruse them well:
Not one of those but had a noble father.
   Hel.   Gentlemen,
Heaven hath through me restored the King to health.
   All.   We understand it, and thank Heaven for you.
   Hel.   I am a simple maid; and therein wealthiest,
That, I protest, I simply am a maid,—
Please it your majesty, I have done already:
The blushes in my cheeks thus whisper me,
'We blush that thou shouldst choose; but, if
         refused,
Let the white death sit on thy cheek for ever:
We'll ne'er come there again.'
   King.   Make choice; and see,
Who shuns thy love, shuns all his love in me.
   Hel.   Now, Dian, from thy altar do I fly,
And to imperial Love, that god most high,
Do my sighs stream.—Sir, will you hear my suit?
   First Lord.   And grant it.
   Hel.   Thanks, sir: all the rest is mute.
   Laf.   I had rather be in this choice, than throw ames-ace
for my life.
   Hel.   The honour, sir, that flames in your fair eyes,
Before I speak, too threateningly replies:
Love make your fortunes twenty times above
Her that so wishes, and her humble love!
   Sec. Lord.   No better, if you please.
   Hel.   My wish receive,
Which great Love grant! and so I take my leave.
   Laf.   Do all they deny her? An they were sons of
mine, I'd have them whipped, or I would send them to
the Turk to make eunuchs of.
   Hel.   [*To Third Lord*] Be not afraid that I your hand
        should take;
I'll never do you wrong for your own sake:
Blessing upon your vows! and in your bed
Find fairer fortune, if you ever wed!
   Laf.   These boys are boys of ice, they'll none have her:

sure, they are bastards to the English: the French ne'er
got them.
    Hel.   You are too young, too happy, and too good,
To make yourself a son out of my blood.
    Fourth Lord.   Fair one, I think not so.
    Laf.   There's one grape yet,—I am sure, thy father
drank wine.—But if thou be'st not as ass, I am a youth of
fourteen: I have known thee already.
    Hel. [*To Bertram*] I dare not say, I take you; but
           I give
Me, and my service, ever whilst I live,
Into your guiding power.—This is the man.
    King.   Why, then, young Bertram, take her; she's
thy wife.
    Ber.   My wife, my liege! I shall beseech your highness,
In such a business give me leave to use
The help of mine own eyes.
    King.   Know'st thou not, Bertram,
What she has done for me?
    Ber.   Yes, my good lord;
But never hope to know why I should marry her.
    King.   Thou know'st, she has raised me from my sickly
           bed.
    Ber.   But follows it, my lord, to bring me down
Must answer for your raising? I know her well:
She had her breeding at my father's charge.
A poor physician's daughter my wife!—Disdain
Rather corrupt me ever!
    King.   'T is only title thou disdain'st in her, the which
I can build up. Strange is it, that our bloods,
Of colour, weight, and heat, poured all together,
Would quite confound distinction, yet stand off
In differences so mighty. If she be
All that is virtuous—save what thou dislik'st,
A poor physician's daughter—thou dislik'st
Of virtue for the name; but do not so:
From lowest place when virtuous things proceed,
The place is dignified by the doer's deed:
Where great additions swell't, and virtue none.
It is a dropsied honour. Good alone
Is good without a name; vileness is so:
The property by what it is should go,
Not by the title. She is young, wise, fair;
In these to nature she's immediate heir,
And these breed honour: that is honour's scorn
Which challenges itself as honour's born,
And is not like the sire: honours thrive,
When rather from our acts we them derive,
Than our foregoers. The mere word's a slave,
Deboshed on every tomb; on every grave,

A lying trophy; and as oft is dumb,
Where dust and damned oblivion is the tomb
Of honoured bones indeed.   What should be said?
If thou canst like this creature as a maid,
I can create the rest: virtue, and she,
Is her own dower; honour and wealth from me.
   Ber.   I cannot love her, nor will strive to do't.
   King.   Thou wrong'st thyself, if thou shouldst strive to
        choose.
   Hel.   That you are well restored, my lord, I'm glad.
Let the rest go.
   King.   My honour's at the stake, which to defeat
I must produce my power.   Here, take her hand;
Proud scornful boy, unworthy this good gift,
That dost in vile misprision shackle up
My love, and her desert; that canst not dream,
We, poising us in her defective scale,
Shall weigh, thee to the beam; that wilt not know,
It is in us to plant thine honour where
We please to have it grow.   Check thy contempt:
Obey our will, which travails in thy good:
Believe not thy disdain, but presently
Do thine own fortunes that obedient right
Which both thy duty owes, and our power claims;
Or I will throw thee from my care for ever
Into the staggers and the careless lapse
Of youth and ignorance; both my revenge and hate
Loosing upon thee, in the name of justice,
Without all terms of pity.   Speak: thine answer.
   Ber.   Pardon, my gracious lord, for I submit
My fancy to your eyes.   When I consider
What great creation, and what dole of honour,
Flies where you bid it, I find that she, which late
Was in my nobler thoughts most base, is now
The praised of the king; who, so ennobled,
Is, as't were, born so.
   King.   Take her by the hand,
And tell her she is thine: to whom I promise
A counterpoise, if not to thy estate,
A balance more replete.
   Ber.   I take her hand.
   King.   Good fortune and the favour of the king
Smile upon this contract; whose ceremony
Shall seem expedient on the now-born brief,
And be performed to-night: the solemn feast
Shall more attend upon the coming space,
Expecting absent friends.   As thou lov'st her,
Thy love's to me religious, else, does err.
                    [*Exeunt all but Lafeu and Parolles*
   Laf.   Do you hear, monsieur? a word with you.

33

Par. Your pleasure, sir?

Laf. Your lord and master did well to make his recantation.

Par. Recantation?—My lord? my master?

Laf. Ay; is it not a language I speak?

Par. A most harsh one, and not to be understood without bloody succeeding. My master?

Laf. Are you companion to the Count Rousillon?

Par. To any count; to all counts; to what is man.

Laf. To what is count's man: count's master is of another style.

Par. You are too old, sir; let it satisfy you, you are too old.

Laf. I must tell thee, sirrah, I write man; to which title age cannot bring thee.

Par. What I dare too well do, I dare not do.

Laf. I did think thee, for two ordinaries, to be a pretty wise fellow: thou didst make tolerable vent of thy travel: it might pass; yet the scarfs, and the bannerets about thee, did manifoldly dissuade me from believing thee a vessel of too great a burden. I have now found thee: when I lose thee again, I care not, yet art thou good for nothing but taking up, and that thou'rt scarce worth.

Par. Hadst thou not the privilege of antiquity upon thee,—

Laf. Do not plunge thyself too far in anger, lest thou hasten thy trial; which if—Lord have mercy on thee for a hen! So, my good window of lattice, fare thee well: thy casement I need not open, for I look through thee. Give me thy hand.

Par. My lord, you give me most egregious indignity.

Laf. Ay, with all my heart; and thou art worthy of it.

Par. I have not, my lord, deserved it.

Laf. Yes, good faith, every drachm of it: And I will not bate thee a scruple.

Par. Well, I shall be wiser.

Laf. E'en as soon as thou canst, for thou hast to pull at a smack o' the contrary. If ever thou be'st bound in thy scarf, and beaten, thou shalt find what it is to be proud of thy bondage. I have a desire to hold my acquaintance with thee, or rather my knowledge, that I may say, in the default, he is a man I know.

Par. My lord, you do me most insupportable vexation.

Laf. I would it were hell-pains for thy sake, and my poor doing eternal: for doing I am past;—as I will by thee, in what motion age will give me leave.   [*Exit*

Par. Well, thou hast a son shall take this disgrace off me, scurvy, old, filthy, scurvy lord!—Well, I must be patient; there is no fettering of authority. I'll beat him,

by my life, if I can meet him with any convenience, an he
were double and double a lord.   I'll have no more pity
of his age, than I would have of—I'll beat him: an if I
could but meet him again!

Re-enter LAFEU

Laf.   Sirrah, your lord and master's married: there's
news for you; you have a new mistress.
Par.   I most unfeignedly beseech your lordship to make
some reservation of your wrongs: he is my good lord:
whom I serve above is my master.
Laf.   Who? God?
Par.   Ay, sir.
Laf.   The devil it is, that's thy master.   Why does
thou garter up thy arms o' this fashion? dost make hose
of thy sleeves? do other servants so?   Thou wert best
set thy lower part where thy nose stands.   By mine
honour, if I were but two hours younger, I'd beat thee:
methinks't, thou art a general offence, and every man
should beat thee; I think, thou wast created for men to
breathe themselves upon thee.
Par.   This is hard and undeserved measure, my lord.
Laf.   Go to, sir; you were beaten in Italy for picking
a kernel out of a pomegranate: you are a vagabond, and
no true traveller.   You are more saucy with lords and
honourable personages, than the commission of your birth
and virtue gives you heraldry.   You are not worth another
word, else I'd call you knave.   I leave you.   [*Exit*
Par.   Good, very good; it is so then:—good, very
good.   Let it be concealed awhile.

Re-enter BERTRAM

Ber.   Undone, and forfeited to cares for ever!
Par.   What is the matter, sweet-heart?
Ber.   Although before the solemn priest I have sworn,
I will not bed her.
Par.   What, what, sweet-heart?
Ber.   O my Parolles, they have married me!—
I'll to the Tuscan wars, and never bed her.
Par.   France is a dog-hole, and it no more merits
The tread of a man's foot.   To the wars!
Ber.   There's letters from my mother: what the
                                          import is
I know not yet.
Par.   Ay, that would be known.   To the wars, my boy!
                                          to the wars!
He wears his honour in a box, unseen,
That hugs his kicky-wicky here at home,
Spending his manly marrow in her arms,

35

Which should sustain the bound and high curvet
Of Mars's fiery steed.   To other regions!
France is a stable; we, that dwell in it, jades;
Therefore to the war!
   Ber.   It shall be so: I'll send her to my house.
Acquaint my mother with my hate to her,
And wherefore I am fled; write to the king
That which I durst not speak.   His present gift
Shall furnish me to those Italian fields,
Where noble fellows strike.   War is no strife
To the dark house and the detested wife.
   Par.   Will this capriccio hold in thee, art sure?
   Ber.   Go with me to my chamber, and advise me.
I'll send her straight away: away to-morrow.
I'll to the wars, she to her single sorrow.
   Par.   Why, these balls bound; there's noise in it; 't
      is hard.
A young man married is a man that's marred:
Therefore away, and leave her: bravely go;
The king has done you wrong; but hush, 't is so.   [*Exeunt*

SCENE IV.—Paris.   Another Room in the Palace

Enter HELENA *and Clown*

   Hel.   My mother greets me kindly: is she well?
   Clo.   She is not well; but yet she has her health: she's
very merry; but yet she is not well: but thanks be given,
she's very well, and wants nothing i' the world; but yet
she is not well.
   Hel.   If she be very well, what does she ail, that she's
not very well?
   Clo.   Truly, she's very well, indeed, but for two things.
   Hel.   What two things?
   Clo.   One, that she's not in heaven, whither God send
her quickly! the other, that she's in earth, from whence
God send her quickly!

Enter PAROLLES

   Par.   Bless you, my fortunate lady!
   Hel.   I hope, sir, I have your good will to have mine
own good fortunes.
   Par.   You had my prayers to lead them on; and to
keep them on, have them still.—O, my knave! How
does my old lady?
   Clo.   So that you had her wrinkles, and I her money,
I would she did as you say.
   Par.   Why, I say nothing.

Clo.   Marry, you are the wiser man; for many a man's tongue shakes out his master's undoing.   To say nothing, to do nothing, to know nothing, and to have nothing, is to be a great part of your title, which is within a very little of nothing.

Par.   Away! thou 'rt a knave.

Clo.   You should have said, sir, before a knave 'thou'rt a knave'; that is, before me thou'rt a knave: this had been truth, sir.

Par.   Go to, thou art a witty fool; I have found thee.

Clo.   Did you find me in yourself, sir, or were you taught to find me?   The search, sir, was profitable; and much fool may you find in you, even to the world's pleasure, and the increase of laughter.

Par.   A good knave i' faith, and well fed.—
Madam, my lord will go away to-night;
A very serious business calls on him.
The great prerogative and rite of love,
Which, as your due, time claims, he does acknowledge,
But puts it off to a compelled restraint;
Whose want, and whose delay, is strewed with sweets,
Which they distil now in the curbéd time
To make the coming hour o'erflow with joy,
And pleasure drown the brim.

Hel.   What's his will else?

Par.   That you will take your instant leave o' the king,
And make this haste as your own good proceeding,
Strengthened with what apology you think
May make it probable need.

Hel.   What more commands he?

Par.   That, having this obtained, you presently
Attend his further pleasure.

Hel.   In everything I wait upon his will.

Par.   I shall report it so.

Hel.   I pray you.—Come, sirrah.
                                                   [*Exeunt*

SCENE V.—Another Room in the Same

Enter LAFEU *and* BERTRAM

Laf.   But, I hope, your lordship thinks not him a soldier.

Ber.   Yes, my lord, and of very valiant approof.

Laf.   You have it from his own deliverance.

Ber.   And by other warranted testimony.

Laf.   Then my dial goes not true.   I took this lark for a bunting.

Ber.   I do assure you, my lord, he is very great in knowledge, and accordingly valiant.

37

Laf. I have then sinned against his experience, and transgressed against his valour; and my state that way is dangerous, since I cannot yet find in my heart to repent. Here he comes. I pray you, make us friends: I will pursue the amity.

Enter PAROLLES

Par. [*To Bertram*] These things shall be done, sir.
Laf. Pray you, sir, who's his tailor?
Par. Sir?
Laf. O, I know him well. Ay, sir; he, sir, is a good workman, a very good tailor.
Ber. [*Aside to Parolles*] Is she gone to the king?
Par. She is.
Ber. Will she away to-night?
Par. As you'll have her.
Ber. I have writ my letters, casketed my treasure,
Given order for our horses; and to-night,
When I should take possession of the bride,
End ere I do begin.
Laf. A good traveller is something at the latter end of a dinner, but one that lies three-thirds, and uses a known truth to pass a thousand nothings with, should be once heard, and thrice beaten.—God save you, captain.
Ber. Is there any unkindness between my lord and you, monsieur?
Par. I know not how I have deserved to run into my lord's displeasure.
Laf. You have made shift to run into 't, boots and spurs and all, like him that leaped into the custard, and out of it you'll run again, rather than suffer question for your residence.
Ber. It may be you have mistaken him, my lord.
Laf. And shall do so ever, though I took him at his prayers. Fare you well, my lord; and believe this of me, there can be no kernel in this light nut; the soul of this man is his clothes: trust him not in matter of heavy consequence; I have kept of them tame, and know their natures.—Farewell, monsieur: I have spoken better of you, than you have or will deserve at my hand; but we must do good against evil.   [*Exit*
Par. An idle lord, I swear.
Ber. I think so.
Par. Why, do you not know him?
Ber. Yes, I do know him well; and common speech
Gives him a worthy pass. Here comes my clog.

Enter HELENA

Hel. I have, sir, as I was commanded from you,
Spoke with the king, and have procured his leave

For present parting; only he desires
Some private speech with you.
  Ber.   I shall obey his will.
You must not marvel, Helen, at my course,
Which holds not colour with the time, nor does
The ministration and required office
On my particular: prepared I was not
For such a business; therefore am I found
So much unsettled. This drives me to entreat you
That presently you take your way for home;
And rather muse than ask why I entreat you;
For my respects are better than they seem,
And my appointments have in them a need
Greater than shows itself at the first view,
To you that know them not. This to my mother.
         [Giving a letter
'T will be two days ere I shall see you: so,
I leave you to your wisdom.
  Hel.   Sir, I can nothing say,
But that I am your most obedient servant.
  Ber. Come, come, no more of that.
  Hel.   And ever shall
With true observance seek to eke out that
Wherein toward me my homely stars have failed
To equal my great fortune.
  Ber.   Let that go:
My haste is very great. Farewell: hie home.
  Hel. Pray, sir, your pardon.
  Ber.   Well, what would you say?
  Hel. I am not worthy of the wealth I owe;
Nor dare I say 't is mine, and yet it is;
But, like a timorous thief, most fain would steal
What law does vouch mine own.
  Ber.   What would you have?
  Hel. Something, and scarce so much:—nothing, in-
    deed.—
I would not tell you what I would, my lord:—
Faith, yes;—
Strangers and foes do sunder and not kiss.
  Ber. I pray you, stay not, but in haste to horse.
  Hel. I shall not break your bidding, good my lord.
  Ber. Where are my other men, monsieur?—Farewell.
         [Exit Helena
Go thou toward home; where I will never come,
Whilst I can shake my sword, or hear the drum.—
Away! and for our flight.
  Par.   Bravely, coragio! *[Exeunt*

ACT THREE

SCENE I.—Florence. A Room in the DUKE's Palace

Flourish. Enter the DUKE OF FLORENCE, *attended; two French Lords, and Soldiers*

Duke.   So that, from point to point, now have you heard
The fundamental reasons of this war,
Whose great decision hath much blood let forth,
And more thirsts after.
First Lord.   Holy seems the quarrel
Upon your grace's party; black and fearful
On the opposer's.
Duke.   Therefore we marvel much our cousin France
Would, in so just a business shut his bosom
Against our borrowing prayers.
Sec. Lord.   Good my lord,
The reasons of our state I cannot yield
But like a common and an outward man
That the great figure of a council frames
By self-unable motion: therefore dare not
Say what I think of it, since I have found
Myself in my uncertain grounds to fail
As often as I guessed.
Duke.   Be it his pleasure.
Sec. Lord.   But I am sure, the younger of our nature,
That surfeit on their ease, will day by day
Come here for physic.
Duke.   Welcome shall they be,
And all the honours that can fly from us
Shall on them settle.   You know your places well;
When better fall, for your avails they fell.
To-morrow to the field.   [*Flourish. Exeunt*

SCENE II.—Rousillon. A Room in the COUNTESS's Palace

Enter COUNTESS *and Clown*

Count.   It hath happened all as I would have had it,
save that he comes not along with her.
Col.   By my troth, I take my young lord to be a very
melancholy man.
Count.   By what observance, I pray you?
Clo.   Why, he will look upon his boot, and sing; mend
the ruff, and sing; ask questions, and sing; pick his teeth,

and sing.   I know a man, that had this trick of melancholy, sold a goodly manor for a song.

Count.   Let me see what he writes, and when he means to come.

Clo.   I have no mind to Isbel, since I was at court.   Our old ling and our Isbel's o' the country are nothing like your old ling and your Isbel's o' the court: the brains of my Cupid's knocked out, and I begin to love, as an old man loves money, with no stomach.

Count.   What have we here?

Clo.   E'en that you have there.   [*Exit*

Count.   [*Reads*]   "I have sent you a daughter-in-law: she had recovered the king, and undone me.   I have wedded her, not bedded her; and sworn to make the *not* eternal.   You shall hear I am run away: know it before the report come.   If there be breadth enough in the world, I will hold a long distance.   My duty to you.

Your unfortunate son,
BERTRAM."

This is not well: rash and unbridled boy,
To fly the favours of so good a king!
To pluck his indignation on thy head,
By the misprising of a maid too virtuous
For the contempt of empire!

Re-enter Clown

Clo.   O madam! yonder is heavy news within, between two soldiers and my young lady.

Count.   What is the matter?

Clo.   Nay, there is some comfort in the news, some comfort: your son will not be killed so soon as I thought he would.

Count.   Why should he be killed?

Clo.   So say I, madam, if he run away, as I hear he does: the danger is in standing to't; that's the loss of men, though it be the getting of children.   Here they come will tell you more; for my part, I only hear your son was run away.   [*Exit*

Enter HELENA and two Gentlemen

First Gent.   Save you, good madam.

Hel.   Madam, my lord is gone, for ever gone.

Sec. Gent.   Do not say so.

Count.   Think upon patience.—Pray you, gentlemen,—
I have felt so many quirks of joy and grief,
That the first face of neither, on the start,
Can woman me unto't:—where is my son, I pray you?

Sec. Gent.   Madam, he's gone to serve the Duke of Florence.

We met him thitherward; for thence we came,
And, after some despatch in hand at court,
Thither we bend again.
    Hel.   Look on his letter, madam: here's my passport.
[*Reads*] 'When thou canst get the ring upon my finger,
which never shall come off, and show me a child begotten
of thy body, that I am father to, then call me husband:
but in such a *then* I write a *never*.' This is a dreadful
sentence.
    Count.   Brought you this letter, gentlemen?
    First Gent.   Ay, madam;
And, for the contents' sake, are sorry for our pains.
    Count.   I prithee, lady, have a better cheer;
If thou engrossest all the griefs are thine,
Thou robb'st me of a moiety.   He was my son,
But I do wash his name out of my blood,
And thou art all my child.—Towards Florence is he?
    Sec. Gent.   Ay, madam.
    Count.   And to be a soldier?
    Sec. Gent.   Such is his noble purpose; and, believe 't,
The duke will lay upon him all the honour
That good convenience claims.
    Count.   Return you thither?
    First Gent.   Ay, madam, with the swiftest wing of speed.
    Hel.   [*Reads*] 'Till I have no wife, I have nothing in
France.'
'T is bitter.
    Count.   Find you that there?
    Hel.   Ay, madam.
    First Gent.   'T is but the boldness of his hand,
Which haply, his heart was not consenting to.
    Count.   Nothing in France, until he have no wife!
There's nothing here that is too good for him,
But only she; and she deserves a lord
That twenty such rude boys might tend upon,
And call her hourly, mistress.   Who was with him?
    First Gent.   A servant only, and a gentleman
Which I have sometime known.
    Count.   Parolles was it not?
    First Gent.   Ay, my good lady, he.
    Count.   A very tainted fellow, and full of wickedness.
My son corrupts a well-derivéd nature
With his inducement.
    First Gent.   Indeed, good lady,
The fellow has a deal of that too much
Which holds him much to have.
    Count.   Y'are welcome, gentlemen.
I will entreat you, when you see my son,
To tell him, that his sword can never win
The honour that he loses: more I'll entreat you

Written to bear along.
   Sec. Gent.   We serve you, madam,
In that and all your worthiest affairs.
   Count.   Not so, but as we change our courtesies.
Will you draw near?

                     [Exeunt Countess and Gentlemen
   Hel. 'Till I have no wife, I have nothing in France.'
Nothing in France, until he has no wife!
Thou shalt have none, Rousillon, none in France;
Then hast thou all again. Poor lord! is't I
That chase thee from thy country, and expose
Those tender limbs of thine to the event
Of the none-sparing war? and is it I
That drive thee from the sportive court, where thou
Wast shot at with fair eyes, to be the mark
Of smoky muskets? O you leaden messengers
That ride upon the violent speed of fire,
Fly with false aim; move the still-piercing air
That sings with piercing; do not touch my lord!
Whoever shoots at him, I set him there;
Whoever charges on his forward breast,
I am the caitiff that do hold him to it;
And, though I kill him not, I am the cause
His death was so effected. Better 't were,
I met the ravin lion when he roared
With sharp constraint of hunger: better 't were,
That all the miseries which nature owes
Were mine at once. No, come thou home, Rousillon,
Whence honour but of danger wins a scar,
As oft it loses all: I will be gone.
My being here it is that holds thee hence:
Shall I stay here to do 't? no, no, although
The air of Paradise did fan the house,
And angels officed all: I will be gone,
That pitiful rumour may report my flight,
To consolate thine ear. Come, night; end, day!
For with the dark, poor thief, I'll steal away.   *[Exit*

SCENE III.—Florence. Before the DUKE'S Palace

Flourish. Enter the DUKE OF FLORENCE, BERTRAM,
    PAROLLES, *Lords, Officers, Soldiers, and others*

   Duke. The general of our horse thou art; and we,
Great in our hope, lay our best love and credence
Upon thy promising fortune.
   Ber.   Sir, it is
A charge too heavy for my strength; but yet

We'll strive to bear it, for your worthy sake,
To the extreme edge of hazard.   *Then go thou forth,*
    Duke.
And fortune play upon thy prosperous helm,
As thy auspicious mistress!
    Ber.   This very day,
Great Mars, I put myself into thy file;
Make me but like my thoughts, and I shall prove
A lover of thy drum, hater of love.   [*Exeunt*

SCENE IV.—Rousillon. A Room in the COUNTESS'S
Palace

Enter COUNTESS *and her Steward*

    Count. Alas! and would you take the letter of her?
Might you not know she would do as she has done,
By sending me a letter? Read it again.

    Stew. [*Reads*] '*I am Saint Jaques' pilgrim, thither gone.*
    Ambitious love hath so in me offended,
That bare-foot plod I the cold ground upon,
    With sainted vow my faults to have amended.

Write, write, that, from the bloody course of war,
    My dearest master, your dear son, may hie:
Bless him at home in peace, whilst I from far
    His name with zealous fervour sanctify.

His taken labours bid him me forgive:
    I, his despiteful Juno, sent him forth
From courtly friends, with camping foes to live,
    Where death and danger dogs the heels of worth:

He is too good and fair for Death and me.
Whom I myself embrace, to set him free.'

    Count. Ah, what sharp stings are in her mildest words!—
Rinaldo, you ne'er lacked advice so much
As letting her pass so: had I spoke with her
I could have well diverted her intents,
Which thus she hath prevented.
    Stew.   Pardon me, madam:
If I had given you this at over-night,
She might have been o'erta'en; and yet she writes,
Pursuit would be but vain.
    Count.   What angel shall
Bless this unworthy husband? he cannot thrive,

Unless her prayers, whom Heaven delights to hear
And loves to grant, reprieve him from the wrath
Of greatest justice.—Write, write, Rinaldo,
To this unworthy husband of his wife:
Let every word weigh heavy of her worth,
That he does weigh too light: my greatest grief,
Though little he do feel it, set down sharply.
Despatch the most convenient messenger.—
When, haply, he shall hear that she is gone,
He will return; and hope I may, that she,
Hearing so much, will speed her foot again,
Led hither by pure love. Which of them both
Is dearest to me I have no skill in sense
To make distinction.—Provide this messenger.—
My heart is heavy, and mine age is weak;
Grief would have tears, and sorrow bids me speak.

                                              [*Exeunt*

SCENE V.—Without the Walls of Florence

A tucket afar off. Enter an old Widow of Florence, DIANA,
     VIOLENTA, MARIANA, *and other Citizens*

Wid. Nay, come; for if they do approach the city,
we shall lose all the sight.
Dia. They say, the French count has done most honourable service.
Wid. It is reported that he has taken their greatest
commander, and that with his own hand he slew the
duke's brother. We have lost our labour; they are gone
a contrary way: hark! you may know by their trumpets.
Mar. Come; let's return again, and suffice ourselves
with the report of it. Well, Diana, take heed of this
French earl: the honour of a maid is her name, and no
legacy is so rich as honesty.
Wid. I have told my neighbour how you have been
solicited by a gentleman his companion.
Mar. I know that knave; hang him! one Parolles:
a filthy officer he is in those suggestions for the young earl.
—Beware of them Diana; their promises, enticements,
oaths, tokens, and all these engines of lust, are not the
things they go under: many a maid hath been seduced
by them; and the misery is, example that so terrible
shows in the wreck of maidenhood cannot for all that
dissuade succession, but that they are limed with the
twigs that threaten them. I hope I need not to advise you
further; but, I hope, your own grace will keep you where
you are, though there were no further danger known, but
the modesty which is so lost.

Dia.   You shall not need to fear me.

Wid.   I hope so.—Look, here comes a pilgrim: I know she will lie at my house; thither they send one another. I'll question her.—

Enter HELENA, *in the dress of a Pilgrim*

God save you, pilgrim!—whither are you bound?

Hel.   To Saint Jaqués le Grand.

Where do the palmers lodge, I do beseech you?

Wid.   At the Saint Francis, here beside the port.

Hel.   Is this the way?

Wid.   Ay, marry, is't.—Hark you!

[*A march afar off*

They come this way.—If you will tarry, holy pilgrim,
But till the troops come by,
I will conduct you where you shall be lodged:
The rather, for I think I know your hostess
As ample as myself.

Hel.   Is it yourself?

Wid.   If you shall please so, pilgrim.

Hel.   I thank you, and will stay upon your leisure.

Wid.   You came, I think, from France?

Hel.   I did so.

Wid.   Here you shall see a countryman of yours,
That has done worthy service.

Hel.   His name, I pray you.

Dia.   The Count Rousillon: know you such a one?

Hel.   But by the ear, that hears most nobly of him;
His face I know not.

Dia.   Whatsoe'er he is,
He's bravely taken here.   He stole from France,
As't is reported, for the king had married him
Against his liking.   Think you it is so?

Hel.   Ay, surely, mere the truth: I know his lady.

Dia.   There is a gentleman that serves the count,
Reports but coarsely of her.

Hel.   What's his name?

Dia.   Monsieur Parolles.

Hel.   O, I believe with him;
In argument of praise, or to the worth
Of the great count himself, she is too mean
To have her name repeated: all her deserving
Is a reservéd honesty, and that
I have not heard examined.

Dia.   Alas, poor lady!
'T is a hard bondage to become the wife
Of a detesting lord.

Wid.   Ay, right; good creature, wheresoe'er she is,
Her heart weighs sadly.   This young maid might do her

A shrewd turn, if she pleased.
Hel.   How do you mean?
May be, the amorous count solicits her
In the unlawful purpose.
Wid.   He does indeed;
And brokes with all that can in such a suit
Corrupt the tender honour of a maid:
But she is armed for him, and keeps her guard
In honestest defence.
Mar.   The gods forbid else!

Enter, with drum and colours, a party of the Florentine army,
BERTRAM, *and* PAROLLES

Wid.   So, now they come.—
That is Antonio, the duke's eldest son;
That, Escalus.
Hel.   Which is the Frenchman?
Dia.   He;
That with the plume: 't is a most gallant fellow;
I would he loved his wife.   If he were honester,
He were much goodlier; is 't not a handsome gentleman?
Hel.   I like him well.
Dia.   'T is pity, he is not honest.   Yond's that same
                  knave
That leads him to these places: were I his lady,
I'd poison that vile-rascal.
Hel.   Which is he?
Dia.   That   jack-an-apes   with   scarfs.   Why   is   he
melancholy?
Hel.   Perchance he's hurt i' the battle.
Par.   Lose our drum! well.
Mar.   He's shrewdly vexed at something.   Look, he
has spied us.
Wid.   Marry, hang you!
Mar.   And your courtesy for a ring-carrier!
                  [*Exeunt Bertram, Parolles, Officers and
                                          Soldiers*
Wid.   The troop is past.   Come, pilgrim, I will bring
                  you
Where you shall host: of enjoined penitents
There's four or five, to Great Saint Jacqués bound,
Already at my house.
Hel.   I humbly thank you.
Please it this matron and this gentle maid
To eat with us to-night, the charge and thanking
Shall be for me; and, to requite you further,
I will bestow some precepts of this virgin
Worthy the note.
Both.   We'll take your offer kindly. [*Exeunt*

SCENE VI.—Camp before Florence

Enter BERTRAM *and the two French Lords*

First Lord. Nay, good my lord, put him to't: let him have his way.

Sec. Lord. If your lordship find him not a hilding, hold me no more in your respect.

First Lord. On my life, my lord, a bubble.

Ber. Do you think I am so far deceived in him?

First Lord. Believe it, my lord: in mine own direct knowledge, without any malice, but to speak of him as my kinsman, he's a most notable coward, an infinite and endless liar, an hourly promise-breaker, the owner of no one good quality worthy your lordship's entertainment.

Sec. Lord. It were fit you knew him, lest, reposing too far in his virtue which he hath not, he might, at some great and trusty business in a main danger, fail you.

Ber. I would I knew in what particular action to try him.

Sec. Lord. None better than to let him fetch off his drum, which you hear him so confidently undertake to do.

First Lord. I, with a troop of Florentines, will suddenly surprise him: such I will have whom, I am sure, he knows not from the enemy. We will bind and hoodwink him so, that he shall suppose no other but that he is carried into the leaguer of the adversaries, when we bring him to our own tents. Be but your lordship present at his examination: if he do not, for the promise of his life, and in the highest compulsion of base fear, offer to betray you, and deliver all the intelligence in his power against you, and that with the divine forfeit of his soul upon oath, never trust my judgment in anything.

Sec. Lord. O for the love of laughter, let him fetch his drum: he says he has a stratagem for't. When your lordship sees the bottom of his success in't, and to what metal this counterfeit lump of ore will be melted, if you give him not John Drum's entertainment, your inclining cannot be removed. Here he comes.

First Lord. O, for the love of laughter, hinder not the honour of his design: let him fetch off his drum in any hand.

Enter PAROLLES

Ber. How now, monsieur? this drum sticks sorely in your disposition.

Sec. Lord. A pox on't! let it go: 't is but a drum.

Par. But a drum! Is't but a drum? A drum so lost! —There was an excellent command, to charge in with our horse upon our own wings and to rend our own soldiers!

48

Sec. Lord. That was not to be blamed in the command of the service: it was a disaster of war that Cæsar himself could not have prevented, if he had been there to command.

Ber. Well, we cannot greatly condemn our success: some dishonour we had in the loss of that drum; but it is not to be recovered.

Par. It might have been recovered.

Ber. It might; but it is not now.

Par. It is to be recovered. But that the merit of service is seldom attributed to the true and exact performer, I would have that drum or another, or *hic jacet*.

Ber. Why, if you have a stomach to 't, monsieur, if you think your mystery in stratagem can bring this instrument of honour again into his native quarter, be magnanimous in the enterprise, and go on; I will grace the attempt for a worthy exploit: if you speed well in it, the duke shall both speak of it and extend to you what further becomes his greatness, even to the utmost syllable of your worthiness.

Par. By the hand of a soldier, I will undertake it.

Ber. But you must not now slumber in it.

Par. I'll about it this evening: and I will presently pen down my dilemmas, encourage myself in my certainty, put myself into my mortal preparation, and by midnight look to hear further from me.

Ber. May I be bold to acquaint his grace you are gone about it?

Par. I know not what the success will be, my lord; but the attempt I vow.

Ber. I know thou art valiant, and, to the possibility of thy soldiership, will subscribe for thee. Farewell.

Par. I love not many words.   [*Exit*

First Lord. No more than a fish loves water.—Is not this a strange fellow, my lord, that so confidently seems to undertake this business, which he knows is not to be done, damns himself to do, and dares better be damned than to do 't?

Sec. Lord. You do not know him, my lord, as we do: certain it is, that he will steal himself into a man's favour, and for a week escape a great deal of discoveries; but when you find him out, you have him ever after.

Ber. Why, do you think, he will make no deed at all of this, that so seriously he does address himself unto?

First Lord. None in the world; but return with an invention, and clap upon you two or three probable lies. But we have almost embossed him, you shall see his fall to-night; for, indeed, he is not for your lordship's respect.

Sec. Lord. We'll make you some sport with the fox, ere we case him. He was first smoked by the old Lord Lafeu: when his disguise and he is parted, tell me what

a sprat you shall find him, which you shall see this very
night.
 First Lord. I must go look my twigs: he shall be
  caught.
 Ber. Your brother, he shall go along with me.
 First Lord. As't please your lordship: I'll leave you.
              [Exit
 Ber. Now will I lead you to the house, and show you
The lass I spoke of.
 Sec. Lord.   But, you say, she's honest.
 Ber. That's all the fault. I spoke with her but once,
And found her wondrous cold; but I sent to her,
By this same coxcomb that we have i' the wind,
Tokens and letters which she did re-send;
And this is all I have done. She's a fair creature;
Will you go see her?
 Sec. Lord. With all my heart, my lord.

              [Exeunt

SCENE VII.—Florence. A Room in the Widow's House

Enter HELENA *and Widow*

 Hel. If you misdoubt me that I am not she,
I know not how I shall assure you further,
But I shall lose the grounds I work upon.
 Wid. Though my estate be fallen, I was well born,
Nothing acquainted with these businesses,
And would not put my reputation now
In any staining act.
 Hel.   Nor would I wish you.
First, give me trust, the count he is my husband,
And what to your sworn counsel I have spoken,
Is so, from word to word; and then you cannot
By the good aid that I of you shall borrow
Err in bestowing it.
 Wid.   I should believe you;
For you have showed me that which well approves
You are great in fortune.
 Hel.   Take this purse of gold,
And let me buy your friendly help thus far,
Which I will over-pay, and pay again,
When I have found it. The count he woos your daughter,
Lays down his wanton siege before her beauty,
Resolved to carry her: let her, in fine, consent,
As we'll direct her how't is best to bear it.
Now, his important blood will naught deny
That she'll demand: a ring the county wears,
That downward hath succeeded in his house

From son to son, some four or five descents
Since the first father wore't: this ring he holds
In most rich choice; yet, in his idle fire,
To buy his will, it would not seem too dear,
Howe'er repented after.
  Wid.   Now I see
The bottom of your purpose.
  Hel. You see it lawful then. It is no more
But that your daughter, ere she seems as won,
Desires this ring, appoints him an encounter,
In fine, delivers me to fill the time,
Herself most chastely absent. After this,
To marry her, I'll add three thousand crowns
To what is past already.
  Wid.   I have yielded.
Instruct my daughter how she shall perséver,
That time and place with this deceit so lawful
May prove coherent. Every night he comes
With musics of all sorts, and songs composed
To her unworthiness: it nothing steads us
To chide him from our eaves, for he persists,
As if his life lay on't.
  Hel.   Why then, to-night
Let us assay our plot; which, if it speed,
Is wicked meaning in a lawful deed,
And lawful meaning in a lawful act
Where both not sin, and yet a sinful fact.
But let's about it.
             [Exeunt

ACT FOUR

SCENE I.—Without the Florentine Camp

Enter First French Lord, with five or six Soldiers in ambush

  First Lord. He can come no other way but by this
hedge-corner. When you sally upon him, speak what
terrible language you will: though you understand it not
yourselves, no matter; for we must not seem to understand
him, unless some one among us, whom we must produce
for an interpreter.
  First Sold. Good captain, let me be the interpreter.
  First Lord. Art not acquainted with him? knows
he not thy voice?
  First Sold. No, sir, I warrant you.
  First Lord. But what linsey-woolsey hast thou to speak
to us again?
  First Sold. Even such as you speak to me.

First Lord. He must think us some band of strangers i' the adversary's entertainment. Now, he hath a smack of all neighbouring languages; therefore, we must every one be a man of his own fancy, not to know what we speak one to another, so we seem to know, is to know straight our purpose: chough's language, gabble enough, and good enough. As for you, interpreter, you must seem very politic. But couch, ho! here he comes, to beguile two hours in a sleep, and then to return and swear the lies he forges.

Enter PAROLLES

Par. Ten o'clock: within these three hours 't will be time enough to go home. What shall I say I have done? It must be a very plausive invention that carries it. They begin to smoke me, and disgraces have of late knocked too often at my door. I find, my tongue is too foolhardy; but my heart hath the fear of Mars before it and of his creatures, nor daring the reports of my tongue.

First Lord. [*Aside*] This is the first truth that e'er thine own tongue was guilty of.

Par. What the devil should move me to undertake the recovery of this drum, being not ignorant of the impossibility, and knowing I had no such purpose? I must give myself some hurts, and say, I got them in exploit. Yet slight ones will not carry it: they will say, 'Came you off with so little?' and great ones I dare not give. Wherefore? what's the instance? Tongue, I must put you into a butter-woman's mouth, and buy myself another of Bajazet's mule, if you prattle me into these perils.

First Lord. [*Aside*] Is it possible, he should know what he is, and be that he is?

Par. I would the cutting of my garments would serve the turn, or the breaking of my Spanish sword.

First Lord. [*Aside*] We cannot afford you so.

Par. Or the baring of my beard, and to say, it was in stratagem.

First Lord. [*Aside*] 'T would not do.

Par. Or to drown my clothes, and say, I was stripped.

First Lord. [*Aside*] Hardly serve.

Par. Though I swore I leaped from the window of the citadel—

First Lord. [*Aside*] How deep?

Par. Thirty fathom.

First Lord. [*Aside*] Three great oaths would scarce make that be believed.

Par. I would I had any drum of the enemy's: I would swear I recovered it.

First Lord. [*Aside*] You shall hear one anon.

Par. A drum now of the enemy's!   [*Alarum within*
First Lord. *Throca movousus, cargo, cargo, cargo.*
All. *Cargo, cargo, villianda par corbo, cargo.*
Par. O! ransom, ransom!—Do not hide mine eyes.
                               [*They seize and blindfold him*
First Sold. *Boskos thromuldo boskos.*
Par. I know, you are the Muskos' regiment;
And I shall lose my life for want of language.
If there be here German, or Dane, Low Dutch,
Italian, or French, let him speak to me:
I will discover that which shall undo
The Florentine.
First Sold. *Boskos vauvado:*—
I undersand thee, and can speak thy tongue:—
Kerelybonto:—Sir,
Betake thee to thy faith, for seventeen poniards
Are at thy bosom.
Par.   O!
First Sold.   O, pray, pray, pray!—
Manka revania dulche.
First Lord.   *Oscorbi dulchos volivorco.*
First Sold. The general is content to spare thee yet,
And, hoodwinked as thou art, will lead thee on
To gather from thee: haply, thou may'st inform
Something to save thy life.
Par.   O, let me live,
And all the secrets of our camp I'll show,
Their force, their purposes; nay, I'll speak that
Which you will wonder at.
First Sold.   But wilt thou faithfully?
Par. If I do not, damn me.
First Sold.   *Acordolinta.*—
Come on, thou art granted space.
                          [*Exit, with Parolles guarded*
First Lord. Go, tell the Count Rousillon, and my brother,
We have caught the woodcock, and will keep him muffled,
Till we do hear from them.
Sec. Sold.   Captain, I will.
First Lord. 'A will betray us all unto ourselves.
Inform on that.
Sec. Sold. So I will, sir.
First Lord. Till then, I'll keep him dark, and safely
        locked.   [*Exeunt*

SCENE II.—Florence. A Room in the Widow's House

Enter BERTRAM *and* DIANA

Ber. They told me, that your name was Fontibell.

53

Dia.   No, my good lord, Diana.
Ber.   Titled goddess,
And worth it, with addition! But, fair soul,
In your fine frame hath love no quality?
If the quick fire of youth light not your mind,
You are no maiden, but a monument:
When you are dead, you should be such a one
As you are now, for you are cold and stern;
And now you should be as your mother was
When your sweet self was got.
Dia.   She then was honest.
Ber.   So should you be.
Dia.   No:
My mother did but duty; such, my lord,
As you owe to your wife.
Ber.   No more o' that!
I pr'ythee, do not strive against my vows.
I was compelled to her; but I love thee
By love's own sweet constraint, and will for ever
Do thee all rights of service.
Dia.   Ay, so you serve us,
Till we serve you; but when you have our roses,
You barely leave our thorns to prick ourselves,
And mock us with our bareness.
Ber.   How have I sworn!
Dia.   'T is not the many oaths that make the truth,
But the plain single vow, that is vowed true.
What is not holy, that we swear not by,
But take the Highest to witness: then, pray you, tell me,
If I should swear by Jove's great attributes
I loved you dearly, would you believe my oaths
When I did love you ill? This has no holding,
To swear by him whom I protest to love
That I will work against him. Therefore, your oaths
Are words, and poor conditions, but unsealed;
At least in my opinion.
Ber.   Change it, change it.
Be not so holy-cruel: love is holy,
And my integrity ne'er knew the crafts
That you do charge men with. Stand no more off,
But give thyself unto my sick desires,
Who then recover: say, thou art mine, and ever
My love, as it begins, shall so perséver.
Dia.   I see, that men make ropes in such a case,
That we'll forsake ourselves. Give me that ring.
Ber.   I'll lend it thee, my dear; but have no power
To give it from me.
Dia.   Will you not, my lord?
Ber.   It is an honour 'longing to our house,
Bequeathéd down from many ancestors,

Which were the greatest obloquy i' the world
In me to lose.
    Dia.   Mine honour's such a ring.
My chastity's the jewel of our house,
Bequeathéd down from many ancestors,
Which were the greatest obloquy i' the world
In me to lose.   Thus, your own proper wisdom
Brings in the champion honour on my part
Against your vain assault.
    Ber.   Here, take my ring:
My house, mine honour, yea, my life, be thine,
And I'll be bid by thee.
    Dia.   When midnight comes, knock at my chamber-
window:
I'll order take, my mother shall not hear.
Now will I charge you in the band of truth,
When you have conquered my yet maiden bed,
Remain there but an hour, nor speak to me.
My reasons are most strong; and you shall know them,
When back again this ring shall be delivered:
And on your finger, in the night, I'll put
Another ring, that what in time proceeds
May token to the future our past deeds.
Adieu till then; then, fail not. You have won
A wife of me, though there my hope be done.
    Ber. A heaven on earth I have won by wooing thee.
                                      [Exit
    Dia.   For which live long to thank both Heaven and me?
You may so in the end—
My mother told me just how he would woo,
As if she sat in's heart; she says, all men
Have the like oaths. He had sworn to marry me,
When his wife's dead; therefore I'll lie with him
When I am buried. Since Frenchmen are so braid,
Marry that will, I live and die a maid:
Only, in this disguise, I think't no sin
To cozen him that would unjustly win.   *[Exit*

SCENE III.—The Florentine Camp

Enter two French Lords, and two or three Soldiers

    First Lord.   You have not given him his mother's letter?
    Sec. Lord.   I have delivered it an hour since: there is
something in't that stings his nature, for on the reading
it he changed almost into another man.
    First Lord.   He has much worthy blame laid upon him,
for shaking off so good a wife and so sweet a lady.
    Sec. Lord.   Especially he hath incurred the everlasting

displeasure of the king, who had even tuned his bounty to sing happiness to him. I will tell you a thing, but you shall let it dwell darkly within you.

First Lord. When you have spoken it, 't is dead, and I am the grave of it.

Sec. Lord. He hath perverted a young gentlewoman, here in Florence, of a most chaste renown, and this night he fleshes his will in the spoil of her honour: he hath given her his monumental ring, and thinks himself made in the unchaste composition.

First Lord. Now, God delay our rebellion: as we are ourselves, what things are we!

Sec. Lord. Merely our own traitors: and as in the common course of all treasons we still see them reveal themselves till they attain to their abhorred ends, so he that in this action contrives against his own nobility, in his proper stream o'erflows himself.

First Lord. Is it not meant damnable in us, to be trumpeters of our unlawful intents? We shall not then have his company to-night?

Sec. Lord. Not till after midnight, for he is dieted to his hour.

First Lord. That approaches apace: I would gladly have him see his company anatomised, that he might take a measure of his own judgments, wherein so curiously he had set this counterfeit.

Sec. Lord. We will not meddle with him till he come, for his presence must be the whip of the other.

First Lord. In the meantime, what hear you of these wars?

Sec. Lord. I hear there is an overture of peace.

First Lord. Nay, I assure you, a peace concluded.

Sec. Lord. What will Count Rousillon do then? will he travel higher, or return again into France?

First Lord. I perceive by this demand, you are not altogether of his counsel.

Sec. Lord. Let it be forbid, sir; so should I be a great deal of his act.

First Lord. Sir, his wife some two months since fled from his house: her pretence is a pilgrimage to Saint Jaques le Grand, which holy undertaking with most austere sanctimony she accomplished; and, there residing, the tenderness of her nature became as a prey to her grief; in fine, made a groan of her last breath, and now she sings in heaven.

Sec. Lord. How is this justified?

First Lord. The stronger part of it by her own letters; which makes her story true, even to the point of her death: her death itself, which could not be her office to say is come, was faithfully confirmed by the rector of the place.

Sec. Lord. Hath the count all this intelligence?

First Lord. Ay, and the particular confirmations, point from point, to the full arming of the verity.

Sec. Lord. I am heartily sorry that he'll be glad of this.

First Lord. How mightily, sometimes, we make us comforts of our losses!

Sec. Lord. And how mightily, some other times, we drown our gain in tears. The great dignity that his valour hath here acquired for him, shall at home be encountered with a shame as ample.

First Lord. The web of our life is of a mingled yarn, good and ill together: our virtues would be proud if our faults whipped them not; and our crimes would despair if they were not cherished by our virtues.

Enter a Servant

How now? where's your master?

Serv. He met the duke in the street, sir, of whom he hath taken a solemn leave; his lordship will next morning for France. The duke hath offered him letters of commendations to the king.

Sec. Lord. They shall be no more than needful there, if they were more than they can commend.

First Lord. They cannot be too sweet for the king's tartness. Here's his lordship now.

Enter BERTRAM

How now, my lord! is't not after midnight?

Ber. I have to-night despatched sixteen businesses, a month's length a-piece, by an abstract of success: I have conge'd with the duke, done my adieu with his nearest, buried a wife, mourned for her, writ to my lady mother I am returning, entertained my convoy; and between these main parcels of despatch effected many nicer needs: the last was the greatest, but that I have not ended yet.

Sec. Lord. If the business be of any difficulty, and this morning your departure hence, it requires haste of your lordship.

Ber. I mean, the business is not ended, as fearing to hear of it hereafter. But shall we have this dialogue between the fool and the soldier? Come, bring forth this counterfeit model: he has deceived me, like a double-meaning prophesier.

Sec. Lord. Bring him forth. [*Exeunt Soldiers*] He has sat i' the stocks all night, poor gallant knave.

Ber. No matter; his heels have deserved it, in usurping his spurs so long. How does he carry himself?

First Lord. I have told your lordship already; the stocks carry him. But, to answer you as you would be

57

understood, he weeps like a wench that had shed her milk. He hath confessed himself to Morgan, whom he supposes to be a friar, from the time of his remembrance to this very instant disaster of his sitting i' the stocks; and what think you he hath confessed?

Ber. Nothing of me, has 'a?

Sec. Lord. His confession is taken, and it shall be read to his face: if your lordship be in 't, as I believe you are, you must have the patience to hear it.

Re-enter Soldiers, with PAROLLES

Ber. A plague upon him! muffled? he can say nothing of me: hush! hush!

First Lord. Hoodman comes!—*Porto tartarossa.*

First Sold. He calls for the tortures: what will you say without 'em?

Par. I will confess what I know without constraint: if ye pinch me like a pasty, I can say no more.

First Sold. Bosko chimurcho.

Sec. Lord. Boblibindo chicurmurcho.

First Sold. You are a merciful general.—Our general bids you answer to what I shall ask you out of a note.

Par. And truly, as I hope to live.

First Sold. 'First, demand of him, how many horse the duke is strong.' What say you to that?

Par. Five or six thousand; but very weak and un-serviceable: the troops are all scattered, and the com-manders very poor rogues, upon my reputation and credit, and as I hope to live.

First Sold. Shall I set down your answer so?

Par. Do: I'll take the sacrament on 't, how and which way you will.

Ber. All's one to him. What a past-saving slave is this!

First Lord. You are deceived, my lord: this is Monsieur Parolles, the gallant militarist—that was his own phrase—that had the whole theory of war in the knot of his scarf, and the practice in the chape of his dagger.

Sec. Lord. I will never trust a man again for keeping his sword clean; nor believe he can have everything in him by wearing his apparel neatly.

First Sold. Well, that's set down.

Par. Five or six thousand horse, I said—I will say true—or thereabouts, set down,—for I'll speak truth.

First Lord. He's very near the truth in this.

Ber. But I con him no thanks for 't, in the nature he delivers it.

Par. Poor rogues, I pray you, say.

First Sold. Well, that's set down.

Par. I humbly thank you, sir. A truth's a truth: the rogues are marvellously poor.

First Sold. 'Demand of him, of what strength they are afoot.' What say you to that?

Par. By my troth, sir, if I were to live this present hour, I will tell true. Let me see: Spurio, a hundred and fifty; Sebastian, so many; Corambus, so many; Jaques, so many; Guiltian, Cosmo, Lodowick, and Gratii, two hundred fifty each; mine own company, Chitopher, Vaumond, Bentii, two hundred fifty each: so that the muster file, rotten and sound, upon my life, amounts not to fifteen thousand poll; half of the which dare not shake the snow from off their cassocks lest they shake themselves to pieces.

Ber. What shall be done to him?

First Lord. Nothing, but let him have thanks.—Demand of him my condition, and what credit I have with the duke.

First Sold. Well, that's set down. 'You shall demand of him, whether one Captain Dumain be i' the camp, a Frenchman; what his reputation is with the duke; what his valour, honesty, and expertness in wars; on whether he thinks it were not possible with well-weighing sums of gold to corrupt him to a revolt.' What say you to this? what do you know of it?

Par. I beseech you, let me answer to the particular of the inter'gatories: demand them singly.

First Sold. Do you know this Captain Dumain?

Par. I know him: he was a botcher's 'prentice in Paris, from whence he was whipped for getting the shrieve's fool with child; a dumb innocent, that could not say him nay.   [*Dumain lifts up his hand in anger*

Ber. Nay, by your leave, hold your hands; though I know, his brains are forfeit to the next tile that falls.

First Sold. Well, is this captain in the Duke of Florence's camp?

Par. Upon my knowledge he is, and lousy.

First Lord. Nay, look not so upon me; we shall hear of your lordship anon.

First Sold. What is his reputation with the duke?

Par. The duke knows him for no other but a poor officer of mine, and writ to me this other day to turn him out o' the band: I think I have his letter in my pocket.

First Sold. Marry, we'll search.

Par. In good sadness, I do not know: either it is there, or it is upon a file, with the duke's other letters, in my tent.

First Sold. Here't is: here's a paper; shall I read it to you?

Par. I do not know if it be it or no.

Ber. Our interpreter does it well.

First Lord. Excellently.
First Sold. [*Reads*] '*Dian, the count's a fool, and full of gold,*'—
Par. That is not the duke's letter, sir: that is an advertisement to a proper maid in Florence, one Diana, to take heed of the allurement of one Count Rousillon, a foolish idle boy, but, for all that, very ruttish. I pray you, sir, put it up again.
First Sold. Nay, I'll read it first, by your favour.
Par. My meaning, in't, I protest, was very honest in the behalf of the maid: for I knew the young count to be a dangerous and lascivious boy, who is a whale to virginity, and devours up all the fry it finds.
Ber. Damnable, both-sides rogue!
First Sold. [*Reads*] '*When he swears oaths, bid him drop gold, and take it;*
After he scores, he never pays the score:
Half won is match well made: match, and well make it:
He ne'er pays after debts; take it before,
And say, a soldier, Dian, told thee this.
Men are to mell with, boys are not to kiss;
For count of this, the count's a fool, I know it,
Who pays before, but not when he does owe it.
Thine, as he vowed to thee in thine ear,
                                    PAROLLES.'
Ber. He shall be whipped through the army, with this rhyme in's forehead.
Sec. Lord. This is your devoted friend, sir; the manifold linguist, and the armipotent soldier.
Ber. I could endure anything before but a cat, and now he's a cat to me.
First Sold. I perceive, sir, by our general's looks, we shall be fain to hang you.
Par. My life, sir, in any case! Not that I am afraid to die; but that, my offences being many, I would repent out the remainder of nature. Let me live, sir, in a dungeon, i' the stocks, or anywhere, so I may live.
First Sold. We'll see what may be done, so you confess freely: therefore, once more to this Captain Dumain. You have answered to his reputation with the duke, and to his valour: what is his honesty?
Par. He will steal, sir, an egg out of a cloister; for rapes and ravishments he parallels Nessus. He professes not keeping of oaths; in breaking them he is stronger than Hercules. He will lie, sir, with such volubility, that you would think truth were a fool. Drunkenness is his best virtue; for he will be swinedrunk, and in his sleep he does little harm, save to his bed-clothes about him; but they know his conditions, and lay him in straw. I have but little more to say, sir, of his honesty: he has every-

60

thing that an honest man should not have; what an honest man should have, he has nothing.

First Lord. I begin to love him for this.

Ber. For this description of thine honesty? A pox upon him! for me he is more and more a cat.

First Sold. What say you to his expertness in war?

Par. Faith, sir, he has led the drum before the English tragedians,—to belie him, I will not,—and more of his soldiership I know not; except, in that country, he had the honour to be the officer at a place there called Mile End, to instruct for the doubling of files: I would do the man what honour I can, but of this I am not certain.

First Lord. He hath out-villained villainy so far, that the rarity redeems him.

Ber. A pox on him! he's a cat still.

First Sold. His qualities being at this poor price, I need not ask you, if gold will corrupt him to revolt.

Par. Sir, for a cardecue he will sell the fee-simple of his salvation, the inheritance of it; and cut the entail from all remainders, and a perpetual succession for it perpetually.

First Sold. What's his brother, the other Captain Dumain?

Sec. Lord. Why does he ask him of me?

First Sold. What's he?

Par. E'en a crow o' the same nest; not altogether so great as the first in goodness, but greater a great deal in evil. He excels his brother for a coward, yet his brother is reputed one of the best that is. In a retreat he outruns any lackey; marry, in coming on he has the cramp.

First Sold. If your life be saved, will you undertake to betray the Florentine?

Par. Ay, and the captain of his horse, Count Rousillon.

First Sold. I'll whisper with the general, and know his pleasure.

Par. [*Aside*] I'll no more drumming; a plague of all drums! Only to seem to deserve well, and to beguile the supposition of that lascivious young boy the count, have I run into this danger. Yet who would have suspected an ambush, where I was taken?

First Sold. There is no remedy, sir, but you must die. The general says, you, that have so traitorously discovered the secrets of your army, and made such pestiferous reports of men very nobly held, can serve the world for no honest use; therefore you must die. Come, headsman, off with his head.

Par. O Lord, sir, let me live, or let me see my death!

First Sold. That shall you, and take your leave of all your friends. [*Unmuffling him*

So, look about you: know you any here?

61

Ber.   Good morrow, noble captain.

Sec. Lord.   God bless you, Captain Parolles.

First Lord.   God save you, noble captain.

Sec. Lord.   Captain, what greeting will you to my Lord Lafeu? I am for France.

First Lord.   Good captain, will you give me a copy of the sonnet you writ to Diana in behalf of the Count Rousillon? an I were not a very coward, I'd compel it of you; but fare you well.

> [*Exeunt Bertram, Frenchmen, etc.*

First Sold.   You are undone, captain; all but your scarf, that has a knot on't yet.

Par.   Who cannot be crushed with a plot?

First Sold.   If you could find out a country where but women were, that had received so much shame, you might begin an impudent nation. Fare you well, sir; I am for France too: we shall speak of you there.   [*Exit*

Par.   Yet am I thankful: if my heart were great,
'T would burst at this. Captain I'll be no more;
But I will eat and drink, and sleep as soft
As captain shall: simply the thing I am
Shall make me live. Who knows himself a braggart,
Let him fear this; for it will come to pass,
That every braggart shall be found an ass.
Rust, sword! cool, blushes! and, Parolles, live
Safest in shame! being fooled, by foolery thrive!
There's place and means for every man alive!
I'll after them.   [*Exit*

SCENE IV.—Florence.   A Room in the Widow's House

Enter HELENA, *Widow, and* DIANA

He.   That you may well perceive I have not wronged you,
One of the greatest in the Christian world
Shall be my surety: fore whose throne, 't is needful,
Ere I can perfect mine intents, to kneel.
Time was, I did him a desiréd office,
Dear almost as his life; which gratitude
Through flinty Tartar's bosom would peep forth
And answer thanks. I duly am informed,
His grace is at Marseilles; to which place
We have convenient convoy. You must know,
I am supposéd dead: the army breaking,
My husband hies him home; where, Heaven aiding,
And by the leave of my good lord the king,
We'll be before our welcome.

Wid.   Gentle madam,
You never had a servant, to whose trust

Your business was more welcome.
    Hel.   Nor you, mistress,
Ever a friend, whose thoughts more truly labour
To recompense your love.   Doubt not, but Heaven
Hath brought me up to be your daughter's dower,
As it hath fated her to be my motive
And helper to a husband.   But, O strange men
That can such sweet use make of what they hate,
When saucy trusting of the cozened thoughts
Defiles the pitchy night!   So lust doth play
With what it loathes, for that which is away.
But more of this hereafter.—You, Diana,
Under my poor instructions, yet must suffer
Something in my behalf.
    Dia.   Let death and honesty
Go with your impositions, I am yours
Upon your will to suffer.
    Hel.   Yet, I pray you:
But with the word, the time will bring on summer,
When briars shall have leaves as well as thorns,
And be as sweet as sharp.   We must away;
Our waggon is prepared, and time revives us:
All's well that ends well: still the fine's the crown;
Whate'er the course, the end is the renown.   [*Exeunt*

SCENE V.—Rousillon. A Room in the COUNTESS's
Palace

Enter COUNTESS, LAFEU, *and Clown*

    Laf. No, no, no; your son was misled with a snipt-
taffeta fellow there, whose villainous saffron would have
made all the unbaked and doughy youth of a nation in his
colour: your daughter-in-law had been alive at this hour,
and your son here at home, more advanced by the king
than by that red-tailed humble-bee I speak of.
    Count. I would I had not known him. It was the death
of the most virtuous gentlewoman that ever Nature had
praise for creating: if she had partaken of my flesh, and
cost me the dearest groans of a mother, I could not have
owed her a more rooted love.
    Laf. 'T was a good lady, 't was a good lady: we may
pick a thousand salads, ere we light on such another herb.
    Clo. Indeed, sir, she was the sweet-marjoram of the
salad, or rather the herb of grace.
    Laf. They are not salad-herbs, you knave; they are
nose-herbs.
    Clo. I am no great Nebuchadnezzar, sir; I have not
much skill in grass.

63

Laf. Whether dost thou profess thyself, a knave or a fool?

Clo. A fool, sir, at a woman's service, and a knave at a man's.

Laf. Your distinction?

Clo. I would cozen the man of his wife, and do his service.

Laf. So you were a knave at his service, indeed.

Clo. And I would give his wife my bauble, sir, to do her service.

Laf. I will subscribe for thee, thou art both knave and fool.

Clo. At your service.

Laf. No, no, no.

Clo. Why, sir, if I cannot serve you, I can serve as great a prince as you are.

Laf. Who's that? a Frenchman?

Clo. 'Faith, sir, 'a has an English name; but his phisnomy is more hotter in France than there.

Laf. What prince is that?

Clo. The black prince, sir; *alias*, the prince of darkness; *alias*, the devil.

Laf. Hold thee, there's my purse. I give thee not this to suggest thee from thy master thou talkest of: serve him still.

Clo. I am a woodland fellow, sir, that always loved a great fire; and the master I speak of ever keeps a good fire. But, sure, he is the prince of the world; let his nobility remain in's court. I am for the house with the narrow gate, which I take to be too little for pomp to enter: some, that humble themselves, may; but the many will be too chill and tender, and they'll be for the flowery way, that leads to the broad gate and the great fire.

Laf. Go thy ways, I begin to be aweary of thee; and I tell thee so before, because I would not fall out with thee. Go thy ways: let my horses be well looked to, without any tricks.

Clo. If I put any tricks upon 'em, sir, they shall be jades' tricks, which are their own right by the law of nature.   [*Exit*

Laf. A shrewd knave, and an unhappy.

Count. So he is. My lord, that's gone, made himself much sport out of him: by his authority he remains here, which he thinks is a patent for his sauciness; and, indeed, he has no pace, but runs where he will.

Laf. I like him well; 't is not amiss. And I was about to tell you, since I heard of the good lady's death, and that my lord your son was upon his return home, I moved the king, my master, to speak in the behalf of my daughter;

which, in the minority of them both, his majesty, out of a self-gracious remembrance, did first propose. His highness hath promised me to do it; and to stop up the displeasure he hath conceived against your son, there is no fitter matter. How does your ladyship like it?

Count. With very much content, my lord; and I wish it happily effected.

Laf. His highness comes post from Marseilles, of as able body as when he numbered thirty: he will be here to-morrow, or I am deceived by him that in such intelligence hath seldom failed.

Count. It rejoices me that I hope I shall see him ere I die. I have letters that my son will be here to-night: I shall beseech your lordship to remain with me till they meet together.

Laf. Madam, I was thinking with what manners I might safely be admitted.

Count. You need but plead your honourable privilege.

Laf. Lady, of that I have made a bold charter; but, I thank my God, it holds yet.

Re-enter Clown

Clo. O madam! yonder's my lord your son with a patch of velvet on's face: whether there be a scar under it or no, the velvet knows; but't is a goodly patch of velvet. His left cheek is a cheek of two pile and a half, but his right cheek is worn bare.

Laf. A scar nobly got, or a noble scar, is a good livery of honour; so, belike, is that.

Clo. But it is your carbonadoed face.

Laf. Let us go see your son, I pray you; I long to talk with the young noble soldier.

Clo. 'Faith, there's a dozen of 'em, with delicate fine hats, and most courteous feathers which bow the head and nod at every man.   [*Exeunt*

ACT FIVE

SCENE I.—Marseilles.   A Street

Enter HELENA, *Widow, and* DIANA, *with two Attendants*

Hel.   But this exceeding posting, day and night,
Must wear your spirits low: we cannot help it;
But, since you have made the days and nights as one,
To wear your gentle limbs in my affairs,
Be bold you do so grow in my requital
As nothing can uproot you.   In happy time;

65

Enter a Gentleman

This man may help me to his majesty's ear,
If he would spend his power.—God save you, sir.
   Gent. And you.
   Hel. Sir, I have seen you in the court of France.
   Gent. I have been sometimes there.
   Hel. I do presume, sir, that you are not fallen
From the report that goes upon your goodness;
And therefore, goaded with most sharp occasions
Which lay nice manners by, I put you to
The use of your own virtues, for the which
I shall continue thankful.
   Gent.   What's your will?
   Hel. That it will please you
To give this poor petition to the king,
And aid me, with that store of power you have,
To come into his presence.
   Gent. The king's not here.
   Hel.   Not here, sir?
   Gent.   Not, indeed:
He hence removed last night, and with more haste
Than is his use.
   Wid.   Lord, how we lose our pains!
   Hel. All's well that ends well yet,
Though time seem so adverse, and means unfit.—
I do beseech you, whither is he gone?
   Gent. Marry, as I take it, to Rousillon;
Whither I am going.
   Hel.   I do beseech you, sir,
Since you are like to see the king before me,
Commend the paper to his gracious hand;
Which, I presume, shall render you no blame,
But rather make you thank your pains for it.
I will come after you, with what good speed
Our means will make us means.
   Gent.   This I'll do for you.
   Hel. And you shall find yourself to be well thanked,
Whate'er falls more.—We must to horse again:—
Go, go, provide.   *[Exeunt*

SCENE II.—Rousillon. The Inner Court of the
COUNTESS's Palace

Enter Clown and PAROLLES

   Par. Good Monsieur Lavatch, give my Lord Lafeu
this letter. I have ere now, sir, been better known to you,
when I have held familiarity with fresher clothes; but

66

I am now, sir, muddied in Fortune's mood, and smell some-
what strong of her strong displeasure.

Clo. Truly, Fortune's displeasure is but sluttish; if it
smell so strongly as thou speakest of, I will henceforth
eat no fish of Fortune's buttering. Pr'ythee, allow the
wind.

Par. Nay, you need not to stop your nose, sir: I spake
but by a metaphor.

Clo. Indeed, sir, if your metaphor stink, I will stop my
nose; or against any man's metaphor. Pr'ythee, get
thee further.

Par. Pray you, sir, deliver me this paper.

Clo. Foh! pr'ythee, stand away: a paper from
Fortune's close-stool to give to a nobleman! Look, here
he comes himself.

Enter LAFEU

Here is a pur of Fortune's, sir, or of Fortune's cat (but
not a musk-cat), that has fallen into the unclean fishpond
of her displeasure, and, as he says, is muddied withal.
Pray you, sir, use the carp as you may, for he looks like a
poor, decayed, ingenious, foolish, rascally knave. I do
pity his distress in my smiles of comfort, and leave him to
your lordship.   [*Exit*

Par. My lord, I am a man whom Fortune hath cruelly
scratched.

Laf. And what would you have me to do? 'T is too
late to pare her nails now. Wherein have you played the
knave with Fortune, that she should scratch you, who of
herself is a good lady and would not have knaves thrive
long under her? There's a cardecue for you. Let the
justices make you and Fortune friends; I am for other
business.

Par. I beseech your honour to hear me one single word.

Laf. You beg a single penny more: come, you shall
ha''t; save your word.

Par. My name, my good lord, is Parolles.

Laf. You beg more than one word then,—Cox my
passion! give me your hand.—How does your drum?

Par. O my good lord! you were the first that found
me.

Laf. Was I, in sooth? and I was the first that lost
thee.

Par. It lies in you, my lord, to bring me in some grace,
for you did bring me out.

Laf. Out upon thee, knave! dost thou put upon me
at once both the office of God and the devil? one brings
thee in grace, and the other brings thee out. [*Trumpets
sound*] The king's coming; I know by his trumpets.—
Sirrah, inquire further after me: I had talk of you last

night. Though you are a fool and a knave, you shall eat:
go to, follow.
Par. I praise God for you.   [*Exeunt*

SCENE III.—The Same. A Room in the COUNTESS's
Palace

Flourish. Enter KING, COUNTESS, LAFEU, *Lords,
Gentlemen, Guards, etc.*

King. We lost a jewel of her, and our esteem
Was made much poorer by it: but your son,
As mad in folly, lacked the sense to know
Her estimation home.
Count.   'T is past, my liege;
And I beseech your majesty to make it
Natural rebellion, done i' the blaze of youth,
When oil and fire too strong for reason's force
O'erbears it and burns on.
King.   My honoured lady,
I have forgiven and forgotten all,
Though my revenges were high bent upon him,
And watched the time to shoot.
Laf.   This I must say,—
But first I beg my pardon,—the young lord
Did to his majesty, his mother, and his lady,
Offence of mighty note, but to himself
The greatest wrong of all: he lost a wife,
Whose beauty did astonish the survey
Of richest eyes; whose words all ears took captive;
Whose dear perfection hearts that scorned to serve
Humbly called mistress.
King.   Praising what is lost
Makes the remembrance dear.—Well, call him hither.
We are reconciled, and the first view shall kill
All repetition.—Let him not ask our pardon:
The nature of his great offence is dead,
And deeper than oblivion we do bury
The incensing relics of it: let him approach,
A stranger, no offender; and inform him,
So 't is our will he should.
Gent.   I shall, my liege.   [*Exit*
King. What says he to your daughter? have you
    spoke?
Laf. All that he is hath reference to your highness.
King. Then shall we have a match. I have letters
    sent me
That set him high in fame.

Enter BERTRAM

Laf.   He looks well on't.
  King.   I am not a day of season,
For thou may'st see a sunshine and a hail
In me at once; but to the brightest beams
Distracted clouds give way: so stand thou forth;
The time is fair again.
  Ber.   My high-repented blames,
Dear sovereign, pardon to me.
  King.   All is whole;
Not one word more of the consuméd time.
Let's take the instant by the forward top,
For we are old, and on our quick'st decrees
The inaudible and noiseless foot of Time
Steals ere we can effect them.   You remember
The daughter of this lord?
  Ber.   Admiringly, my liege.
I stuck my choice upon her, ere my heart
Durst make too bold a herald of my tongue:
Where the impression of mine eye infixing,
Contempt his scornful perspective did lend me
Which warped the line of every other favour,
Scorned a fair colour, or expressed it stolen,
Extended or contracted all proportions
To a most hideous object.   Thence it came,
That she whom all men praised and whom myself,
Since I have lost, have loved, was in mine eye
The dust that did offend it.
  King.   Well excused:
That thou didst love her, strikes some scores away
From the great compt.   But love that comes too late,
Like a remorseful pardon slowly carried,
To the great sender turns a sour offence,
Crying, 'That's good that's gone.'   Our rasher faults
Make trivial price of serious things we have,
Not knowing them until we know their grave:
Oft our displeasures, to ourselves unjust,
Destroy our friends and after weep their dust:
Our own love, waking, cries to see what's done,
While shameful hate sleeps out the afternoon.
Be this sweet Helen's knell, and now forget her.
Send forth your amorous token for fair Maudlin:
The main consents are had; and here we'll stay
To see our widower's second marriage to-day.
  Count.   Which better than the first, O dear Heaven,
                                              bless!
Or, ere they meet, in me, O Nature, cess!
  Laf.   Come on, my son, in whom my house's name
Must be digested, give a favour from you,

To sparkle in the spirits of my daughter,
That she may quickly come.   [*Bertram gives a ring*]
          —By my old beard,
And every hair that's on't, Helen, that's dead,
Was a sweet creature; such a ring as this,
The last that e'er I took her leave at court,
I saw upon her finger.

Ber.   Hers it was not.

King. Now, pray you, let me see it; for mine eye,
While I was speaking, oft was fastened to't.—
This ring was mine; and, when I gave it Helen,
I bade her, if her fortunes ever stood
Necessitied to help, that by this token
I would relieve her. Had you that craft to reave her
Of what should stead her most?

Ber.   My gracious sovereign,
Howe'er it pleases you to take it so,
The ring was never hers.

Count.   Son, on my life,
I have seen her wear it; and she reckoned it
At her life's rate.

Laf.   I am sure I saw her wear it.

Ber. You are deceived: my lord, she never saw it.
In Florence was it from a casement thrown me,
Wrapped in a paper, which contained the name
Of her that threw it. Noble she was, and thought
I stood ingaged: but when I had subscribed
To mine own fortune, and informed her fully,
I could not answer in that course of honour
As she had made the overture, she ceased,
In heavy satisfaction, and would never
Receive the ring again.

King.   Plutus himself,
That knows the tinct and multiplying medicine,
Hath not in nature's mystery more science
Than I have in this ring: 't was mine, 't was Helen's,
Whoever gave it you. Then, if you know
That you are well acquainted with yourself,
Confess 't was hers, and by what rough enforcement
You got it from her. She called the saints to surety,
That she would never put it from her finger,
Unless she gave it to yourself in bed,
Where you have never come, or sent it us
Upon her great disaster.

Ber.   She never saw it.

King. Thou speak'st it falsely, as I love mine honour,
And mak'st conjectural fears to come into me,
Which I would fain shut out. If it should prove
That thou art so inhuman,—'t will not prove so;—
And yet I know not:—thou didst hate her deadly,

And she is dead; which nothing, but to close
Her eyes myself, could win me to believe
More than to see this ring.—Take him away.—

                        [Guards seize Bertram

My fore-past proofs, how'er the matter fall,
Shall tax my fears of little vanity,
Having vainly feared too little.—Away with him!
We'll sift this matter further.
   Ber.   If you shall prove
This ring was ever hers, you shall as easy
Prove that I husbanded her bed in Florence,
Where yet she never was.   *[Exit, guarded*

Enter a Gentleman

   King.   I am wrapped in dismal thinkings.
   Gent.   Gracious sovereign,
Whether I have been to blame, or no, I know not:
Here's a petition from a Florentine
Who hath, for four or five removes, come short
To tender it herself.   I undertook it,
Vanquished thereto by the fair grace and speech
Of the poor suppliant, who by this, I know,
Is here attending: her business looks in her
With an importing visage, and she told me,
In a sweet verbal brief, it did concern
Your highness with herself.
   King.   [*Reads*]   ' *Upon his many protestations to marry
me, when his wife was dead, I blush to say it, he won me.
Now is the Count Rousillon a widower: his vows are for-
feited to me, and my honour's paid to him. He stole from
Florence, taking no leave, and I follow him to his country
for justice. Grant it me, O king! in you it best lies: other-
wise a seducer flourishes, and a poor maid is undone.*
                           DIANA CAPILET.'
   Laf.   I will buy me a son-in-law in a fair, and toll: for
this, I'll none of him.
   King.   The heavens have thought well on thee, Lafeu,
To bring forth this discovery.—Seek these suitors:—
Go speedily, and bring again the count.
             [Exeunt Gentleman and some Attendants
I am feared, the life of Helen, lady,
Was foully snatched.
   Count.   Now, justice on the doers!

Re-enter BERTRAM, *guarded*

   King.   I wonder, sir, sith wives are monsters to you,
And that you fly them as you swear them lordship,
Yet you desire to marry.—

Re-enter Gentleman, with Widow and DIANA

                               What woman's that?

    Dia.   I am, my lord, a wretched Florentine,
Derivéd from the ancient Capilet:
My suit, as I do understand, you know,
And therefore know how far I may be pitied.

    Wid.   I am her mother, sir, whose age and honour
Both suffer under this complaint we bring,
And both shall cease, without your remedy.

    King.   Come hither, count. Do you know these
           women?

    Ber.   My lord, I neither can nor will deny
But that I know them. Do they charge me further?

    Dia.   Why do you look so strange upon your wife?

    Ber.   She's none of mine, my lord.

    Dia.   If you shall marry,
You give away this hand, and that is mine;
You give away heaven's vows, and those are mine;
You give away myself, which is known mine;
For I by vow am so embodied yours,
That she which marries you must marry me;
Either both, or none.

    Laf.   [*To Bertram*] Your reputation comes too short
for my daughter: you are no husband for her.

    Ber.   My lord, this is a fond and desperate creature,
Whom sometime I have laughed with. Let your highness
Lay a more noble thought upon mine honour
Than for to think that I would sink it here.

    King.   Sir, for my thoughts, you have them ill to friend
Till your deeds gain them; fairer prove your honour
Than in my thought it lies.

    Dia.   Good my lord,
Ask him upon his oath, if he does think
He had not my virginity.

    King.   What say'st thou to her?

    Ber.   She's impudent, my lord;
And was a common gamester to the camp.

    Dia.   He does me wrong, my lord: if I were so,
He might have bought me at a common price:
Do not believe him. O, behold this ring,
Whose high respect, and rich validity,
Did lack a parallel; yet, for all that,
He gave it to a commoner o' the camp,
If I be one.

    Count.   He blushes, and 't is it:
Of six preceding ancestors, that gem
Conferred by testament to the sequent issue,
Hath it been owed and worn. This is his wife:
That ring's a thousand proofs.

King.   Methought, you said,
You saw one here in court could witness it.
    Dia.   I did, my lord, but loath am to produce
So bad an instrument: his name's Parolles.
    Laf.   I saw the man to-day, if man he be.
    King.   Find him, and bring him hither.
                                   [*Exit an Attendant*
    Ber.   What of him?
He's quoted for a most perfidious slave,
With all the spots o' the world taxed and deboshed,
Whose nature sickens but to speak a truth.
Am I or that or this for what he'll utter,
That will speak anything?
    King.   She hath that ring of yours.
    Ber.   I think, she has: certain it is, I liked her
And boarded her i' the wanton way of youth.
She knew her distance, and did angle for me,
Madding my eagerness with her restraint,
As all impediments in fancy's course
Are motives of more fancy; and, in fine,
Her infinite cunning, with her modern grace,
Subdued me to her rate: she got the ring,
And I had that which any inferior might
At market-price have bought.
    Dia.   I must be patient;
You, that turned off a first so noble wife,
May justly diet me. I pray you yet,—
Since you lack virtue, I will lose a husband,—
Send for your ring; I will return it home,
And give me mine again.
    Ber.   I have it not.
    King.   What ring was yours, I pray you?
    Dia.   Sir, much like
The same upon your finger.
    King.   Know you this ring? this ring was his of late.
    Dia.   And this was it I gave him, being a-bed.
    King.   The story then goes false, you threw it him
Out of a casement.
    Dia.   I have spoken the truth.

Re-enter Attendant with PAROLLES

    Ber.   My lord, I do confess, the ring was hers.
    King.   You boggle shrewdly, every feather starts you.—
Is this the man you speak of?
    Dia.   Ay, my lord.
    King.   Tell me, sirrah, but tell me true, I charge you,
Not fearing the displeasure of your master—
Which, on your just proceeding, I'll keep off—
By him and by this woman here, what know you?

Par. So please your majesty, my master hath been
an honourable gentleman: tricks he hath had in him,
which gentleman have.

King. Come, come, to the purpose. Did he love this
woman?

Par. Faith, sir, he did love her; but how?

King. How, I pray you?

Par. He did love her, sir, as a gentleman loves a woman.

King. How is that?

Par. He loved her, sir, and loved her not.

King. As thou art a knave, and no knave. What an
equivocal companion is this!

Par. I am a poor man, and at your majesty's command.

Laf. He's a good drum, my lord, but a naughty orator.

Dia. Do you know, he promised me marriage?

Par. Faith, I know more than I'll speak.

King. But wilt thou not speak all thou know'st?

Par. Yes, so please your majesty. I did go between
them, as I said; but more than that, he loved her,—for,
indeed, he was mad for her, and talked of Satan, and of
limbo, and of Furies, and I know not what: yet I was
in that credit with them at that time, that I knew of their
going to bed, and of other motions, as promising her
marriage, and things that would derive me ill will to speak
of: therefore, I will not speak what I know.

King. Thou hast spoken all already, unless thou canst
say they are married. But thou art too fine in thy
evidence; therefore, stand aside.—
This ring, you say, was yours?

Dia.   Ay, my good lord.

King. Where did you buy it? or who gave it you?

Dia. It was not given me, nor I did not buy it.

King. Who lent it you?

Dia.   It was not lent me neither.

King. Where did you find it then?

Dia.   I found it not.

King. If it were yours by none of all these ways,
How could you give it him?

Dia.   I never gave it him.

Laf. This woman's an easy glove, my lord: she goes
off and on at pleasure.

King. This ring was mine: I gave it his first wife.

Dia. It might be yours or hers, for aught I know.

King. Take her away: I do not like her now.
To prison with her; and away with him.—
Unless thou tell'st me where thou hadst this ring
Thou diest within this hour.

Dia.   I'll never tell you.

King. Take her away.

Dia.   I'll put in bail, my liege.

King. I think thee now some common customer.
Dia. By Jove, if ever I knew man, 't was you.
King. Wherefore hast thou accused him all this while?
Dia. Because he's guilty, and he is not guilty.
He knows I am no maid, and he'll swear to 't:
I'll swear I am a maid, and he knows not.
Great king, I am no strumpet, by my life!
I am either maid, or else this old man's wife.
                              [*Pointing to Lafeu*
King. She does abuse our ears. To prison with her!
Dia. Good mother, fetch my bail.   [*Exit Widow*
—Stay, royal sir:
The jeweller that owes the ring is sent for,
And he shall surety me. But for this lord,
Who hath abused me, as he knows himself,
Though yet he never harmed me, here I quit him.
He knows himself my bed he hath defiled
And at that time he got his wife with child:
Dead though she be, she feels her young one kick.
So there's my riddle,—one that's dead is quick;
And now behold the meaning.

Re-enter Widow, with HELENA

King.   Is there no exorcist
Beguiles the truer office of mine eyes?
Is't real, that I see?
Hel.   No, my good lord;
'T is but the shadow of a wife you see;
The name, and not the thing.
Ber.   Both, both! O, pardon!
Hel. O my good lord, when I was like this maid,
I found you wondrous kind. There is your ring;
And, look you, here's your letter; this it says:
"When from my finger you can get this ring,
And are by me with child," etc.—This is done.
Will you be mine, now you are doubly won?
Ber. If she, my liege, can make me know this clearly,
I'll love her dearly, ever, ever dearly.
Hel. If it appear not plain, and prove untrue,
Deadly divorce step between me and you!—
O my dear mother, do I see you living?
Laf. Mine eyes smell onions, I shall weep anon.—
[*To* PAROLLES] Good Tom Drum, lend me a handker-
chief: so, I thank thee. Wait on me home, I'll make sport
with thee: let thy courtesies alone, they are scurvy ones.
King. Let us from point to point this story know,
To make the even truth in pleasure flow.
[*To* DIANA] If thou be'st yet a fresh uncropped flower,
Choose thou thy husband, and I'll pay thy dower;

For I can guess, that by thy honest aid
Thou kept'st a wife herself, thyself a maid.—
Of that, and all the progress, more and less,
Resolvedly more leisure shall express:
All yet seems well; and if it end so meet,
The bitter past, more welcome is the sweet.   [*Flourish*

EPILOGUE

King.   The king's a beggar now the play is done.
All is well ended, if this suit be won—
That you express content; which we will pay
With strife to please you, day exceeding day:
Ours be your patience then, and yours our parts;
Your gentle hands lend us, and take our hearts. [*Exeunt*

ANTONY AND CLEOPATRA

DRAMATIS PERSONÆ

MARK ANTONY
OCTAVIUS CÆSAR } *triumvirs*
M. ÆMIL. LEPIDUS

SEXTUS POMPEIUS

DOMITIUS ENOBARBUS
VENTIDIUS
EROS
SCARUS } *friends of Antony*
DEBCETAS
DEMETRIUS
PHILO

MECÆNAS
AGRIPPA
DOLABELLA
PROCULEIUS } *friends of Cæsar*
THYREUS
GALLUS

MENAS
MENECRATES } *friends of Pompey*
VARRIUS

TAURUS, *lieutenant-general to Cæsar*
CANIDIUS, *lieutenant-general to Antony*
SILIUS, *an officer under Ventidius*
EUPHRONIUS, *an ambassador from Antony to Cæsar*
ALEXAS, MARDIAN, SELEUCUS, *and* DIOMEDES, *attendants on Cleopatra*

A Soothsayer, A Clown
CLEOPATRA, *queen of Egypt*
OCTAVIA, *sister to Cæsar, and wife to Antony*
CHARMIAN *and* IRAS, *attendants on Cleopatra*

Officers, Soldiers, Messengers, and other Attendants

SCENE—*In several Parts of the Roman Empire*

78

ANTONY AND CLEOPATRA

ACT ONE

SCENE I.—Alexandria. A Room in CLEOPATRA'S Palace.

Enter DEMETRIUS *and* PHILO

Phi. Nay, but this dotage of our general's
O'erflows the measure: those his goodly eyes,
That o'er the files and musters of the war
Have glowed like plated Mars', now bend, now turn
The office and devotion of their view
Upon a tawny front: his captain's heart,
Which in the scuffles of great fights hath burst
The buckles on his breast, renegades all temper,
And is become the bellows and the fan
To cool a gipsy's lust. Look where they come.

Flourish. Enter ANTONY *and* CLEOPATRA, *with their Train;
Eunuchs fanning her*

Take but good note, and you shall see in him
The triple pillar of the world transformed
Into a strumpet's fool: behold and see.
  Cleo. If it be love indeed, tell me how much.
  Ant. There's beggary in the love that can be reckoned.
  Cleo. I'll set a bourn how far to be beloved.
  Ant. Then must thou needs find out new heaven, new
    earth.

Enter an Attendant

  Att. News, my good lord, from Rome.
  Ant.   Grates me:—the sum.
  Cleo. Nay, hear them, Antony:
Fulvia, perchance, is angry; or, who knows
If the scarce-bearded Cæsar have not sent
His powerful mandate to you, 'Do this, or this;
Take in that kingdom, and enfranchise that;
Perform't, or else we damn thee.'
  Ant.   How, my love!
  Cleo. Perchance,—nay, and most like,—
You must not stay here longer, your dismission

Is come from Cæsar; therefore hear it, Antony.—
Where's Fulvia's process? Cæsar's, I would say? both?—
Call in the messengers.—As I am Egypt's queen,
Thou blushest, Antony, and that blood of thine
Is Cæsar's homager; else so thy cheek pays shame
When shrill-tongued Fulvia scolds.—The messengers!
   Ant. Let Rome in Tiber melt, and the wide arch
Of the ranged empire fall! Here is my space.
Kingdoms are clay: our dungy earth alike
Feeds beast as man: the nobleness of life
Is to do thus; when such a mutual pair   [*Embracing*
And such a twain can do't, in which I bind,
On pain of punishment, the world to weet
We stand up peerless.
   Cleo.   Excellent falsehood!
Why did he marry Fulvia, and not love her?—
I'll seem the fool I am not; Antony
Will be himself.
   Ant.   But stirred by Cleopatra.—
Now, for the love of Love and her soft hours,
Let's not confound the time with conference harsh:
There's not a minute of our lives should stretch
Without some pleasure now:—what sport to-night?
   Cleo. Hear the ambassadors.
   Ant.   Fie, wrangling queen!
Whom everything becomes,—to chide, to laugh,
To weep; whose every passion fully strives
To make itself, in thee, fair and admired!
No messenger but thine; and all alone,
To-night we'll wander through the streets, and note
The qualities of people. Come, my queen;
Last night you did desire it.—Speak not to us.
       [*Exeunt Antony and Cleopatra, with their Train*
   Dem. Is Cæsar with Antonius prized so slight?
   Phi. Sir, sometimes, when he is not Antony,
He comes too short of that great property
Which still should go with Antony.
   Dem.   I am full sorry,
That he approves the common liar, who
Thus speaks of him at Rome; but I will hope
Of better deeds to-morrow. Rest you happy!   [*Exeunt*

SCENE II.—Alexandria. Another Room in CLEOPATRA'S Palace

Enter CHARMIAN, IRAS, ALEXAS, *and a Soothsayer*

   Char. Lord Alexas, sweet Alexas, most anything Alexas, almost most absolute Alexas, where's the sooth-

sayer that you praised so to the queen?   O, that I knew
this husband, which, you say, must charge his horns with
garlands!

Alex.   Soothsayer!
Sooth.   Your will?
Char.   Is this the man?—Is't you, sir, that know
things?
Sooth.   In nature's infinite book of secrecy
A little I can read.
Alex.   Show him your hand.

Enter ENOBARBUS

Eno.   Bring in the banquet quickly; wine enough
Cleopatra's health to drink.
Char.   Good sir, give me good fortune.
Sooth.   I make not, but foresee.
Char.   Pray then, foresee me one.
Sooth.   You shall be yet far fairer than you are.
Char.   He means in flesh.
Iras.   No, you shall paint when you are old.
Char.   Wrinkles forbid!
Alex.   Vex not his prescience; be attentive.
Char.   Hush!
Sooth.   You shall be more beloving, than beloved.
Char.   I had rather heat my liver with drinking.
Alex.   Nay, hear him.
Char.   Good now, some excellent fortune!   Let me be
married to three kings in a forenoon, and widow them all:
let me have a child at fifty, to whom Herod of Jewry may
do homage; find me to marry me with Octavius Cæsar,
and companion me with my mistress.
Sooth.   You shall outlive the lady whom you serve.
Char.   O excellent!   I love long life better than figs.
Sooth.   You have seen and proved a fairer former fortune
Than that which is to approach.
Char.   Then, belike, my children shall have no names:—
pr'ythee, how many boys and wenches must I have?
Sooth.   If every of your wishes had a womb,
And fertile every wish, a million.
Char.   Out, fool!   I forgive thee for a witch.
Alex.   You think none but your sheets are privy to your
wishes.
Char.   Nay, come, tell Iras hers.
Alex.   We'll know all our fortunes.
Eno.   Mine, and most of our fortunes, to-night, shall
be—drunk to bed.
Iras.   There's a palm presages chastity, if nothing else.
Char.   Even as the o'erflowing Nilus presageth famine.
Iras.   Go, you wild bedfellow, you cannot soothsay.

Char. Nay, if an oily palm be not a fruitful prognosti-
cation, I cannot scratch mine ear.—Pr'ythee, tell her but
a worky-day fortune.
Sooth. Your fortunes are alike.
Iras. But how? but how? give me particulars.
Sooth. I have said.
Iras. Am I not an inch of fortune better than she?
Char. Well, if you were but an inch of fortune better
than I, where would you choose it?
Iras. Not in my husband's nose.
Char. Our worser thoughts heavens mend! Alexas,—
come, his fortune, his fortune!—O, let him marry a woman
that cannot go, sweet Isis, I beseech thee; and let her die
too, and give him a worse; and let worse follow worse,
till the worst of all follow him laughing to his grave, fifty-
fold a cuckold! Good Isis, hear me this prayer, though
thou deny me a matter of more weight; good Isis, I
beseech thee!
Iras. Amen. Dear goddess, hear that prayer of the
people; for, as it is a heart-breaking to see a handsome
man loose-wived, so it is a deadly sorrow to behold a foul
knave uncuckolded: therefore, dear Isis, keep decorum,
and fortune him accordingly!
Char. Amen.
Alex. Lo, now, if it lay in their hands to make me a
cuckold, they would make themselves whores but they'd
do't.
Eno. Hush! here comes Antony.
Char.   Not he; the queen.

Enter CLEOPATRA

Cleo. Saw you my lord?
Eno. No, lady.
Cleo. Was he not here?
Char. No, madam.
Cleo. He was disposed to mirth; but, on the sudden,
A Roman thought hath struck him.—Enobarbus,—
Eno. Madam?
Cleo. Seek him, and bring him hither.—Where's
          Alexas?
Alex. Here, at your service.—My lord approaches.
Cleo. We will not look upon him: go with us.
          [*Exeunt Cleopatra, Enobarbus, Alexas, Iras,*
                    Charmian, Soothsayer, and Attendants

Enter ANTONY, *with a Messenger and Attendants*

Mess. Fulvia thy wife first came into the field.
Ant. Against my brother Lucius?
Mess. Ay:

But soon that war had end, and the time's state
Made friends of them, jointing their force 'gainst Cæsar;
Whose better issue in the war, from Italy,
Upon the first encounter, drave them.
    Ant.   Well, what worst?
    Mess.   The nature of bad news infects the teller.
    Ant.   When it concerns the fool, or coward.—On:
Things, that are past, are done with me.—'T is thus:
Who tells me true, though in his tale lie death,
I hear him as he flattered.
    Mess.   Labienus—
This is stiff news—hath with his Parthian force
Extended Asia; from Euphrates
His conquering banner shook from Syria
To Lydia and to Ionia: whilst—
    Ant.   Antony, thou wouldst say,—
    Mess.   O, my lord!
    Ant.   Speak to me home, mince not the general tongue:
Name Cleopatra as she is called in Rome;
Rail thou in Fulvia's phrase; and taunt my faults
With such full license as both truth and malice
Have power to utter. O, then we bring forth weeds
When our quick minds lie still; and our ills told us
Is as our earing. Fare thee well awhile.
    Mess.   At your noble pleasure.   [*Exit*
    Ant.   From Sicyon, ho, the news! Speak there!
    First Att.   The man from Sicyon,—is there such an one?
    Sec. Att.   He stays upon your will.
    Ant.   Let him appear.—
These strong Egyptian fetters I must break,
Or lose myself in dotage.

              Enter another Messenger

                      What are you?
    Sec. Mess.   Fulvia thy wife is dead.
    Ant.   Where died she?
    Sec. Mess.   In Sicyon:
Her length of sickness, with what else more serious
Importeth thee to know, this bears.   [*Giving a letter*
    Ant.   Forbear me.—
                        [*Exit Messenger*
There's a great spirit gone! Thus did I desire it:
What our contempts do often hurl from us,
We wish it ours again; the present pleasure,
By revolution lowering, does become
The opposite of itself: she's good, being gone;
The hand could pluck her back, that shoved her on.
I must from this enchanting queen break off:
Ten thousand harms more than the ills I know,
My idleness doth hatch.—How now, Enobarbus!

Re-enter ENOBARBUS

Eno. What's your pleasure, sir?

Ant. I must with haste from hence.

Eno. Why, then, we kill all our women: we see how mortal an unkindness is to them; if they suffer our departure, death's the word.

Ant. I must be gone.

Eno. Under a compelling occasion, let women die: it were pity to cast them away for nothing; though, between them and a great cause, they should be esteemed nothing. Cleopatra, catching but the least noise of this, dies instantly: I have seen her die twenty times upon far poorer moment: I do think there is mettle in death which commits some loving act upon her, she hath such a celerity in dying.

Ant. She is cunning past man's thought.

Eno. Alack, sir, no; her passions are made of nothing but the finest part of pure love: we cannot call her winds and waters sighs and tears; they are greater storms and tempests than almanacs can report; this cannot be cunning in her; if it be, she makes a shower of rain as well as Jove.

Ant. 'Would I had never seen her!

Eno. O, sir, you had then left unseen a wonderful piece of work; which not to have been blessed withal would have discredited your travel.

Ant. Fulvia is dead.

Eno. Sir?

Ant. Fulvia is dead.

Eno. Fulvia!

Ant. Dead.

Eno. Why, sir, give the gods a thankful sacrifice. When it pleaseth their deities to take the wife of a man from him, it shows to man the tailors of the earth: comforting therein, that when old robes are worn out, there are members to make new. If there were no more women but Fulvia, then had you indeed a cut, and the case to be lamented: this grief is crowned with consolation; your old smock brings forth a new petticoat;—and, indeed, the tears live in an onion that should water this sorrow.

Ant. The business she hath broached in the state
Cannot endure my absence.

Eno. And the business you have broached here cannot be without you; especially that of Cleopatra's, which wholly depends on your abode.

Ant. No more light answers. Let our officers
Have notice what we purpose. I shall break
The cause of our expedience to the queen,
And get her love to part. For not alone
The death of Fulvia, with more urgent touches,

Do strongly speak to us; but the letters too
Of many our contriving friends in Rome
Petition us at home.   Sextus Pompeius
Hath given the dare to Cæsar, and commands
The empire of the sea: our slippery people—
Whose love is never linked to the deserver
Till his deserts are past—begin to throw
Pompey the Great and all his dignities
Upon his son, who, high in name and power,
Higher than both in blood and life, stands up
For the main soldier; whose quality, going on,
The sides o' the world may danger.   Much is breeding,
Which, like the courser's hair, hath yet but life,
And not a serpent's poison.   Say, our pleasure,
To such whose place is under us, requires
Our quick remove from hence.
    Eno.   I shall do it.   [*Exeunt*

Scene III.—Alexandria. Another Room in Cleopatra's Palace

Enter CLEOPATRA, CHARMIAN, IRAS, *and* ALEXAS

    Cleo.   Where is he?
    Char.   I did not see him since.
    Cleo.   See where he is, who's with him, what he does:—
I did not send you:—If you find him sad,
Say, I am dancing; if in mirth, report
That I am sudden sick: quick, and return.

                            [*Exit Alexas*
    Char.   Madam, methinks, if you did love him dearly,
You do not hold the method to enforce
The like from him.
    Cleo.   What should I do, I do not?
    Char.   In each thing give him way, cross him in nothing.
    Cleo.   Thou teachest like a fool the way to lose him.
    Char.   Tempt him not so too far; I wish, forbear:
In time we hate that which we often fear.
But here comes Antony.
    Cleo.   I'm sick and sullen.

Enter ANTONY

    Ant.   I am sorry to give breathing to my purpose.
    Cleo.   Help me away, dear Charmian; I shall fall:
It cannot be thus long, the sides of nature
Will not sustain it.
    Ant.   Now, my dearest queen,—
    Cleo.   Pray you, stand further from me.

Ant.   What's the matter?
Cleo.   I know, by that same eye, there's some good news.
What says the married woman?—You may go:
Would she had never given you leave to come!
Let her not say, 't is I that keep you here,—
I have no power upon you; hers you are.
    Ant.   The gods best know,—
    Cleo.   O, never was there queen
So mightily betrayed! yet at the first
I saw the treasons planted.
    Ant.   Cleopatra,—
    Cleo.   Why should I think you can be mine and true,
Though you in swearing shake the thronéd gods,
Who have been false to Fulvia?   Riotous madness,
To be entangled with those mouth-made vows
Which break themselves in swearing!
    Ant.   Most sweet queen,—
    Cleo.   Nay, pray you, seek no colour for your going,
But bid farewell, and go: when you sued staying,
Then was the time for words: no going then;—
Eternity was in our lips and eyes,
Bliss in our brows bent; none our parts so poor,
But was a race of heaven: they are so still,
Or thou, the greatest soldier of the world,
Art turned the greatest liar.
    Ant.   How now, lady!
    Cleo.   I would I had thy inches; thou shouldst know
There were a heart in Egypt.
    Ant.   Hear me, queen:
The strong necessity of time commands
Our services awhile; but my full heart
Remains in use with you.   Our Italy
Shines o'er with civil swords: Sextus Pompeius
Makes his approaches to the port of Rome:
Equality of two domestic powers
Breed scrupulous faction: the hated, grown to strength,
Are newly grown to love: the condemned Pompey,
Rich in his father's honour, creeps apace
Into the hearts of such as have not thrived
Upon the present state, whose numbers threaten;
And quietness, grown sick of rest, would purge
By any desperate change.   My more particular,
And that which most with you should safe my going,
Is Fulvia's death.
    Cleo.   Though age from folly could not give me freedom
It does from childishness:—can Fulvia die?
    Ant.   She's dead, my queen.
Look here, and, at thy sovereign leisure, read
The garboils she awakened; at the last, best,
See, when and where she died.

Cleo.   O most false love,
Where be the sacred vials thou shouldst fill
With sorrowful water?   Now I see, I see,
In Fulvia's death, how mine received shall be.
    Ant.   Quarrel no more, but be prepared to know
The purposes I bear; which are, or cease,
As you shall give the advice.   By the fire
That quickens Nilus' slime, I go from hence,
Thy soldier, servant; making peace or war
As thou affect'st.
    Cleo.   Cut my lace, Charmian, come;—
But let it be:—I am quickly ill, and well,
So Antony loves.
    Ant.   My precious queen, forbear;
And give true evidence to his love, which stands
An honourable trial.
    Cleo.   So Fulvia told me.
I pr'ythee, turn aside, and weep for her;
Then bid adieu to me, and say the tears
Belong to Egypt: good now, play one scene
Of excellent dissembling, and let it look
Like perfect honour.
    Ant.   You'll heat my blood: no more.
    Cleo.   You can do better yet; but this is meetly.
    Ant.   Now, by my sword,—
    Cleo.   And target.—Still he mends;
But this is not the best.   Look, pr'ythee, Charmian,
How this Herculean Roman does become
The carriage of his chafe.
    Ant.   I'll leave you, lady.
    Cleo.   Courteous lord, one word
Sir, you and I must part,—but that's not it:
Sir, you and I have loved,—but there's not it;
That you know well: something it is I would,—
O, my oblivion is a very Antony,
And I am all forgotten.
    Ant.   But that your royalty
Holds idleness your subject, I should take you
For idleness itself.
    Cleo.   'T is sweating labour
To bear such idleness so near the heart
As Cleopatra this.   But, sir, forgive me;
Since my becomings kill me, when they do not
Eye well to you: your honour calls you hence;
Therefore be deaf to my unpitied folly,
And all the gods go with you!   Upon your sword
Sit laurel victory, and smooth success
Be strewed before your feet!
    Ant.   Let us go.   Come;
Our separation so abides and flies,

That thou, residing here, go'st yet with me,
And I, hence fleeting, here remain with thee.
Away!   [*Exeunt*

SCENE IV.—Rome.   A Room in CÆSAR'S House

Enter OCTAVIUS CÆSAR, LEPIDUS, *and Attendants*

Cæs.   You may see, Lepidus, and henceforth know,
It is not Cæsar's natural wise to hate
Our great competitor.   From Alexandria
This is the news:—he fishes, drinks, and wastes
The lamps of night in revel;   is not more manlike
Than Cleopatra, nor the queen of Ptolemy
More womanly than he;   hardly gave audience, or
Vouchsafed to think he had partners: you shall find there
A man, who is the abstract of all faults
That all men follow.
Lep.   I must not think there are
Evils enow to darken all his goodness:
His faults, in him, seem as the spots of heaven,
More fiery by night's blackness;   hereditary,
Rather than purchased;   what he cannot change,
Than what he chooses.
Cæs.   You are too indulgent.   Let us grant, it is not
Amiss to tumble on the bed of Ptolemy;
To give a kingdom for a mirth;   to sit
And keep the turn of tippling with a slave;
To reel the streets at noon, and stand the buffet
With knaves that smell of sweat: say, this becomes him,—
As his composure must be rare indeed,
Whom these things cannot blemish,—yet must Antony
No way excuse his soils, when we do bear
So great weight in his lightness.   If he filled
His vacancy with his voluptuousness,
Full surfeits and the dryness of his bones
Call on him for't;   but, to confound such time
That drums him from his sport, and speaks as loud
As his own state and ours,—'t is to be chid
As we rate boys who, being mature in knowledge,
Pawn their experience to their present pleasure
And so rebel to judgment.

Enter a Messenger

Lep.   Here's more news.
Mess.   Thy biddings have been done;   and every hour,
Most noble Cæsar, shalt thou have report
How't is abroad.   Pompey is strong at sea;

And it appears, he is beloved of those
That only have feared Cæsar: to the ports
The discontents repair, and men's reports
Give him much wronged.
    Cæs.   I should have known no less.
It hath been taught us from the primal state,
That he which is was wished, until he were;
And the ebbed man ne'er loved till ne'er worth love,
Comes deared by being lacked. This common body,
Like to a vagabond flag upon the stream,
Goes to and back, lackeying the varying tide,
To rot itself with motion.
    Mess.   Cæsar, I bring thee word,
Menecrates and Menas, famous pirates,
Make the sea serve them, which they ear and wound
With keels of every kind: many hot inroads
They make in Italy; the borders maritime
Lack blood to think on't, and flush youth revolt:
No vessel can peep forth, but't is as soon
Taken as seen; for Pompey's name strikes more
Than could his war resisted.
    Cæs.   Antony,
Leave thy lascivious wassails. When thou once
Wast beaten from Modena, where thou slew'st
Hirtius and Pansa, consuls, at thy heel
Did famine follow; whom thou fought'st against,
Though daintily brought up, with patience more
Than savages could suffer: thou didst drink
The stale of horses, and the gilded puddle
Which beasts would cough at: thy palate then did deign
The roughest berry on the rudest hedge;
Yea, like the stag, when snow the pasture sheets,
The barks of trees thou browsed'st; on the Alps,
It is reported thou didst eat strange flesh,
Which some did die to look on; and all this—
It wounds thine honour, that I speak it now—
Was borne so like a soldier, that thy cheek
So much as lanked not.
    Lep.   'T is pity of him.
    Cæs.   Let his shames quickly
Drive him to Rome: 't is time we twain
Did show ourselves i' the field; and, to that end,
Assemble we immediate council: Pompey
Thrives in our idleness.
    Lep.   To-morrow, Cæsar,
I shall be furnished to inform you rightly
Both what by sea and land I can be able
To front this present time.
    Cæs.   Till which encounter,
It is my business too. Farewell.

Lep.   Farewell, my lord.   What you shall know mean-
time
Of stirs abroad, I shall beseech you, sir,
To let me be partaker.
   Cæs.   Doubt not, sir;
I knew it for my bond.   [*Exeunt*

SCENE V.—Alexandria.   A room in CLEOPATRA's Palace

Enter CLEOPATRA, CHARMIAN, IRAS, *and* MARDIAN

   Cleo.   Charmian,—
   Char.   Madam?
   Cleo.   Ha, ha!—
Give me to drink mandragora.
   Char.   Why, madam?
   Cleo.   That I might sleep out this great gap of time,
My Antony is away.
   Char.   You think of him too much.
   Cleo.   O, 't is treason!
   Char.   Madam, I trust, not so.
   Cleo.   Thou, eunuch Mardian!
   Mar.   What's your highness' pleasure?
   Cleo.   Not now to hear thee sing; I take no pleasure
In aught an eunuch has.   'T is well for thee,
That, being unseminar'd, thy freer thoughts
May not fly forth of Egypt.   Hast thou affections?
   Mar.   Yes, gracious madam.
   Cleo.   Indeed?
   Mar.   Not in deed, madam; for I can do nothing,
But what indeed is honest to be done;
Yet have I fierce affections, and think,
What Venus did with Mars.
   Cleo.   O Charmian!
Where think'st thou he is now?   Stands he, or sits he?
Or does he walk?   or is he on his horse?
O happy horse, to bear the weight of Antony!
Do bravely, horse, for wott'st thou whom thou mov'st?
The demi-Atlas of this earth, the arm
And burgonet of men.—He's speaking now,
Or murmuring, 'Where's my serpent of old Nile?'
For so he calls me.   Now I feed myself
With most delicious poison.—Think on me,
That am with Phœbus' amorous pinches black,
And wrinkled deep in time?   Broad-fronted Cæsar,
When thou wast here above the ground, I was
A morsel for a monarch; and great Pompey
Would stand, and make his eyes grow in my brow;
There would he anchor his aspéct and die
With looking on his life.

Enter ALEXAS

Alex.   Sovereign of Egypt, hail!
Cleo. How much unlike art thou Mark Antony!
Yet, coming from him, that great medicine hath
With his tinct gilded thee.—
How goes it with my brave Mark Antony?
   Alex. Last thing he did, dear queen,
He kissed—the last of many doubled kisses—
This orient pearl.—His speech sticks in my heart.
   Cleo. Mine ear must pluck it thence.
   Alex.   'Good friend,' quoth he,
'Say, the firm Roman to great Egypt sends
This treasure of an oyster; at whose foot,
To mend the petty present I will piece
Her opulent throne with kingdoms: all the east,
Say thou, shall call her mistress.' So he nodded,
And soberly did mount an arrogant steed,
Who neighed so high, that what I would have spoke
Was beastly dumbed by him.
   Cleo.   What, was he sad, or merry?
   Alex. Like to the time o' the year between the extremes
Of hot and cold: he was nor sad, nor merry.
   Cleo. O well-divided disposition!—Note him,
Note him, good Charmian, 't is the man; but note him:
He was not sad,—for he would shine on those
That make their looks by his; he was not merry,—
Which seemed to tell them, his remembrance lay
In Egypt with his joy; but between both:
O heavenly mingle!—Be'st thou sad, or merry,
The violence of either thee becomes,
So does it no man else.—Mett'st thou my posts?
   Alex. Ay, madam, twenty several messengers.
Why do you send so thick?
   Cleo.   Who's born that day
When I forget to send to Antony
Shall die a beggar.—Ink and paper, Charmian.—
Welcome, my good Alexas.—Did I, Charmian,
Ever love Cæsar so?
   Char.   O, that brave Cæsar!
   Cleo. Be choked with such another emphasis!
Say, the brave Antony.
   Char.   The valiant Cæsar!
   Cleo. By Isis, I will give thee bloody teeth,
If thou with Cæsar paragon again
My man of men.
   Char.   By your most gracious pardon,
I sing but after you.
   Cleo.   My salad days,
When I was green in judgment:—cold in blood,

To say as I said then!—But come, away;
Get me ink and paper:
He shall have every day a several greeting,
Or I'll unpeople Egypt.   [*Exeunt*

ACT TWO

Scene I.—Messina. A Room in Pompey's House

Enter Pompey, Menecrates, *and* Menas

Pom. If the great gods be just, they shall assist
The deeds of justest men.
Mene.   Know, worthy Pompey,
That what they do delay, they not deny.
Pom. Whiles we are suitors to their throne, decays
The thing we sue for.
Mene.   We, ignorant of ourselves,
Beg often our own harms, which the wise powers
Deny us for our good; so find we profit
By losing of our prayers.
Pom.   I shall do well:
The people love me, and the sea is mine;
My powers are crescent, and my auguring hope
Says it will come to the full. Mark Antony
In Egypt sits at dinner, and will make
No wars without doors: Cæsar gets money where
He loses hearts: Lepidus flatters both,
Of both is flattered; but he neither loves,
Nor either cares for him.
Men.   Cæsar and Lepidus
Are in the field: a mighty strength they carry.
Pom. Where have you this? 't is false.
Men.   From Silvius, sir.
Pom. He dreams: I know they are in Rome together,
Looking for Antony. But all the charms of love,
Salt Cleopatra, soften thy waned lip!
Let witchcraft join with beauty, lust with both!
Tie up the libertine in a field of feasts,
Keep his brain fuming; Epicurean cooks
Sharpen with cloyless sauce his appetite,
That sleep and feeding may prorogue his honour
Even till a Lethe'd dulness!

Enter Varrius

                          How now, Varrius?
Var. This is most certain that I shall deliver:—
Mark Antony is every hour in Rome

Expected; since he went from Egypt, 't is
A space for further travel.
    Pom.   I could have given less matter
A better ear.—Menas, I did not think
This amorous surfeiter would have donned his helm
For such a petty war: his soldiership
Is twice the other twain.   But let us rear
The higher our opinion, that our stirring
Can from the lap of Egypt's widow pluck
The ne'er lust-wearied Antony.
    Men.   I cannot hope,
Cæsar and Antony shall well greet together:
His wife that's dead did trespasses to Cæsar;
His brother warred upon him; although, I think,
Not moved by Antony.
    Pom.   I know not, Menas,
How lesser enmities may give way to greater.
Were 't not that we stand up against them all,
'T were pregnant they should square between themselves
For they have entertainéd cause enough
To draw their swords: but how the fear of us
May cement their divisions, and bind up
The petty difference, we yet not know.
Be 't as our gods will have 't!   It only stands
Our lives upon to use our strongest hands.
Come, Menas.   *[Exeunt*

SCENE II.—Rome. A Room in the House of LEPIDUS

Enter ENOBARBUS *and* LEPIDUS

    Lep. Good Enobarbus, 't is a worthy deed,
And shall become you well, to entreat your captain
To soft and gentle speech.
    Eno.   I shall entreat him
To answer like himself: if Cæsar move him,
Let Antony look over Cæsar's head,
And speak as loud as Mars. By Jupiter,
Were I the wearer of Antonius' beard,
I would not shave 't to-day.
    Lep.   'T is not a time
For private stomaching.
    Eno.   Every time
Serves for the matter that is then born in 't.
    Lep. But small to greater matters must give way.
    Eno. Not if the small come first.
    Lep.   Your speech is passion:
But, pray you, stir no embers up. Here comes
The noble Antony.

Enter ANTONY *and* VENTIDIUS

Eno.   And yonder, Cæsar.

Enter CÆSAR, MECÆNAS, *and* AGRIPPA

Ant. If we compose well here, to Parthia:
Hark ye, Ventidius.
Cæs.   I do not know,
Mecænas; ask Agrippa.
Lep.   Noble friends,
That which combined us was most great, and let not
A leaner action rend us. What's amiss,
May it be gently heard; when we debate
Our trivial difference loud, we do commit
Murder in healing wounds. Then, noble partners,—
The rather, for I earnestly beseech,—
Touch you the sourest points with sweetest terms,
Nor curstness grow to the matter.
Ant.   'T is spoken well.
Were we before our armies, and to fight,
I should do thus.
Cæs. Welcome to Rome.
Ant. Thank you.
Cæs. Sit.
Ant. Sit, sir.
Cæs. Nay, then.
Ant. I learn, you take things ill which are not so;
Or being, concern you not.
Cæs.   I must be laughed at,
If, or for nothing, or a little, I
Should say myself offended; and with you
Chiefly i' the world; more laughed at that I should
Once name you derogately, when to sound your name
It not concerned me.
Ant.   My being in Egypt, Cæsar,
What was't to you?
Cæs. No more than my residing here at Rome
Might be to you in Egypt: yet, if you there
Did practise on my state, your being in Egypt
Might be my question.
Ant.   How intend you, practised?
Cæs. You may be pleased to catch at mine intent
By what did here befall me. Your wife and brother
Made wars upon me, and their contestation
Was theme for you, you were the word of war.
Ant. You do mistake your business; my brother never
Did urge me in his act: I did inquire it,
And have my learning from some true reports,
That drew their swords with you. Did he not rather
Discredit my authority with yours;

And make the wars alike against my stomach,
Having alike your cause? Of this my letters
Before did satisfy you. If you'll patch a quarrel
As matter whole you've not to make it with,
It must not be with this.
    Cæs.   You praise yourself
By laying defects of judgment to me; but
You patched up your excuses.
    Ant.   Not so, not so;
I know you could not lack, I am certain on't,
Very necessity of this thought, that I,
Your partner in the cause 'gainst which he fought,
Could not with graceful eyes attend those wars
Which fronted mine own peace. As for my wife,
I would you had her spirit in such another:
The third o' the world is yours, with which a snaffle
You may pace easy, but not such a wife.
    Eno. Would we had all such wives, that the men might
Go to wars with the women!
    Ant. So much uncurbable, her garboils, Cæsar,
Made out of her impatience,—which not wanted
Shrewdness of policy too,—I grieving grant
Did you too much disquiet: for that, you must
But say, I could not help it.
    Cæs.   I wrote to you
When rioting in Alexandria; you
Did pocket up my letters, and with taunts
Did gibe my missive out of audience.
    Ant.   Sir,
He fell upon me ere admitted: then
Three kings I had newly feasted, and did want
Of what I was i' the morning; but, next day,
I told him of myself; which was as much
As to have asked him pardon. Let this fellow
Be nothing of our strife; if we contend,
Out of our question wipe him.
    Cæs.   You have broken
The article of your oath, which you shall never
Have tongue to charge me with.
    Lep.   Soft, Cæsar!
    Ant. No, Lepidus, let him speak:
The honour's sacred which he talks on now,
Supposing that I lacked it. But on, Cæsar;
The article of my oath,—
    Cæs. To lend me arms and aid when I required them,
The which you both denied.
    Ant.   Neglected, rather;
And then, when poisoned hours had bound me up
From mine own knowledge. As nearly as I may,
I'll play the penitent to you; but mine honesty

Shall not make poor my greatness, nor my power
Work without it.   Truth is, that Fulvia,
To have me out of Egypt, made wars here;
For which myself, the ignorant motive, do
So far ask pardon as befits mine honour
To stoop in such a case.
    Lep.   'T is nobly spoken.
    Mec.   If it might please you to enforce no further
The griefs between ye: to forget them quite
Were to remember that the present need
Speaks to atone you.
    Lep.   Worthily spoken, Mecænas.
    Eno.   Or, if you borrow one another's love for the
instant, you may, when you hear no more words of Pompey,
return it again: you shall have time to wrangle in when
you have nothing else to do.
    Ant.   Thou art a soldier only: speak no more.
    Eno.   That truth should be silent, I had almost forgot.
    Ant.   You wrong this presence; therefore, speak no
              more.
    Eno.   Go then; your considerate stone.
    Cæs.   I do not much dislike the matter, but
The manner of his speech; for't cannot be
We shall remain in friendship, our conditions
So differing in their acts. Yet, if I knew
What hoop should hold us stanch, from edge to edge
O' the world I would pursue it.
    Agr.   Give me leave Cæsar,—
    Cæs.   Speak, Agrippa.
    Agr.   Thou hast a sister by the mother's side,
Admired Octavia: great Mark Antony
Is now a widower.
    Cæs.   Say not so, Agrippa:
If Cleopatra heard you, your reproof
Were well deserved of rashness.
    Ant.   I am not married, Cæsar: let me hear
Agrippa further speak.
    Agr.   To hold you in perpetual amity,
To make you brothers, and to knit your hearts
With an unslipping knot, take Antony
Octavia to his wife; whose beauty claims
No worse a husband than the best of men,
Whose virtue and whose general graces speak
That which none else can utter.   By this marriage,
All little jealousies, which now seem great,
And all great fears, which now import their dangers,
Would then be nothing: truths would be tales,
Where now half tales be truths: her love to both
Would each to other, and all loves to both,
Draw after her.   Pardon what I have spoke;

For 't is a studied, not a present thought,
By duty ruminated.
    Ant.   Will Cæsar speak?
    Cæs.   Not till he hears how Antony is touched
With what is spoke already.
    Ant.   What power is in Agrippa,
If I would say, 'Agrippa, be it so,'
To make this good?
    Cæs.   The power of Cæsar, and
His power unto Octavia.
    Ant.   May I never
To this good purpose, that so fairly shows,
Dream of impediment!—Let me have thy hand:
Further this act of grace, and from this hour
The heart of brothers govern in our loves
And sway our great designs!
    Cæs.   There is my hand.
A sister I bequeath you, whom no brother
Did ever love so dearly: let her live
To join our kingdoms and our hearts; and never
Fly off our loves again!
    Lep.   Happily, Amen!
    Ant.   I did not think to draw my sword 'gainst Pompey;
For he hath laid strange courtesies and great
Of late upon me: I must thank him only,
Lest my remembrance suffer ill report;
At heel of that, defy him.
    Lep.   Time calls upon 's:
Of us must Pompey presently be sought,
Or else he seeks out us.
    Ant.   Where lies he?
    Cæs.   About the Mount Misenum.
    Ant.   What's his strength
By land?
    Cæs.   Great and increasing; but by sea
He is an absolute master.
    Ant.   So's the fame.
Would we had spoke together! Haste we for it:
Yet, ere we put ourselves in arms, despatch we
The business we have talked of.
    Cæs.   With most gladness;
And to invite you to my sister's view,
Whither straight I'll lead you.
    Ant.   Let us, Lepidus,
Not lack your company.
    Lep.   Noble Antony,
Not sickness should detain me.
         [Flourish. Exeunt Cæsar, Antony, and Lepidus
    Mec.   Welcome from Egypt, sir.
    Eno.   Half the heart of Cæsar, worthy Mecænas!—

My honourable friend, Agrippa!—
    Agr. Good Enobarbus!
    Mec. We have cause to be glad, that matters are so well
digested. You stayed well by it in Egypt.
    Eno. Ay, sir; we did sleep day out of countenance,
and made the night light with drinking.
    Mec. Eight wild-boars roasted whole at a breakfast,
and but twelve persons there; is this true?
    Eno. This was but as a fly by an eagle: we had much
more monstrous matter of feast, which worthily deserved
noting.
    Mec. She's a most triumphant lady, if report be square
to her.
    Eno. When she first met Mark Antony, she pursed up
his heart, upon the river of Cydnus.
    Agr. There she appeared indeed; or my reporter
devised well for her.
    Eno. I will tell you.
The barge she sat in, like a burnished throne,
Burned on the water: the poop was beaten gold;
Purple the sails, and so perfuméd that
The winds were love-sick with them; the oars were silver,
Which to the tune of flutes kept stroke, and made
The water which they beat to follow faster,
As amorous of their strokes. For her own person,
It beggared all description: she did lie
In her pavilion—cloth-of-gold of tissue—
O'er-picturing that Venus where we see
The fancy outwork nature: on each side her
Stood pretty dimpled boys, like smiling Cupids,
With divers-coloured fans, whose wind did seem
To glow the delicate cheeks which they did cool
And what they undid did.
    Agr. O, rare for Antony!
    Eno. Her gentlewomen, like the Nereides,
So many mermaids, tended her i' th' eyes,
And made their bends adornings: at the helm
A seeming mermaid steers; the silken tackle
Swell with the touches of those flower-soft hands,
That yarely frame the office. From the barge
A strange invisible perfume hits the sense
Of the adjacent wharfs. The city cast
Her people out upon her; and Antony,
Enthroned i' the market-place, did sit alone,
Whistling to the air; which, but for vacancy,
Had gone to gaze on Cleopatra, too,
And made a gap in nature.
    Agr.   Rare Egyptian!
    Eno. Upon her landing, Antony sent to her,
Invited her to supper: she replied,

It should be better he became her guest,
Which she entreated. Our courteous Antony,
Whom ne'er the word of 'No' woman heard speak,
Being barbered ten times o'er, goes to the feast;
And for his ordinary pays his heart
For what his eyes eat only.
    Agr.   Royal wench!
She made great Cæsar lay his sword to bed;
He ploughed her, and she cropped.
    Eno.   I saw her once,
Hop forty paces through the public street;
And having lost her breath, she spoke, and panted,
That she did make defect perfection,
And, breathless, power breathe forth.
    Mec. Now Antony must leave her utterly.
    Eno. Never; he will not:
Age cannot wither her, nor custom stale
Her infinite variety. Other women cloy
The appetites they feed; but she makes hungry
Where most she satisfies: for vilest things
Become themselves in her; that the holy priests
Bless her when she is riggish.
    Mec. If beauty, wisdom, modesty, can settle
The heart of Antony, Octavia is
A blessèd lottery to him.
    Agr.   Let us go.—
Good Enobarbus, make yourself my guest
Whilst you abide here.
    Eno.   Humbly, sir, I thank you.
                               [Exeunt

SCENE III.—Rome. A Room in CÆSAR's House

Enter CÆSAR, ANTONY, OCTAVIA *between them;*
and Attendants

    Ant. The world and my great office will sometimes
Divide me from your bosom.
    Octa.   All which time,
Before the gods my knee shall bow my prayers
To them for you.
    Ant.   Good night, sir.—My Octavia,
Read not my blemishes in the world's report:
I have not kept my square; but that to come
Shall all be done by the rule. Good night, dear lady.—
    Octa. Good night, sir.
    Cæs. Good night.   *[Exeunt Cæsar and Octavia*

Enter a Soothsayer

    Ant. Now, sirrah,—you do wish yourself in Egypt?

Sooth. Would I had never come from thence, nor you
    thither!
Ant. If you can, your reason?
Sooth. I see it in my motion, have it not in my tongue:
    but yet hie you to Egypt again.
Ant. Say to me,
Whose fortunes shall rise higher, Cæsar's or mine?
Sooth. Cæsar's.
Therefore, O Antony, stay not by his side:
Thy demon—that's thy spirit which keeps thee—is
Noble, courageous, high, unmatchable,
Where Cæsar's is not; but near him thy angel
Becomes a fear, as being o'erpowered: therefore
Make space enough between you.
Ant.   Speak this no more.
Sooth. To none but thee; no more, but when to thee
If thou dost play with him at any game,
Thou'rt sure to lose; and, of that natural luck,
He beats thee 'gainst the odds: thy lustre thickens,
When he shines by. I say again, thy spirit
Is all afraid to govern thee near him,
But, he away, 't is noble.
Ant.   Get thee gone:
Say to Ventidius, I would speak with him.—
                        [Exit Soothsayer
He shall to Parthia.—Be it art of hap,
He hath spoken true: the very dice obey him;
And in our sports my better cunning faints
Under his chance: if we draw lots, he speeds;
His cocks do win the battle still of mine,
When it is all to nought; and his quails ever
Beat mine, inhooped, at odds. I will to Egypt:
And though I make this marriage for my peace,
I' the east my pleasure lies.

Enter Ventidius

                    O, come, Ventidius,
You must to Parthia: your commission's ready;
Follow me, and receive't.   *[Exeunt*

SCENE IV.—Rome. A Street

Enter Lepidus, Mecænas, *and* Agrippa

Lep. Trouble yourselves no further: pray you, hasten
Your generals after.
Agr.   Sir, Mark Antony
Will e'en but kiss Octavia, and we'll follow.

Lep. Till I shall see you in your soldier's dress,
Which will become you both, farewell.
 Mec.   We shall,
As I conceive the journey, be at the Mount
Before you, Lepidus.
 Lep.   Your way is shorter;
My purposes do draw me much about:
You'll win two days upon me.
 Mec., Agr.   Sir, good success!
 Lep. Farewell.   [*Exeunt*

SCENE V.—Alexandria. A Room in the Palace

Enter CLEOPATRA, CHARMIAN, IRAS, *and* ALEXAS

 Cleo. Give me some music,—music, moody food
Of us that trade in love.
 Attend.   The music, ho!

Enter MARDIAN

 Cleo. Let it alone; let's to billiards: come, Charmian.
 Char. My arm is sore; best play with Mardian.
 Cleo. As well a woman with an eunuch played,
As with a woman.—Come, you'll play with me, sir?
 Mar. As well as I can, madam.
 Cleo. And when good will is showed, though 't come
    too short,
The actor may plead pardon. I'll none now.—
Give me mine angle,—we'll to the river: there,
My music playing far off, I will betray
Tawny-finned fishes; my bended hook shall pierce
Their slimy jaws; and, as I draw them up,
I'll think them every one an Antony,
And say, 'Ah, ha! you're caught!'
 Char.   'T was merry when
You wagered on your angling; when your diver
Did hang a salt-fish on his hook, which he
With fervency drew up.
 Cleo.   That time—O times!—
I laughed him out of patience; and that night
I laughed him into patience: and next morn,
Ere the ninth hour, I drunk him to his bed;
Then put my tires and mantles on him, whilst
I wore his sword Philippan.

Enter a Messenger

          O, from Italy?—
Ram thou thy fruitful tidings in mine ears,
That long time have been barren.

Mess.   Madam, madam,—
Cleo.   Antony's dead!—if thou say so, villain,
Thou kill'st thy mistress: but well and free,
If thou so yield him, there is gold and here
My bluest veins to kiss,—a hand that kings
Have lipped, and trembled kissing.
Mess.   First, madam, he is well.
Cleo.   Why, there's more gold
But, sirrah, mark, we use
To say, the dead are well: bring it to that,
The gold I give thee will I melt and pour
Down thy ill-uttering throat.
Mess.   Good madam, hear me.
Cleo.   Well, go to, I will;
But there's no goodness in thy face: if Antony
Be free, and healthful, why so tart a favour
To trumpet such good tidings? if not well,
Thou shouldst come like a Fury crowned with snakes,
Not like a formal man.
Mess.   Will't please you hear me?
Cleo.   I have a mind to strike thee, ere thou speak'st:
Yet, if thou say, Antony lives, is well,
Or friends with Cæsar, or not captive to him,
I'll set thee in a shower of gold, and hail
Rich pearls upon thee.
Mess.   Madam, he's well.
Cleo.   Well said.
Mess.   And friends with Cæsar.
Cleo.   Thou'rt an honest man.
Mess.   Cæsar and he are greater friends than ever.
Cleo.   Make thee a fortune from me.
Mess.   But, yet madam,—
Cleo.   I do not like 'but yet,' it does allay
The good precedence; fie upon 'but yet!'
'But yet' is as a gaoler to bring forth
Some monstrous malefactor.   Pr'ythee, friend,
Pour out the pack of matter to mine ear,
The good and bad together: he's friends with Cæsar;
In state of health, thou say'st; and, thou say'st, free.
Mess.   Free, madam? no: I made no such report:
He's bound unto Octavia.
Cleo.   For what good turn?
Mess.   For the best turn i' the bed.
Cleo.   I am pale, Charmian.
Mess.   Madam, he's married to Octavia.
Cleo.   The most infectious pestilence upon thee!
                                    [*Strikes him down*
Mess.   Good madam, patience.
Cleo.   What say you?—
                                    [*Strikes him again*

Hence, horrible villain! or I'll spurn thine eyes
Like balls before me; I'll unhair thy head.
                   [She hales him up and down
Thou shalt be whipped with wire, and stewed in brine,
Smarting in lingering pickle.
   Mess.   Gracious madam,
I, that do bring the news, made not the match.
   Cleo. Say, 't is not so, a province I will give thee,
And make thy fortunes proud: the blow thou hadst
Shall make thy peace for moving me to rage;
And I will boot thee with what gift beside
Thy modesty can beg.
   Mess.   He's married, madam.
   Cleo. Rogue, thou hast lived too long.

                            [Draws a knife
   Mess.   Nay, then I'll run—
What mean you, madam? I have made no fault.
                                 [Exit
   Char. Good madam, keep yourself within yourself:
The man is innocent.
   Cleo. Some innocents 'scape not the thunderbolt.—
Melt Egypt into Nile! and kindly creatures
Turn all to serpents!—Call the slave again:—
Though I am mad, I will not bite him:—Call.
   Char. He is afeared to come.
   Cleo.   I will not hurt him.—
                         [Exit Charmian
These hands do lack nobility, that they strike
A meaner than myself; since I myself
Have given myself the cause.—

Re-enter CHARMIAN *and Messenger*

                         Come hither, sir.
Though it be honest, it is never good
To bring bad news: give to a gracious message
An host of tongues; but let ill tidings tell
Themselves when they be felt.
   Mess. I have done my duty.
   Cleo.   Is he married?
I cannot hate thee worser than I do,
If thou again say, Yes.
   Mess.   He's married, madam.
   Cleo. The gods confound thee! dost thou hold there
       still?
   Mess. Should I lie, madam?
   Cleo.   O, I would, thou didst,
So half my Egypt were submerged, and made
A cistern for scaled snakes. Go, get thee hence:
Hadst thou Narcissus in thy face, to me

Thou wouldst appear most ugly.   He is married?
   Mess.   I crave your highness' pardon.
   Cleo.   He is married?
   Mess.   Take no offence that I would not offend you:
To punish me for what you make me do,
Seems much unequal.   He is married to Octavia.
   Cleo.   O, that his fault should make a knave of thee,
That art not what thou'rt sure of!—Get thee hence:
The merchandise which thou hast brought from Rome
Are all too dear for me: lie they upon thy hand,
And be undone by 'em!   [*Exit Messenger*
   Char.   Good your highness, patience.
   Cleo.   In praising Antony, I have dispraised Cæsar.
   Char.   Many times, madam.
   Cleo.   I am paid for't now.
Lead me from hence;
I faint:—O Iris!   Charmian!—'T is no matter.—
Go to the fellow, good Alexas; bid him
Report the feature of Octavia, her years,
Her inclination, let him not leave out
The colour of her hair: bring me word quickly.—
                                                [*Exit Alexas*
Let him for ever go:—let him not—Charmian,
Though he be painted one way like a Gorgon,
The other way's a Mars.—[*To* MARDIAN] Bid you Alexas
Bring me word, how tall she is.—Pity me, Charmian,
But do not speak to me.—Lead me to my chamber.
                                                [*Exeunt*

SCENE VI.—Near Misenum

Flourish. Enter POMPEY *and* MENAS, *at one side, with
   drum and trumpet; at another* CÆSAR, LEPIDUS,
   ANTONY, ENOBARBUS, MECÆNAS, with Soldiers
   marching*

   Pom.   Your hostages I have, so have you mine;
And we shall talk before we fight.
   Cæs.   Most meet
That first we come to words; and therefore have we
Our written purposes before us sent;
Which if thou hast considered, let us know
If 't will tie up thy discontented sword,
And carry back to Sicily much tall youth
That else must perish here.
   Pom.   To you all three,
The senators alone of this great world,
Chief factors for the gods,—I do not know
Wherefore my father should revengers want,
Having a son, and friends; since Julius Cæsar,

Who at Philippi the good Brutus ghosted,
There saw you labouring for him.   What was it,
That moved pale Cassius to conspire?   And what
Made the all-honoured, honest Roman, Brutus,
With the armed rest, courtiers of beauteous freedom,
To drench the Capitol, but that they would
Have one man but a man?   And that is it
Hath made me rig my navy; at whose burden
The angered ocean foams; with which I meant
To scourge the ingratitude that despiteful Rome
Cast on my noble father.

  Cæs.   Take your time.

  Ant. Thou canst not fear us, Pompey, with thy sails;
We'll speak with thee at sea; at land, thou know'st
How much we do o'er-count thee.

  Pom.   At land, indeed,
Thou dost o'er-count me of my father's house:
But, since the cuckoo builds not for himself,
Remain in 't as thou may'st.

  Lep.   Be pleased to tell us,—
For this is from the present,—how you take
The offers we have sent you.

  Cæs.   There's the point.

  Ant. Which do not be entreated to, but weigh
What it is worth embraced.

  Cæs.   And what may follow
To try a larger fortune.

  Pom.   You have made me offer
Of Sicily, Sardinia; and I must
Rid all the sea of pirates; then, to send
Measures of wheat to Rome: this 'greed upon
To part with unhacked edges, and bear back
Our targes undinted.

  Cæs., Ant., Lep. That's our offer.

  Pom.   Know then,
I came before you here, a man prepared
To take this offer: but Mark Antony
Put me to some impatience.—Though I lose
The praise of it by telling, you must know,
When Cæsar and your brother were at blows,
Your mother came to Sicily, and did find
Her welcome friendly.

  Ant.   I have heard it, Pompey;
And am well studied for a liberal thanks
Which I do owe you.

  Pom.   Let me have your hand:
I did not think, sir, to have met you here.

  Ant. The beds i' the east are soft; and thanks to you
That called me, timelier than my purpose, hither,—
For I have gained by 't.

Cæs.   Since I saw you last,
There is a change upon you.
Pom.   Well, I know not
What counts harsh fortune casts upon my face;
But in my bosom shall she never come,
To make my heart her vassal.
Lep.   Well met here.
Pom. I hope so, Lepidus.—Thus we are agreed.
I crave our composition may be written,
And sealed between us.
Cæs.   That's the next to do.
Pom. We'll feast each other ere we part; and let's
Draw lots who shall begin.
Ant.   That will I, Pompey.
Pom. No, Antony, take the lot:
But, first or last, your fine Egyptian cookery
Shall have the fame. I have heard, that Julius Cæsar
Grew fat with feasting there.
Ant.   You have heard much.
Pom. I have fair meanings, sir.
Ant.   And fair words to them.
Pom. Then, so much have I heard:
And I have heard, Apollodorus carried—
Eno. No more of that:—he did so.
Pom.   What, I pray you?
Eno. A certain queen to Cæsar in a mattress.
Pom. I know thee now: how far'st thou, soldier?
Eno.   Well;
And well am like to do; for I perceive,
Four feasts are toward.
Pom.   Let me shake thy hand;
I never hated thee. I have seen thee fight,
When I have envied thy behaviour.
Eno.   Sir,
I never loved you much; but I have praised you,
When you have well deserved ten times as much
As I have said you did.
Pom.   Enjoy thy plainness,
It nothing ill becomes thee.—
Aboard my galley I invite you all:
Will you lead, lords?
Cæs., Ant., Lep. Show us the way, sir.
Pom.   Come.
          [*Exeunt Pompey, Cæsar, Antony, Lepidus,
                    Soldiers, and Attendants*
Men. [*Aside*] Thy father, Pompey, would ne'er have
made this treaty.—You and I have known, sir.
Eno. At sea, I think.
Men. We have, sir.
Eno. You have done well by water.

Men. And you by land.

Eno. I will praise any man that will praise me; though it cannot be denied what I have done by land.

Men. Nor what I have done by water.

Eno. Yes; something you can deny for your own safety: you have been a great thief by sea.

Men. And you by land.

Eno. There I deny my land service. But give me your hand, Menas: if our eyes had authority, here they might take two thieves kissing.

Men. All men's faces are true, whatsoe'er their hands are.

Eno. But there is never a fair woman has a true face.

Men. No slander; they steal hearts.

Eno. We came hither to fight with you.

Men. For my part, I am sorry it is turned to a drinking. Pompey doth this day laugh away his fortune.

Eno. If he do, sure, he cannot weep't back again.

Men. You have said, sir. We looked not for Mark Antony here. Pray you, is he married to Cleopatra?

Eno. Cæsar's sister is called Octavia.

Men. True, sir; she was the wife of Caius Marcellus.

Eno. But she is now the wife of Marcus Antonius.

Men. Pray ye, sir?

Eno. 'T is true.

Men. Then is Cæsar and he for ever knit together.

Eno. If I were bound to divine of this unity, I would not prophesy so.

Men. I think, the policy of that purpose made more in the marriage than the love of the parties.

Eno. I think so too: but you shall find the band that seems to tie their friendship together will be the very strangler of their amity: Octavia is of a holy, cold, and still conversation.

Men. Who would not have his wife so?

Eno. Not he, that himself is not so; which is Mark Antony. He will to his Egyptian dish again: then shall the sighs of Octavia blow the fire up in Cæsar; and, as I said before, that which is the strength of their amity, shall prove the immediate author of their variance. Antony will use his affection where it is: he married but his occasion here.

Men. And thus it may be. Come, sir, will you aboard? I have a health for you.

Eno. I shall take it, sir: we have used our throats in Egypt.

Men. Come, let's away.   [*Exeunt*

SCENE VII.—On board POMPEY's Galley, lying near
Misenum

Music.   Enter two or three Servants, with a banquet

First Serv. Here they'll be, man. Some o' their plants
are ill-rooted already; the least wind i' the world will blow
them down.
Sec. Serv. Lepidus is high-coloured.
First Serv. They have made him drink alms-drink.
Sec. Serv. As they pinch one another by the disposition,
he cries out, 'No more;' reconciles them to his entreaty,
and himself to the drink.
First Serv. But it raises the greater war between him
and his discretion.
Sec. Serv. Why, this it is to have a name in great men's
fellowship: I had as lief have a reed that will do me no
service as a partisan I could not heave.
First Serv. To be called into a huge sphere, and not
to be seen to move in 't, are the holes where eyes should
be, which pitifully disaster the cheeks.

A sennet sounded.   Enter CÆSAR, ANTONY, LEPIDUS,
POMPEY, AGRIPPA, MECÆNAS, ENOBARBUS, MENAS,
with other Captains

Ant. Thus do they, sir. They take the flow o' the Nile
By certain scales i' the pyramid; they know,
By the height, the lowness, or the mean, if dearth
Or foison follow. The higher Nilus swells,
The more it promises: as it ebbs, the seedsman
Upon the slime and ooze scatters his grain,
And shortly comes to harvest.
Lep. You have strange serpents there.
Ant. Ay, Lepidus.
Lep. Your serpent of Egypt is bred now of your mud
by the operation of your sun: so is your crocodile.
Ant. They are so.
Pom. Sit,—and some wine!—A health to Lepidus!
Lep. I am not so well as I should be, but I'll ne'er out.
Eno. Not till you have slept; I fear me, you'll be in,
till then.
Lep. Nay, certainly, I have heard, the Ptolemies'
pyramises are very goodly things; without contradiction,
I have heard that.
Men. [*Aside*] Pompey, a word.
Pom. [*Aside*]   Say in mine ear: what is't?
Men. [*Aside*] Forsake thy seat, I do beseech thee,
          captain,

And hear me speak a word.
   Pom. [*Aside*]   Forbear me till anon.—
This wine for Lepidus.
   Lep. What manner o' thing is your crocodile?
   Ant. It is shaped, sir, like itself, and it is as broad as it
hath breadth; it is just so high as it is, and moves with its
own organs; it lives by that which nourisheth it; and the
elements once out of it, it transmigrates.
   Lep. What colour is it of?
   Ant. Of its own colour too.
   Lep. 'T is a strange serpent.
   Ant. 'T is so: and the tears of it are wet.
   Cæs. Will this description satisfy him?
   Ant. With the health that Pompey gives him, else he
is a very epicure.
   Pom. [*To* MENAS, *aside*]   Go hang, sir, hang! Tell me
         of that? away!
Do as I bid you.—Where's this cup I called for?
   Men. [*Aside*] If for the sake of merit thou wilt hear me,
Rise from thy stool.
   Pom. [*Aside*] I think, thou'rt mad. The matter?
                                [*Walks aside*
   Men. I have ever held my cap off to thy fortunes.
   Pom. Thou hast served me with much faith. What's
         else to say?—
Be jolly, lords.
   Ant.   These quick-sands, Lepidus,
Keep off them, for you sink.
   Men. Wilt thou be lord of all the world?
   Pom.   What say'st thou?
   Men. Wilt thou be lord of the whole world? That's
         twice.
   Pom. How should that be?
   Men.   But entertain it,
And, though thou think me poor, I am the man
Will give thee all the world.
   Pom.   Hast thou drunk well?
   Men. No, Pompey, I have kept me from the cup.
Thou art, if thou dar'st be, the earthly Jove:
Whate'er the ocean pales, or sky inclips,
Is thine, if thou wilt ha't.
   Pom.   Show me which way.
   Men. These three world-sharers, these competitors,
Are in thy vessel: let me cut the cable;
And, when we are put off, fall to their throats:
All then is thine.
   Pom. Ah, this thou shouldst have done,
And not have spoke on't. In me, 't is villainy;
In thee, 't had been good service. Thou must know,
'T is not my profit that does lead mine honour;

Mine honour, it.   Repent, that e'er thy tongue
Hath so betrayed thine act: being done unknown,
I should have found it afterwards well done,
But must condemn it now.   Desist, and drink.
   Men.   [*Aside*]   For this,
I'll never follow thy palled fortunes more.
Who seeks, and will not take, when once 't is offered,
Shall never find it more.
   Pom.   This health to Lepidus.
   Ant.   Bear him ashore.—I'll pledge it for him, Pompey.
   Eno.   Here's to thee, Menas.
   Men.   Enobarbus, welcome.
   Pom.   Fill, till the cup be hid.
   Eno.   There's a strong fellow, Menas.
                   [*Pointing to the Attendant who carries
                              off Lepidus*
   Men.   Why?
   Eno.   'A bears the third part of the world, man: see'st
not?
   Men.   The third part then is drunk: 'would it were all,
That is might go on wheels!
   Eno.   Drink thou; increase the reels.
   Men.   Come.
   Pom.   This is not yet an Alexandrian feast.
   Ant.   It ripens towards it.—Strike the vessels, ho!
Here is to Cæsar.
   Cæs.   I could well forbear it.
It's monstrous labour when I wash my brain
And it grows fouler.
   Ant.   Be a child o' the time.
   Cæs.   Possess it, I'll make answer; but I had rather fast
From all, four days, than drink so much in one.
   Eno.   [*To Antony*]   Ha, my brave emperor!
Shall we dance now the Egyptian Bacchanals,
And celebrate our drink?
   Pom.   Let's ha' t' good soldier.
   Ant.   Come, let us all take hands,
Till that the conquering wine hath steeped our sense
In soft and delicate Lethe.
   Eno.   All take hands.—
Make battery to our ears with the loud music;
The while I'll place you: then, the boy shall sing;
The holding every man shall bear, as loud
As his strong sides can volley.
          [*Music plays.   Enobarbus places them hand
                            in hand*

SONG

    *Come, thou monarch of the vine,
    Plumpy Bacchus with pink eyne*

> *In thy vats our cares be drowned,*
> *With thy grapes our hairs be crowned!*
> *Cup us, till the world go round,*
> *Cup us, till the world go round!*

Cæs. What would you more? Pompey, good night.
              Good brother,
Let me request you off: our graver business
Frowns at this levity.—Gentle lords, let's part;
You see, we have burnt our cheeks. Strong Enobarb
Is weaker than the wine; and mine own tongue
Splits what it speaks: the wild disguise hath almost
Antick'd us all. What needs more words? Good-night.—
Good Antony, your hand.
Pom.   I'll try you on the shore.
Ant. And shall, sir. Give's your hand.
Pom.   O Antony!
You have my father's house.—But what? we are friends.
Come down into the boat.
Eno.   Take heed you fall not.—
        [Exeunt Pompey, Cæsar, Antony and
                        Attendants
Menas, I'll not on shore.
Men.   No, to my cabin.—
These drums!—these trumpets, flutes! what!—
Let Neptune hear, we bid a loud farewell
To these great fellows: sound, and be hanged! sound out!
        [A flourish of trumpets, with drums
Eno. Hoo, says 'a!—There's my cap.
Men. Hoo!—Noble captain! come.   *[Exeunt*

ACT THREE

SCENE I.—A Plain in Syria

Enter VENTIDIUS *in triumph with* SILIUS, *and other Romans,*
Officers, and Soldiers; the dead body of PACORUS *borne*
before him

Ven. Now, darting Parthia, art thou struck; and now
Pleased fortune does of Marcus Crassus' death
Make me revenger.—Bear the king's son's body
Before our army.—Thy Pacorus, Orodes,
Pays this for Marcus Crassus.
Sil.   Noble Ventidius,
Whilst yet with Parthian blood thy sword is warm,
The fugitive Parthians follow: spur through Media,
Mesopotamia, and the shelters whither

The routed fly: so thy grand captain Antony
Shall set thee on triumphant chariots, and
Put garlands on thy head.
  Ven.   O Silius, Silius,
I've done enough: a lower place, note well,
May make too great an act: for learn this, Silius,
Better to leave undone, than by our deed acquire
Too high a fame, when him we serve's away.
Cæsar and Antony have ever won
More in their officer than person: Sossius,
One of my place in Syria, his lieutenant,
For quick accumulation of renown
Which he achieved by the minute, lost his favour.
Who does i' the wars more than his captain can,
Becomes his captain's captain; and ambition,
The soldier's virtue, rather makes choice of loss
Than gain which darkens him.
I could do more to do Antonius good,
But 't would offend him; and in his offence
Should my performance perish.
  Sil.   Thou hast, Ventidius, that
Without the which a soldier and his sword
Grants scarce distinction. Thou wilt write to Antony?
  Ven. I'll humbly signify what in his name,
That magical word of war, we have effected;
How, with his banners and his well-paid ranks,
The ne'er-yet-beaten horse of Parthia
We have jaded out o' the field.
  Sil.   Where is he now?
  Ven. He purposeth to Athens; whither, with what
    haste
The weight we must convey with 's will permit,
We shall appear before him.—On, there; pass along.
                [*Exeunt*

SCENE II.—Rome. An Ante-chamber in CÆSAR'S House

Enter AGRIPPA *and* ENOBARBUS, *meeting*

  Agr. What, are the brothers parted?
  Eno. They have despatched with Pompey: he is gone;
The other three are sealing. Octavia weeps
To part from Rome; Cæsar is sad; and Lepidus,
Since Pompey's feast, as Menas says, is troubled
With the green sickness.
  Agr.   'T is a noble Lepidus.
  Eno. A very fine one. O, how he loves Cæsar!
  Agr. Nay, but how dearly he adores Mark Antony!
  Eno. Cæsar? Why, he's the Jupiter of men.

Agr. What's Antony? the god of Jupiter.
Eno. Spake you of Cæsar? How! the nonpareil!
Agr. O Antony! O thou Arabian bird!
Eno. Would you praise Cæsar, say, 'Cæsar;'—go no
further.
Agr. Indeed, he plied them both with excellent praises.
Eno. But he loves Cæsar best;—yet he loves Antony.
Ho! hearts, tongues, figures, scribes, bards, poets, cannot
Think, speak, cast, write, sing, number,—ho!—
His love to Antony. But as for Cæsar,
Kneel down, kneel down, and wonder.
Agr.   Both he loves.
Eno. They are his shards, and he their beetle [*Trumpets
So,*—
This is to horse.—Adieu, noble Agrippa.
Agr. Good fortune, worthy soldier; and farewell.

Enter CÆSAR, ANTONY, LEPIDUS, *and* OCTAVIA

Ant. No further, sir.
Cæs. You take from me a great part of myself;
Use me well in 't.—Sister, prove such a wife
As my thoughts make thee, and as my furthest band
Shall pass on thy approof.—Most noble Antony,
Let not the piece of virtue which is set
Betwixt us as the cement of our love,
To keep it builded, be the ram to batter
The fortress of it; for better might we
Have loved without this mean, if on both parts
This be not cherished.
Ant.   Make me not offended
In your distrust.
Cæs.   I have said.
Ant.   You shall not find,
Though you be therein curious, the least cause
For what you seem to fear. So, the gods keep you,
And make the hearts of Romans serve your ends!
We will here part.
Cæs. Farewell, my dearest sister, fare thee well:
The elements be kind to thee, and make
Thy spirits all of comfort! fare thee well.
Octa. My noble brother!—
Ant. The April's in her eyes; it is love's spring.
And these the showers to bring it on.—Be cheerful.
Octa. Sir, look well to my husband's house; and—
Cæs.   What, Octavia?
Octa.   I'll tell you in your ear.
Ant. Her tongue will not obey her heart, nor can
Her heart inform her tongue,—the swan's down-feather,
That stands upon the swell at the full of tide,

And neither way inclines.
 Eno. [*Aside to Agrippa*] Will Cæsar weep?
 Agr.   He has a cloud in's face.
 Eno. He were the worse for that, were he a horse;
So is he, being a man.
 Agr.   Why, Enobarbus,
When Antony found Julius Cæsar dead,
He cried almost to roaring; and he wept,
When at Philippi he found Brutus slain.
 Eno. That year, indeed, he was troubled with a rheum;
What willingly he did confound he wailed,
Believe 't, till I wept too.
 Cæs.   No, sweet Octavia,
You shall hear from me still: the time shall not
Out-go my thinking on you.
 Ant.   Come, sir, come;
I'll wrestle with you in my strength of love:
Look, here I have you; thus I let you go,
And give you to the gods.
 Cæs.   Adieu; be happy!
 Lep. Let all the number of the stars give light
To thy fair way!
 Cæs. Farewell, farewell.   [*Kisses Octavia*
 Ant.   Farewell.
       [*Trumpets sound. Exeunt*

SCENE III.—Alexandria. A Room in the Palace

Enter CLEOPATRA, CHARMIAN, IRAS, *and* ALEXAS

 Cleo. Where is the fellow?
 Alex.   Half afeared to come.
 Cleo. Go to, go to.—Come hither, sir.

Enter the Messenger

 Alex.   Good majesty,
Herod of Jewry dare not look upon you
But when you are well pleased.
 Cleo.   That Herod's head
I'll have: but how, when Antony is gone
Through whom I might command it?—Come thou near.
 Mess. Most gracious majesty,—
 Cleo.   Didst thou behold
Octavia?
 Mess. Ay, dread queen.
 Cleo.   Where?
 Mess.   Madam, in Rome
I looked her in the face; and saw her led
Between her brother and Mark Antony.

Cleo. Is she as tall as me?
Mess.   She is not, madam.
Cleo. Didst hear her speak? is she shrill-tongued, or
         low?
Mess. Madam, I heard her speak: she is low-voiced.
Cleo. That's not so good. He cannot like her long.
Char. Like her? O Isis! 't is impossible.
Cleo. I think so, Charmian: dull of tongue and
         dwarfish!—
What majesty is in her gait? Remember,
If e'er thou look'dst on majesty.
Mess.   She creeps;
Her motion and her station are as one:
She shows a body rather than a life;
A statue, than a breather.
Cleo.   Is this certain?
Mess. Or I have no observance.
Char.   Three in Egypt
Cannot make better note.
Cleo.   He's very knowing,
I do perceive 't.—There's nothing in her yet.—
The fellow has good judgment.
Char.   Excellent.
Cleo. Guess at her years, I pr'ythee.
Mess.   Madam,
She was a widow—
Cleo.   Widow?—Charmian, hark.
Mess. And I do think she's thirty.
Cleo. Bear'st thou her face in mind? is't long or
         round?
Mess. Round, even to faultiness.
Cleo. For the most part, too, they are foolish that are
         so.—
Her hair, what colour?
Mess. Brown, madam; and her forehead
As low as she would wish it.
Cleo.   There's gold for thee:
Thou must not take my former sharpness ill.
I will employ thee back again: I find thee
Most fit for business. Go, make thee ready;
Our letters are prepared.   [*Exit Messenger*
Char.   A proper man.
Cleo. Indeed, he is so: I repent me much,
That so I harried him. Why, methinks, by him,
This creature's no such thing.
Char.   Nothing, madam.
Cleo. The man has seen some majesty, and should
know.
Char. Hath he seen majesty? Isis else defend
And serving you so long!

Cleo. I have one thing more to ask him yet, good
        Charmian:
But 't is no matter; thou shalt bring him to me
Where I will write.   All may be well enough.
    Char. I warrant you, madam.   *[Exeunt*

SCENE IV.—Athens. A Room in ANTONY'S House

Enter ANTONY *and* OCTAVIA

    Ant. Nay, nay, Octavia, not only that,—
That were excusable, that, and thousands more
Of semblable import,—but he hath waged
New wars 'gainst Pompey; made his will, and read it
To public ear:
Spoke scantly of me: when perforce he could not
But pay me terms of honour, cold and sickly
He vented them; most narrow measure lent me:
When the best hint was given him, he not took 't,
Or did it from his teeth.
    Octa.   O, my good lord,
Believe not all; or, if you must believe,
Stomach not all. A more unhappy lady,
If this division chance, ne'er stood between,
Praying for both parts:
The good gods will mock me presently,
When I shall pray, 'O, bless my lord and husband!'
Undo that prayer, by crying out as loud,
'O, bless my brother!' Husband win, win brother,
Prays, and destroys the prayer; no midway
'Twixt these extremes at all.
    Ant.   Gentle Octavia,
Let your best love draw to that point which seeks
Best to preserve it. If I lose mine honour,
I lose myself: better I were not yours,
Than yours so branchless. But, as you requested,
Yourself shall go between 's: the meantime, lady,
I'll raise the preparation of a war
Shall stay your brother. Make your soonest haste;
So your desires are yours.
    Octa.   Thanks to my lord,
The Jove of power make me, most weak, most weak,
Your reconciler! Wars 'twixt you twain would be,
As if the world should cleave, and that slain men
Should solder up the rift.
    Ant. When it appears to you where this begins,
Turn your displeasure that way; for our faults
Can never be so equal, that your love
Can equally move with them. Provide your going;

Choose your own company, and command what cost
Your heart has mind to.   *[Exeunt*

SCENE V.—Athens. Another Room in ANTONY's House

Enter ENOBARBUS *and* EROS, *meeting*

Eno. How now, friend Eros?
Eros. There's strange news come, sir.
Eno. What, man?
Eros. Cæsar and Lepidus have made wars upon Pompey.
Eno. This is old: what is the success?
Eros. Cæsar, having made use of him in the wars
'gainst Pompey, presently denied him rivality, would not
let him partake in the glory of the action; and not resting
here, accuses him of letters he had formerly wrote to
Pompey; upon his own appeal, seizes him: so the poor
third is up, till death enlarge his confine.
    Eno. Then, world, thou hast a pair of chaps, no more;
And throw between them all the food thou hast,
They'll grind the one the other. Where's Antony?
    Eros. He's walking in the garden—thus: and spurns
The rush that lies before him; cries, 'Fool, Lepidus!'
And threats the throat of that his officer,
That murdered Pompey.
    Eno.   Our great navy's rigged.
    Eros. For Italy and Cæsar. More, Domitius;
My lord desires you presently: my news
I might have told hearafter.
    Eno.   'T will be naught;
But let it be.—Bring me to Antony.
    Eros. Come, sir.   *[Exeunt*

SCENE VI.—Rome. A Room in CÆSAR's House

Enter CÆSAR, AGRIPPA, *and* MECÆNAS

Cæs. Contemning Rome, he has done all this and more
In Alexandria:—here's the manner of't—
I' the market-place, on a tribunal silvered,
Cleopatra and himself in chairs of gold
Were publicly enthroned: at the feet sat
Cæsarion, whom they call my father's son,
And all the unlawful issue that their lust
Since then hath made between them. Unto her
He gave the stablishment of Egypt; made her
Of lower Syria, Cyprus, Lydia,
Absolute queen.

Mec.   This in the public eye?
Cæs.   I' the common show-place, where they exercise.
His sons he there proclaimed the kings of kings;
Great Media, Parthia, and Armenia,
He gave to Alexander; to Ptolemy he assigned
Syria, Cilicia, and Phœnicia.   She
In the habiliments of the goddess Isis
That day appeared; and oft before gave audience,
As 't is reported so.
Mec.   Let Rome be thus
Informed.
Agr.   Who, queasy with his insolence
Already, will their good thoughts call from him.
Cæs.   The people know it; and have now received
His accusations.
Agr.   Whom does he accuse?
Cæs.   Cæsar; and that, having in Sicily
Sextus Pompeius spoiled, we had not rated him
His part o' the isle: then does he say, he lent me
Some shipping unrestored: lastly, he frets
That Lepidus of the triumvirate
Should be deposed; and, being, that we detain
All his revenue.
Agr.   Sir, this should be answered.
Cæs.   'T is done already, and the messenger gone.
I have told him, Lepidus was grown too cruel;
That he his high authority abused,
And did deserve his change: for what I have conquered,
I grant him part; but then, in his Armenia,
And other of his conquered kingdoms, I
Demand the like.
Mec.   He'll never yield to that.
Cæs.   Nor must not then be yielded to in this.

Enter OCTAVIA *with her train*

Octa.   Hail, Cæsar, and my lord! hail, most dear Cæsar!
Cæs.   That ever I should call thee castaway!
Octa.   You have not called me so, nor have you cause.
Cæs.   Why have you stol'n upon us thus? You come
      not
Like Cæsar's sister: the wife of Antony
Should have an army for an usher, and
The neighs of horse to tell of her approach,
Long ere she did appear; the trees by the way
Should have borne men, and expectation fainted,
Longing for what it had not; nay, the dust
Should have ascended to the roof of heaven,
Raised by your populous troops. But you are come
A market-maid to Rome, and have prevented

The ostentation of our love, which, left unshown,
Is often left unloved: we should have met you
By sea and land, supplying every stage
With an augmented greeting.
 Octa.   Good my lord,
To come thus was I not constrained, but did it
On my free will. My lord, Mark Antony,
Hearing that you prepared for war, acquainted
My grievéd ear withal; whereon, I begged
His pardon for return.
 Cæs.   Which soon he granted,
Being an obstruct 'tween his lust and him.
 Octa. Do not say so, my lord.
 Cæs.   I have eyes upon him,
And his affairs come to me on the wind.
Where is he now?
 Octa.   My lord, in Athens.
 Cæs. No, my most wrongéd sister; Cleopatra
Hath nodded him to her. He hath given his empire
Up to a whore; who now are levying
The kings o' the earth for war. He hath assembled
Bocchus, the king of Libya; Archelaus,
Of Cappadocia; Philadelphos, king
Of Paphlagonia; the Thracian king, Adallas;
King Malchus of Arabia; King of Pont;
Herod of Jewry; Mithridates, king
Of Comagene; Polemon and Amintas,
The kings of Mede, and Lycaonia,
With a more larger list of sceptres.
 Octa.   Ah me, most wretched,
That have my heart parted betwixt two friends
That do afflict each other!
 Cæs.   Welcome hither.
Your letters did withhold our breaking forth,
Till we perceived both how you were wrong led,
And we in negligent danger. Cheer your heart.
Be you not troubled with the time, which drives
O'er your content these strong necessities;
But let determined things to destiny
Hold unbewailed their way. Welcome to Rome;
Nothing more dear to me. You are abused
Beyond the mark of thought; and the high gods,
To do you justice, make their ministers
Of us and those that love you. Best of comfort;
And ever welcome to us.
 Agr.   Welcome, lady.
 Mec. Welcome, dear madam.
Each heart in Rome does love and pity you:
Only the adulterous Antony, most large
In his abominations, turns you off;

And gives his potent regiment to a trull,
That noises it against us.
 Octa.   Is it so, sir?
 Cæs. Most certain. Sister, welcome: pray you,
Be ever known to patience: my dear'st sister! [*Exeunt*

SCENE VII.—ANTONY'S Camp, near the Promontory
of Actium

Enter CLEOPATRA *and* ENOBARBUS

 Cleo. I will be even with thee, doubt it not.
 Eno. But why, why, why?
 Cleo. Thou hast forspoke my being in these wars,
And say'st it is not fit.
 Eno.   Well, is it, is it?
 Cleo. If not denounced against us, why should not we
Be there in person?
 Eno. [*Aside*] Well, I could reply:—
If we should serve with horse and mares together,
The horse were merely lost; the mares would bear
A soldier and his horse.
 Cleo.   What is't you say?
 Eno. Your presence needs must puzzle Antony;
Take from his heart, take from his brain, from 's time,
What should not then be spared. He is already
Traduced for levity; and 't is said in Rome
That Phōtinus, an eunuch, and your maids
Manage this war.
 Cleo.   Sink Rome, and their tongues rot
That speak against us! A charge we bear i' the war,
And, as the president of my kingdom, will
Appear there for a man. Speak not against it;
I will not stay behind.
 Eno.   Nay, I have done.
Here comes the emperor.

Enter ANTONY *and* CANIDIUS

 Ant.   Is't not strange, Canidius,
That from Tarentum, and Brundusium,
He could so quickly cut the Ionian sea,
And take in Toryne?—You have heard on't, sweet?
 Cleo. Celerity is never more admired
Than by the negligent.
 Ant.   A good rebuke,
Which might have well becomed the best of men,
To taunt at slackness.—Canidius, we
Will fight with him by sea.

Cleo.   By sea! What else?
Can.   Why will my lord do so?
Ant.   For that he dares us to 't.
Eno.   So hath my lord dared him to single fight.
Can.   Ay, and to wage this battle at Pharsalia,
Where Cæsar fought with Pompey; but these offers,
Which serve not for his vantage, he shakes off;
And so should you.
Eno.   Your ships are not well manned;
Your mariners are muleters, reapers, people
Ingrossed by swift impress: in Cæsar's fleet
Are those that often have 'gainst Pompey fought:
Their ships are yare; yours, heavy. No disgrace
Shall fall you for refusing him at sea,
Being prepared for land.
Ant.   By sea, by sea.
Eno.   Most worthy sir, you therein throw away
The absolute soldiership you have by land;
Distract your army, which doth most consist
Of war-marked footmen; leave unexecuted
Your own renownéd knowledge; quite forego
The way which promises assurance, and
Give up yourself merely to chance and hazard,
From firm security.
Ant.   I'll fight at sea.
Cleo.   I have sixty sails, Cæsar none better.
Ant.   Our overplus of shipping will we burn;
And with the rest, full-manned, from the head of Actium
Beat the approaching Cæsar. But if we fail,
We then can do 't at land.

Enter a Messenger

                        Thy business?
Mess.   The news is true, my lord; he is descried;
Cæsar has taken Toryne.
Ant.   Can he be there in person? 't is impossible;
Strange, that his power should be.—Canidius,
Our nineteen legions thou shalt hold by land,
And our twelve thousand horse:—we'll to our ship.
Away, my Thetis!

Enter a Soldier

                        How now, worthy soldier?
Sold.   O noble emperor, do not fight by sea;
Trust not to rotten planks. Do you misdoubt
This sword, and these my wounds? Let the Egyptians
And the Phœnicians go a-ducking; we
Have used to conquer standing on the earth,
And fighting foot to foot.

121

Ant.   Well, well.—Away!
                    [*Exeunt Antony, Cleopatra, and Enobarbus*
Sold.   By Hercules, I think, I am i' the right.
Can.   Soldier, thou art; but his whole action grows
Not in the power on't: so our leader's led,
And we are women's men.
Sold.   You keep by land
The legions and the horse whole, do you not?
Can.   Marcus Octavius, Marcus Justeius;
Publicola, and Cælius, are for sea;
But we keep whole by land.   This speed of Cæsar's
Carries beyond belief.
Sold.   While he was yet in Rome,
His power went out in such distractions as
Beguiled all spies.
Can.   Who's his lieutenant, hear you?
Sold.   They say, one Taurus.
Can.   Well I know the man.

Enter a Messenger

Mess.   The emperor calls Canidius.
Can.   With news the time's with labour, and throes forth
Each minute some.   [*Exeunt*

Scene VIII.—A plain near Actium

Enter Cæsar, Taurus, *Officers, and others*

Cæs.   Taurus!
Taur.   My lord?
Cæs.   Strike not by land; keep
          whole:
Provoke not battle, till we have done at sea.
Do not exceed the prescript of this scroll:
Our fortune lies upon this jump.   [*Exeunt*

Enter Antony *and* Enobarbus

Ant.   Set we our squadrons on yond side o' the hill,
In eye of Cæsar's battle; from which place
We may the number of the ships behold,
And so proceed accordingly.   [*Exeunt*

Enter Canidius, *marching with his land Army one way over
     the stage; and* Taurus, *the Lieutenant of* Cæsar, *the
     other way.   After their going in, is heard the noise of a
     sea-fight.*
               Alarum.   Re-enter Enobarbus
Eno.   Naught, naught, all naught!   I can behold no
          longer.

                        122

The Antoniad, the Egyptian admiral,
With all their sixty, fly, and turn the rudder:
To see't, mine eyes are blasted.

Enter SCARUS

Scar.   Gods, and goddesses,
All the whole synod of them!
    Eno.   What's thy passion?
    Scar.   The greater cantle of the world is lost
With very ignorance: we have kissed away
Kingdoms and provinces.
    Eno.   How appears the fight?
    Scar.   On our side like the tokened pestilence,
Where death is sure.   Yon ribaudred nag of Egypt,—
Whom leprosy o'ertake!—i' the midst o' the fight,
When vantage like a pair of twins appeared,
Both as the same, or rather ours the elder,—
The breese upon her, like a cow in June,
Hoists sails, and flies.
    Eno.   That I beheld:
Mine eyes did sicken at the sight, and could not
Endure a further view.
    Scar.   She once being loofed,
The noble ruin of her magic, Antony,
Claps on his sea-wing, and like a doting mallard,
Leaving the fight in height, flies after her.
I never saw an action of such shame:
Experience, manhood, honour, ne'er before
Did violate so itself.
    Eno.   Alack, alack!

Enter CANIDIUS

    Can.   Our fortune on the sea is out of breath,
And sinks most lamentably.   Had our general
Been what he knew himself, it had gone well:
O, he has given example for our flight,
Most grossly, by his own.
    Eno.   Ay, are you thereabouts?
Why then, good night, indeed.
    Can.   Towards Peloponnesus are they fled.
    Scar.   'T is easy to't; and there I will attend
What further comes.
    Can.   To Cæsar will I render
My legions, and my horse: six kings already
Show me the way of yielding.
    Eno.   I'll yet follow
The wounded chance of Antony, though my reason
Sits in the wind against me.   [*Exeunt*

SCENE IX.—Alexandria. A Room in the Palace

Enter ANTONY *and Attendants*

Ant. Hark! the land bids me tread no more upon't;
It is ashamed to bear me.—Friends, come hither:
I am so lated in the world, that I
Have lost my way for ever.—I've a ship
Laden with gold; take that; divide it, fly,
And make your peace with Cæsar.
Att.   Fly! not we.
Ant. I have fled myself, and have instructed cowards
To run, and show their shoulders.—Friends, be gone;
I have myself resolved upon a course,
Which has no need of you; be gone:
My treasure's in the harbour, take it.—
I followed that I blush to look upon:
My very hairs do mutiny; for the white
Reprove the brown for rashness, and they them
For fear and doting.—Friends, be gone: you shall
Have letters from me to some friends that will
Sweep your way for you. Pray you, look not sad,
Nor make replies of loathness: take the hint
Which my despair proclaims; let that be left
Which leaves itself: to the sea-side straightway:
I will possess you of that ship and treasure.
Leave me, I pray, a little; pray you now:—
Nay, do so; for, indeed, I have lost command,
Therefore, I pray you.   I'll see you by-and-by.

                                              [*Sits down*

Enter EROS, *and* CLEOPATRA, *led by* CHARMIAN *and* IRAS

Eros. Nay, gentle madam, to him; comfort him.
Iras. Do, most dear queen.
Char. Do! Why, what else?
Cleo. Let me sit down. O Juno!
Ant. No, no, no, no, no.
Eros. See you here, sir?
Ant. O fie, fie, fie!
Char. Madam.—
Iras. Madam; O good empress!—
Eros. Sir, sir,—
Ant. Yes, my lord, yes.—He at Philippi kept
His sword e'en like a dancer; while I struck
The lean and wrinkled Cassius; and 't was I
That the mad Brutus ended: he alone
Dealt on lieutenantry, and no practice had
In the brave squares of war: yet now—No matter.

Cleo.   An, stand by.
Eros.   The queen, my lord, the queen.
Iras.   Go to him, madam, speak to him:
He is unqualitied with very shame.
Cleo.   Well then,—sustain me:—O!
Eros.   Most noble sir, arise; the queen approaches:
Her head's declined, and death will seize her, but
Your comfort makes the rescue.
Ant.   I have offended reputation,—
A most unnoble swerving.
Eros.   Sir, the queen.
Ant.   O, whither hast thou led me, Egypt?   See,
How I convey my shame out of thine eyes
By looking back on what I have left behind
'Stroy'd in dishonour.
Cleo.   O my lord, my lord!
Forgive my fearful sails: I little thought
You would have followed.
Ant   Egypt, thou knew'st too well,
My heart was to thy rudder tied by the strings,
And thou shouldst tow me after: o'er my spirit
Thy full supremacy thou knew'st, and that
Thy beck might from the bidding of the gods
Command me.
Cleo.   O, my pardon!
Ant.   Now I must
To the young man send humble treaties, dodge
And palter in the shifts of lowness, who
With half the bulk o' the world played as I pleased
Making and marring fortunes.   You did know,
How much you were my conqueror; and that
My sword, made weak by my affection, would
Obey it on all cause.
Cleo.   Pardon, pardon!
Ant.   Fall not a tear, I say; one of them rates
All that is won and lost.   Give me a kiss;
Even this repays me.—We sent our schoolmaster;
Is he come back?—Love, I am full of lead.—
Some wine, within there, and our viands!—Fortune knows,
We scorn her most when most she offers blows.

                                        [*Exeunt*

SCENE X.—CÆSAR'S Camp in Egypt

Enter CÆSAR, DOLABELLA, THYREUS, *and others*

Cæs.   Let him appear that's come from Antony.—
Know you him?
Dol.   Cæsar, 't is his schoolmaster:

An argument that he is plucked, when hither
He sends so poor a pinion of his wing,
Which had superfluous kings for messengers
Not many moons gone by.

Enter EUPHRONIUS

Cæs.   Approach, and speak.
   Euph.   Such as I am, I come from Antony:
I was of late as petty to his ends
As is the morn-dew on the myrtle-leaf
To his grand sea.
   Cæs.   Be 't so.   Declare thine office.
   Euph.   Lord of his fortunes he salutes thee, and
Requires to live in Egypt; which not granted,
He lessens his requests, and to thee sues
To let him breathe between the heavens and earth,
A private man in Athens.   This for him.
Next, Cleopatra does confess thy greatness,
Submits her to thy might, and of thee craves
The circle of the Ptolemies for her heirs,
Now hazarded to thy grace.
   Cæs.   For Antony,
I have no ears to his request.   The queen
Of audience, nor desire, shall fail, so she
From Egypt drive her all-disgracéd friend,
Or take his life there: this if she perform,
She shall not sue unheard.   So to them both.
   Euph.   Fortune pursue thee!
   Cæs.   Bring him through the bands.
                                   [*Exit Euphronius*
[*To Thyreus*] To try thy eloquence, now 't is time;
          despatch.
From Antony win Cleopatra: promise,
And in our name, what she requires; add more,
From thine invention, offers.   Women are not
In their best fortunes strong, but what will perjure
The ne'er-touched vestal.   Try thy cunning, Thyreus;
Make thine own edict for thy pains, which we
Will answer as a law.
   Thyr.   Cæsar, I go.
   Cæs.   Observe how Antony becomes his flaw,
And what thou think'st his very action speaks
In every power that moves.
   Thyr.   Cæsar, I shall.   [*Exeunt*

SCENE XI.—Alexandria. A Room in CLEOPATRA'S
Palace

Enter CLEOPATRA, ENOBARBUS, CHARMIAN, *and* IRAS

Cleo. What shall we do, Enobarbus?
Eno.   Think, and die.
Cleo. Is Antony, or we, in fault for this?
Eno. Antony only, that would make his will
Lord of his reason. What though you fled
From that great face of war, whose several ranges
Frighted each other, why should he follow?
The itch of his affection should not then
Have nicked his captainship; at such a point,
When half to half the world opposed, he being
The meréd question. 'T was a shame no less
Than was his loss, to course your flying flags,
And leave his navy gazing.
Cleo.   Pr'ythee, peace.

Enter ANTONY, *with* EUPHRONIUS

Ant. Is that his answer?
Euph. Ay, my lord.
Ant. The queen shall then have courtesy, so she
Will yield us up.
Euph.   He says so.
Ant.   Let her know 't.
To the boy Cæsar send this grizzled head,
And he will fill thy wishes to the brim
With principalities.
Cleo.   That head, my lord?
Ant. To him again. Tell him, he wears the rose
Of youth upon him, from which the world should note
Something particular: his coin, ships, legions,
May be a coward's; whose ministers would prevail
Under the service of a child as soon
As i' the command of Cæsar: I dare him therefore
To lay his gay comparisons apart,
And answer me declined, sword against sword,
Ourselves alone. I'll write it: follow me.
                    [*Exeunt Antony and Euphronius.*
Eno. [*Aside*] Yes, like enough, high-battled Cæsar will
Unstate his happiness, and be staged to the show,
Against a sworder!—I see, men's judgments are
A parcel of their fortunes, and things outward
Do draw the inward quality after them,
To suffer all alike. That he should dream,
Knowing all measures, the full Cæsar will

127

Answer his emptiness!—Cæsar, thou hast subdued
His judgment too.

Enter an Attendant

 Att.   A messenger from Cæsar.
 Cleo. What, no more ceremony?—See my women!—
Against the blown rose may they stop their nose
That kneeled unto the buds.—Admit him, sir.
 Eno. [*Aside*] Mine honesty and I begin to square.
The loyalty well held to fools does make
Our faith mere folly: yet he that can endure
To follow with allegiance a fall'n lord,
Does conquer him that did his master conquer,
And earns a place i' the story.

Enter THYREUS

 Cleo.   Cæsar's will.
 Thyr. Hear it apart.
 Cleo.   None but friends: say boldly.
 Thyr. So, haply, are they friends to Antony.
 Eno. He needs as many, sir, as Cæsar has,
Or needs not us. If Cæsar please, our master
Will leap to be his friend: for us, you know
Whose he is, we are, and that's Cæsar's.
 Thyr.   So.—
Thus then, thou most renowned: Cæsar entreats,
Not to consider in what case thou stand'st,
Further than he is Cæsar.
 Cleo.   Go on: right royal.
 Thyr. He knows that you embrace not Antony
As you did love but as you feared him.
 Cleo.   O!
 Thyr. The scars upon your honour therefore he
Does pity as constrainéd blemishes,
Not as deserved.
 Cleo.   He is a god, and knows
What is most right. Mine honour was not yielded,
But conquered merely.
 Eno. [*Aside*]   To be sure of that,
I will ask Antony.—Sir, sir, thou'rt so leaky
That we must leave thee to thy sinking, for
Thy dearest quit thee.
 Thyr.   Shall I say to Cæsar
What you require of him? for he partly begs
To be desired to give. It much would please him,
That of his fortunes you should make a staff
To lean upon; but it would warm his spirits,
To hear from me you had left Antony,
And put yourself under his shroud,

The universal landlord.
Cleo. What's your name?
Thyr. My name is Thyreus.
Cleo. Most kind messenger,
Say to great Cæsar this: in deputation
I kiss his conqu'ring hand: tell him, I am prompt
To lay my crown at his feet, and there to kneel:
Tell him, from his all-obeying breath I hear
The doom of Egypt.
Thyr. 'T is your noblest course.
Wisdom and fortune combating together,
If that the former dare but what it can,
No chance may shake it. Give me grace to lay
My duty on your hand.
Cleo. Your Cæsar's father oft,
When he hath mused of taking kingdoms in,
Bestowed his lips on that unworthy place
As it rained kisses.

Re-enter ANTONY *and* ENOBARBUS

Ant. Favours, by Jove that thunders!—
What art thou, fellow?
Thyr. One, that but performs
The bidding of the fullest man, and worthiest
To have command obeyed.
Eno. [*Aside*] You will be whipped.
Ant. Approach, there.—Ay, you kite!—Now, gods and
devils!
Authority melts from me: of late, when I cried, 'Ho!'
Like boys unto a muss, kings would start forth,
And cry, 'Your will?' Have you no ears?

Enter *Attendants*

I am Antony yet. Take hence this Jack, and whip him.
Eno. [*Aside*] 'T is better playing with a lion's whelp,
Than with an old one dying.
Ant. Moon and stars!
Whip him.—Were 't twenty of the greatest tributaries
That do acknowledge Cæsar, should I find them
So saucy with the hand of—she here (what's her name,
Since she was Cleopatra?)—Whip him, fellows,
Till, like a boy, you see him cringe his face,
And whine aloud for mercy. Take him hence.
Thyr. Mark Antony,—
Ant. Tug him away: being whipped,
Bring him again.—This Jack of Cæsar's shall
Bear us an errand to him.—
[*Exeunt Attendants with Thyreus*
You were half blasted ere I knew you: ha!

129

Have I my pillow left unpressed in Rome,
Forborne the getting of a lawful race,
And by a gem of women, to be abused
By one that looks on feeders?
 Cleo.   Good my lord,—
 Ant. You have been a boggler ever:—
But when we in our viciousness grow hard,—
O misery on't!—the wise gods seel our eyes;
In our own filth drop our clear judgments; make us
Adore our errors; laugh at's, while we strut
To our confusion.
 Cleo.   O, is 't come to this?
 Ant. I found you as a morsel cold upon
Dead Cæsar's trencher; nay, you were a fragment
Of Cneius Pompey's; besides what hotter hours,
Unregistered in vulgar fame, you have
Luxuriously picked out: for, I am sure,
Though you can guess what temperance should be,
You know not what it is.
 Cleo.   Wherefore is this?
 Ant. To let a fellow that will take rewards,
And say, 'God quit you!' be familiar with
My playfellow, your hand, this kingly seal,
And plighter of high hearts!—O, that I were
Upon the hill of Basan to outroar
The hornéd herd! for I have savage cause;
And to proclaim it civilly, were like
A haltered neck which does the hangman thank
For being yare about him.—

Re-enter Attendants, with THYREUS

         Is he whipped?
 First Att. Soundly, my lord.
 Ant.   Cried he? and begged he pardon?
 First Att. He did ask favour.
 Ant. If that thy father live, let him repent
Thou wast not made his daughter; and be thou sorry
To follow Cæsar in his triumph, since
Thou hast been whipped for following him: henceforth,
The white hand of a lady fever thee;
Shake thou to look on't.   Get thee back to Cæsar,
Tell him thy entertainment: look, thou say,
He makes me angry with him; for he seems
Proud and disdainful, harping on what I am,
Not what he knew I was.   He makes me angry;
And at this time most easy 't is to do 't,
When my good stars that were my former guides
Have empty left their orbs, and shot their fires
Into the abysm of hell.   If he mislike

My speech, and what is done, tell him, he has
Hipparchus, my enfranchéd bondman, whom
He may at pleasure whip, or hang, or torture,
As he shall like, to quit me. Urge it thou:
Hence, with thy stripes, be gone!   [*Exit Thyreus*
  Cleo. Have you done yet?
  Ant.   Alack! our terrene moon
Is now eclipsed, and it portends alone
The fall of Antony.
  Cleo.   I must stay his time.
  Ant. To flatter Cæsar, would you mingle eyes
With one that ties his points?
  Cleo.   Not know me yet?
  Ant. Cold-hearted toward me?
  Cleo.   Ah, dear, if I be so,
From my cold heart let heaven engender hail,
And poison it in the source; and the first stone
Drop in my neck: as it determines, so
Dissolve my life; the next, Cæsarion smite,
Till by degrees the memory of my womb,
Together with my brave Egyptians all,
By the discandying of this pelleted storm,
Lie graveless, till the flies and gnats of Nile
Have buried them for prey!
  Ant.   I am satisfied.
Cæsar sits down in Alexandria, where
I will oppose his fate. Our force by land
Hath nobly held; our severed navy too
Have knit again, and fleet, threat'ning most sealike.
Where hast thou been, my heart?—Dost thou hear, lady?
If from the field I shall return once more
To kiss these lips, I will appear in blood;
I and my sword will earn our chronicle:
There's hope in't yet.
  Cleo.   That's my brave lord!
  Ant. I will be treble-sinewed, hearted, breathed,
And fight maliciously: for when mine hours
Were nice and lucky, men did ransom lives
Of me for jests; but now, I'll set my teeth,
And send to darkness all that stop me.—Come,
Let's have one other gaudy night.—Call to me
All my sad captains: fill our bowls; once more
Let's mock the midnight bell.
  Cleo.   It is my birthday:
I had thought to have held it poor; but, since my lord
Is Antony again, I will be Cleopatra.
  Ant. We will yet do well.
  Cleo. Call all his noble captains to my lord.
  Ant. Do so; we'll speak to them; and to-night I'll
      force

The wine peep through their scars.—Come on, my queen;
There's sap in 't yet. The next time I do fight,
I'll make death love me, for I will contend
Even with his pestilent scythe.

                  [Exeunt Antony, Cleopatra, and Attendants
   Eno. Now he'll outstare the lightning. To be furious,
Is to be frighted out of fear; and, in that mood,
The dove will peck the estridge: and I see still,
A diminution in our captain's brain
Restores his heart. When valour preys on reason,
It eats the sword it fights with. I will seek
Some way to leave him.   *[Exit*

ACT FOUR

Scene I.—Cæsar's Camp at Alexandria

Enter Cæsar, *reading a letter;* Agrippa, Mecænas, *and others*

   Cæs. He calls me boy, and chides, as he had power
To beat me out of Egypt; my messenger
He hath whipped with rods; dares me to personal combat,
Cæsar to Antony. Let the old ruffian know,
I have many other ways to die; meantime,
Laugh at his challenge.
   Mec.   Cæsar must think,
When one so great begins to rage, he's hunted
Even to falling. Give him no breath, but now
Make boot of his distraction. Never anger
Make good guard for itself.
   Cæs.   Let our best heads
Know, that to-morrow the last of many battles
We mean to fight. Within our files there are,
Of those that serve Mark Antony but late,
Enough to fetch him in. See it done;
And feast the army: we have store to do 't,
And they have earned the waste. Poor Antony!

                                    [Exeunt

Scene II.—Alexandria. A Room in Cleopatra's Palace

Enter Antony, Cleopatra, Enobarbus, Charmian, Iras, Alexas, *and others*

   Ant. He will not fight with me, Domitius.
   Eno.   No.

Ant.   Why should he not?
Eno.   He thinks, being twenty times of better fortune,
He is twenty men to one.
    Ant.   To-morrow, soldier,
By sea and land I'll fight; or I will live,
Or bathe my dying honour in the blood
Shall make it live again.   Woo't thou fight well?
    Eno.   I'll strike, and cry, 'Take all.'
    Ant.   Well said; come on—
Call forth my household servants: let's to-night
Be bounteous at our meal.

Enter Servants

                        Give me thy hand,
Thou hast been rightly honest;—so hast thou;—
And thou,—and thou,—and thou:—you've served me well,
And kings have been your fellows.
    Cleo.   [*Aside to Eno.*]   What means this?
    Eno.   [*Aside to Clo.*]   'T is one of those odd tricks
        which sorrow shoots
Out of the mind.
    Ant.   And thou art honest too.
I wish I could be made so many men,
And all of you clapped up together in
An Antony, that I might do you service
So good as you have done.
    Serv.   The gods forbid!
    Ant.   Well, my good fellows, wait on me to-night;
Scant not my cups, and make as much of me,
As when mine empire was your fellow too,
And suffered my command.
    Cleo.   [*Aside to Eno.*]   What does he mean?
    Eno.   [*Aside to Cleo*].   To make his followers weep.
    Ant.   Tend me to-night;
May be, it is the period of your duty:
Haply, you shall not see me more; or if,
A mangled shadow: perchance, to-morrow
You'll serve another master.   I look on you
As one that takes his leave.   Mine honest friends,
I turn you not away; but, like a master
Married to your good service, stay till death:
Tend me to-night two hours, I ask no more,
And the gods yield you for't!
    Eno.   What mean you, sir,
To give them this discomfort?   Look, they weep;
And I, an ass, am onion-eyed: for shame,
Transform us not to women.
    Ant.   Ho, ho, ho!
Now, the witch take me, if I meant it thus!

Grace grow where those drops fall! My hearty friends,
You take me in too dolorous a sense,
For I spake to you for your comfort; did desire you
To burn this night with torches.   Know, my hearts,
I hope well of to-morrow; and will lead you
Where rather I'll expect victorious life
Than death and honour.   Let's to supper, come,
And drown consideration.   [*Exeunt*

SCENE III.—Alexandria.   Before CLEOPATRA's Palace

Enter two Soldiers, to their guard

First Sold.   Brother, good night: to-morrow is the day.
Sec. Sold.   It will determine one way: fare you well.
Heard you of nothing strange about the streets?
First Sold.   Nothing.   What news?
Sec. Sold.   Belike, 't is but a rumour.   Good night to you.
First Sold.   Well, sir, good night.

Enter two other Soldiers

Sec. Sold.   Soldiers, have careful watch.
Third Sold.   And you.   Good night, good night.
                    [*The first two place themselves at their posts*
Fourth Sold.   Here we: [*they take their posts*] and if
                    to-morrow
Our navy thrive, I have an absolute hope
Our landmen will stand up.
Third Sold.   'T is a brave army,
And full of purpose.
                    [*Music of hautboys underground*
Fourth Sold.   Peace! what noise?
First Sold.   List, list!
Sec. Sold.   Hark!
First Sold.   Music i' the air.
Third Sold.   Under the earth.
Fourth Sold.   It signs well, does it not?
Third Sold.   No.
First Sold.   Peace, I say!
What should this mean!
Sec. Sold.   'T is the god Hercules, whom Antony loved,
Now leaves him.
First Sold.   Walk; let's see if other watchmen
Do hear what we do.
                    [*They advance to another post*
Sec. Sold.   How now, masters?
Soldiers.   [*Speaking together*]   How now?
How now? do you hear this?

First Sold.   Ay; is't not strange?
Third Sold. Do you hear, masters? do you hear?
First Sold. Follow the noise so far as we have quarter;
Let's see how't will give off.
Soldiers.   Content. 'T is strange.
                                  [Exeunt

SCENE IV.—Alexandria. A Room in CLEOPATRA'S Palace

Enter ANTONY *and* CLEOPATRA; CHARMIAN, *and others*
attending

Ant. Eros! mine armour, Eros!
Cleo.   Sleep a little.
Ant. No, my chuck.—Eros, come; mine armour, Eros!

Enter EROS, *with armour*

Come, good fellow, put mine iron on:—
If fortune be not ours to-day, it is
Because we brave her.—Come.
Cleo.   Nay, I'll help too.
What's this for?
Ant.   Ah, let be, let be! thou art
The armourer of my heart:—false, false; this, this.
Cleo. Sooth, la, I'll help. Thus it must be.
Ant.   Well well;
We shall thrive now.—Seest thou, my good fellow?
Go, put on thy defences.
Eros.   Briefly, sir.
Cleo. Is not this buckled well?
Ant.   Rarely, rarely:
He that unbuckles this, till we do please
To doff't for repose, shall hear a storm.—
Thou fumblest, Eros; and my queen's a squire
More tight at this than thou. Despatch.—O love,
That thou could see my wars to-day, and knew'st
The royal occupation! thou shouldst see
A workman in't.

Enter an armed Soldier

             Good morrow to thee; welcome:
Thou look'st like him that knows a warlike charge:
To business that we love we rise betime,
And go to't with delight.
Sold.   A thousand, sir,
Early though't be, have on their riveted trim,
And at the port expect you.   *[Shout. Trumpets flourish*

Enter Captains and Soldiers

Capt.   The morn is fair.—Good morrow, general.
All.   Good morrow, general.
Ant.   'T is well blown, lads.
This morning, like the spirit of a youth
That means to be of note, begins betimes.—
So, so; come, give me that: this way; well said.
Fare thee well, dame: whate'er becomes of me,
This is a soldier's kiss. [*Kisses her*] Rebukable,
And worthy shameful cheek it were, to stand
On more mechanic compliment: I'll leave thee
Now, like a man of steel.—You, that will fight,
Follow me close; I'll bring you to't.—Adieu.
                    [*Exeunt Antony, Eros, Officers, and Soldiers*
Char.   Please you, retire to your chamber.
Cleo.   Lead me.
He goes forth gallantly.   That he and Cæsar might
Determine this great war in single fight!
Then Antony—but now—Well, on.   [*Exeunt*

SCENE V.—ANTONY's Camp near Alexandria

Trumpets sound.   Enter ANTONY *and* EROS; *a Soldier
meeting them*

Sold.   The gods make this a happy day to Antony!
Ant.   Would thou, and those thy scars, had once pre-
vailed
To make me fight at land!
Sold.   Hadst thou done so,
The kings that have revolted, and the soldier
That has this morning left thee, would have still
Followed thy heels.
Ant.   Who's gone this morning?
Sold.   Who?
One ever near thee; call for Enobarbus,
He shall not hear thee; or from Cæsar's camp
Say, ' I am none of thine.'
Ant.   What say'st thou?
Sold.   Sir,
He is with Cæsar.
Eros.   Sir, his chests and treasure
He has not with him.
Ant.   Is he gone?
Sold.   Most certain.
Ant.   Go, Eros, send his treasure after; do it;
Detain no jot, I charge thee.   Write to him—
I will subscribe—gentle adieus and greetings:

136

Say, that I wish he never find more cause
To change a master.—O, my fortunes have
Corrupted honest men!—Despatch.—Enobarbus!

[Exeunt

Scene VI.—Cæsar's Camp before Alexandria

Flourish.   Enter Cæsar, *with* Agrippa, Enobarbus,
and others

Cæs.   Go forth, Agrippa, and begin the fight.
Our will is, Antony be took alive;
Make it so known.
  Agr.   Cæsar, I shall.   *[Exit*
  Cæs.   The time of universal peace is near;
Prove this a prosperous day, the three-nooked world
Shall bear the olive freely.

Enter a Messenger

  Mess.   Antony
Is come into the field.
  Cæs.   Go, charge Agrippa
Plant those that have revolted in the van,
That Antony may seem to spend his fury
Upon himself.   *[Exeunt Cæsar and his Train*
  Eno.   Alexas did revolt, and went to Jewry,
On affairs of Antony; there did persuade
Great Herod to incline himself to Cæsar,
And leave his master Antony: for this pains,
Cæsar hath hanged him.   Canidius, and the rest
That fell away, have entertainment, but
No honourable trust.   I have done ill,
Of which I do accuse myself so sorely,
That I will joy no more.

Enter a Soldier of Cæsar's

  Sold.   Enobarbus, Antony
Hath after thee sent all thy treasure, with
His bounty overplus: the messenger
Came on my guard, and at thy tent is now
Unloading of his mules.
  Eno.   I give it you.
  Sold.   Mock not, Enobarbus,
I tell you true: best you safed the bringer
Out of the host; I must attend mine office,
Or would have done't myself.   Your emperor
Continues still a Jove.   *[Exit*
  Eno.   I am alone the villain of the earth,

137

And feel I am so most.   O Antony!
Thou mine of bounty, how wouldst thou have paid
My better service, when my turpitude
Thou dost so crown with gold!   This blows my heart:
If swift thought break it not, a swifter mean
Shall outstrike thought; but thought will do't, I feel.
I fight against thee!—No: I will go seek
Some ditch, wherein to die: the foul'st best fits
My latter part of life.   [*Exit*

SCENE VII.—Field of Battle between the Camps

Alarum.   Drums and trumpets.   Enter AGRIPPA *and others*

   Agr.   Retire, we have engaged ourselves too far.
Cæsar himself has work, and our oppression
Exceeds what we expected.   [*Exeunt*

   Alarum.   Enter ANTONY *and* SCARUS *wounded*

   Scar.   O my brave emperor, this is fought indeed!
Had we done so at first, we had driven them home
With clouts about their heads.
   Ant.   Thou bleed'st apace.
   Scar.   I had a wound here that was like a T,
But now 't is made an H.
   Ant.   Thy do retire.
   Scar.   We'll beat 'em into bench-holes.   I have yet
Room for six scotches more.

Enter EROS

   Eros.   They are beaten, sir; and our advantage serves
For a fair victory.
   Scar.   .   Let us score their backs,
And snatch 'em up, as we take hares, behind:
'T is sport to maul a runner.
   Ant.   I will reward thee
Once for thy sprightly comfort, and ten-fold
For thy good valour.   Come thee on.
   Scar.   I'll halt after.   [*Exeunt*

SCENE VIII.—Under the Walls of Alexandria

Alarum.   Enter ANTONY, *marching;* SCARUS *and Forces*

   Ant.   We have beat him to his camp.   Run one before,
And let the queen know of our gests.—To-morrow,
Before the sun shall see us, we'll spill the blood

That has to-day escaped.   I thank you all;
For doughty-handed are you, and have fought
Not as you served the cause, but as it had been
Each man's like mine: you have shown all Hectors.
Enter the city, clip your wives, your friends,
Tell them your feats; whilst they with joyful tears
Wash the congealment from your wounds, and kiss
The honoured gashes whole.—Give me thy hand:

Enter CLEOPATRA, *attended*

To this great fairy I'll commend thy acts,
Make her thanks bless thee.—O thou day o' the world!
Chain mine armed neck; leap thou, attire and all,
Through proof of harness to my heart, and there
Ride on the pants triumphing.
    Cleo.   Lord of lords!
O infinite virtue! com'st thou smiling from
The world's great snare uncaught?
    Ant.   My nightingale,
We have beat them to their beds.   What, girl! though grey
Do something mingle with our younger brown, yet ha' we
A brain that nourishes our nerves, and can
Get goal for goal of youth.   Behold this man;
Commend unto his lips thy favouring hand:—
Kiss it, my warrior:—he hath fought to-day
As if a god, in hate of mankind, had
Destroyed in such a shape.
    Cleo.   I'll give thee, friend,
An armour all of gold; it was a king's.
    Ant.   He has deserved it, were it carbuncled
Like holy Phœbus' car.—Give me thy hand:
Through Alexandria make a jolly march;
Bear our hacked targets like the men that owe them.
Had out great palace the capacity
To camp this host, we all would sup together,
And drink carouses to the next day's fate,
Which promises royal peril.—Trumpeters,
With brazen din blast you the city's ear:
Make mingle with our rattling tabourines,
That heaven and earth may strike their sounds together,
Applauding our approach.   *[Exeunt*

SCENE IX.—CÆSAR's Camp

Sentinels on their Post

    First Sold.   If we be not relieved within this hour
We must return to the court of guard.   The night

Is shiny and they say we shall embattle
By the second hour i' the morn.
   Sec. Sold.   This last day was
A shrewd one to us.

Enter ENOBARBUS

   Eno.   O, bear me witness, night,—
   Third Sold.   What man is this?
   Sec. Sold.   Stand close, and list him.
   Eno.   Be witness to me, O thou blessed moon,
When men revolted shall upon record
Bear hateful memory, poor Enobarbus did
Before thy face repent!—
   First Sold.   Enobarbus!
   Third Sold.   Peace!
Hark further.
   Eno.   O sovereign mistress of true melancholy,
The poisonous damp of night disponge upon me,
That life, a very rebel to my will,
May hang no longer on me: throw my heart
Against the flint and hardness of my fault,
Which, being dried with grief, will break to powder,
And finish all foul thoughts. O Antony,
Nobler than my revolt is infamous,
Forgive me in thine own particular;
But let the world rank me in register
A master-leaver and a fugitive.
O Antony! O Antony!   *[Dies*
   Sec. Sold.   Let's speak to him.
   First Sold.   Let's hear him; for the things he speaks
May concern Cæsar.
   Third Sold.   Let's do so. But he sleeps.
   First Sold.   Swoons rather; for so bad a prayer as his
Was never yet for sleep.
   Sec. Sold.   Go we to him.
   Third Sold.   Awake, sir, awake! speak to us.
   Sec. Sold.   Hear you, sir?
   First Sold.   The hand of death hath raught him.
          [Drums afar off]   Hark! the drums
Demurely wake the sleepers. Let us bear him
To the court of guard; he is of note: our hour
Is fully out.
   Third Sold.   Come on then;
He may recover yet.   *[Exeunt with the body*

Scene X.—Between the two Camps

Enter Antony *and* Scarus, *with Forces, marching*

   Ant. Their preparation is to-day by sea:
We please them not by land.
   Scar.   For both, my lord.
   Ant. I would, they'd fight i' the fire, or i' the air;
We'd fight there too. But this it is: our foot
Upon the hills adjoining to the city
Shall stay with us: order for sea is given;
They have put forth the haven: . . .
Where their appointment we may best discover,
And look on their endeavour.   *[Exeunt*

Enter Cæsar *and his Forces, marching*

   Cæs. But being charged, we will be still by land,
Which, as I take't, we shall; for his best force
Is forth to man his galleys. To the vales,
And hold our best advantage!   *[Exeunt*

Re-enter Antony *and* Scarus

   Ant. Yet they are not joined. Where yond pine does
      stand,
I shall discover all: I'll bring thee word
Straight how't is like to go.   *[Exit*
   Scar.   Swallows have built
In Cleopatra's sails their nests: the auguries
Say, they know not,—they cannot tell;—look grimly
And dare not speak their knowledge. Antony
Is valiant, and dejected; and, by starts,
His fretted fortunes give him hope, and fear,
Of what he has, and has not.
              [Alarum afar off, as at a sea-fight

Re-enter Antony
   Ant.   All is lost!
This foul Egyptian hath betrayéd me:
My fleet hath yielded to the foe; and yonder
They cast their caps up, and carouse together
Like friends long lost.—Triple-turned whore 't is thou
Hast sold me to this novice, and my heart
Makes only wars on thee.—Bid them all fly;
For when I am revenged upon my charm,
I have done all. Bid them all fly; be gone.   *[Exit Scarus*
O sun, thy uprise shall I see no more:
Fortune and Antony part here; even here

Do we shake hands.—All come to this?—The hearts
That spanieled me at heels, to whom I gave
Their wishes, do discandy, melt their sweets
On blossoming Cæsar; and this pine is barked
That overtopped them all.   Betrayed I am.
O this false soul of Egypt! this grave charm,—
Whose eye becked forth my wars, and called them home,
Whose bosom was my crownet, my chief end,—
Like a right gipsy, hath, at fast and loose,
Beguiled me to the very heart of loss.—
What, Eros! Eros!

Enter CLEOPATRA

                    Ah, thou spell! Avaunt!
   Cleo.   Why is my lord enraged against his love?
   Ant.   Vanish, or I shall give thee thy deserving,
And blemish Cæsar's triumph.   Let him take thee.
And hoist thee up to the shouting plébians:
Follow his chariot, like the greatest spot
Of all thy sex; most monster-like, be shown
For poor'st diminutives, for doits; and let
Patient Octavia plough thy visage up
With her prepared nails.   [*Exit Cleopatra*
          T is well thou'rt gone,
If it be well to live; but better't were
Thou fell'st into my fury, for one death
Might have prevented many.—Eros, ho!—
The shirt of Nessus is upon me: teach me,
Alcides, thou mine ancestor, thy rage:
Let me lodge Lichas on the horns o' the moon;
And with those hands, that grasped the heaviest club,
Subdue my worthiest self.   The witch shall die:
To the young Roman boy she hath sold me, and I fall
Under this plot, she dies for't.—Eros, ho!   [*Exit*

SCENE XI.—Alexandria.   A Room in CLEOPATRA'S
Palace

Enter CLEOPATRA, CHARMIAN, IRAS, and MARDIAN

   Cleo.   Help me, my women!   O! he is more mad
Than Telamon for his shield; the boar of Thessaly
Was never so embossed.
   Char.   To the monument!
There lock yourself, and send him word you are dead.
The soul and body rive not more in parting,
Than greatness going off.
   Cleo.   To the monument!—
Mardian, go tell him I have slain myself;

Say, that the last I spoke was, Antony,
And word it, pr'ythee, piteously.   Hence,
Mardian, and bring me how he takes my death.
To the monument!   [*Exeunt*

SCENE XII.—Another Room in the Palace

Enter ANTONY *and* EROS

Ant.   Eros, thou yet behold'st me?
Eros.   Ay, noble lord.
Ant.   Sometime, we see a cloud that's dragonish,
A vapour sometime like a bear, or lion,
A towered citadel, a pendant rock,
A forkéd mountain, or blue promontory
With trees upon 't, that nod unto the world,
And mock our eyes with air: thou hast seen these signs;
They are black vesper's pageants.
Eros.   Ay, my lord.
Ant.   That which is now a horse, even with a thought
The rack dislimns, and makes it indistinct,
As water is in water.
Eros.   It does, my lord.
Ant.   My good knave, Eros, now thy captain is
Even such a body: here I am Antony;
Yet cannot hold this visible shape, my knave.
I made these wars for Egypt: and the queen,—
Whose heart, I thought, I had, for she had mine,
Which, whilst it was mine, had annexed unto 't
A million more, now lost,—she, Eros, has
Packed cards with Cæsar, and false-played my glory
Unto an enemy's triumph.—
Nay, weep not, gentle Eros; there is left us
Ourselves to end ourselves.

Enter MARDIAN

                              O, thy vile lady!
She has robbed me of my sword.
Mar.   No, Antony;
My mistress loved thee, and her fortunes mingled
With thine entirely.
Ant.   Hence, saucy eunuch: peace!
She hath betrayed me, and shall die the death.
Mar.   Death of one person can be paid but once,
And that she has discharged.   What thou wouldst do,
Is done unto thy hand: the last she spake
Was, 'Antony! most noble Antony!'
Then in the midst a tearing groan did break

143

The name of Antony; it was divided
Between her heart and lips.   She rendered life,
Thy name so buried in her.
  Ant.   Dead then?
  Mar.   Dead.
  Ant.   Unarm, Eros: the long day's task is done,
And we must sleep.—That thou depart'st hence safe,
Does pay thy labour richly; go.   [*Exit Mardian*
         —Off, pluck off:—
The seven-fold shield of Ajax cannot keep
The battery from my heart.   O, cleave, my sides!
Heart, once be stronger than thy continent
Crack thy frail case!—Apace, Eros, apace.—
No more a soldier:—bruiséd pieces, go;
You have been nobly borne.—From me awhile—
                         [*Exit Eros*
I will o'ertake thee, Cleopatra, and
Weep for my pardon.   So it must be, for now
All length is torture: since the torch is out,
Lie down, and stray no farther.   Now all labour
Mars what it does: yea, very force entangles
Itself with strength: seal then, and all is done.—
Eros!—I come, my queen.—Eros!—Stay for me:
Where souls do couch on flowers, we'll hand in hand,
And with our spritely port make the ghosts gaze:
Dido and her Æneas shall want troops,
And all the haunt be ours.—Come, Eros! Eros!

Re-enter EROS

  Eros.   What would my lord?
  Ant.   Since Cleopatra died,
I have lived in such dishonour, that the gods
Detest my baseness.   I, that with my sword
Quartered the world, and o'er green Neptune's back
With ships made cities, condemn myself, to lack
The courage of a woman; less noble mind
Than she, which by her death our Cæsar tells,
' I am conqueror of myself.'   Thou art sworn, Eros,
That when the exigent should come,—which now
Is come, indeed,—when I should see behind me
The inevitable prosecution of
Disgrace and horror, that on my command
Thou then wouldst kill me: do't; the time is come.
Thou strik'st not me, 't is Cæsar thou defeat'st.
Put colour in thy cheek.
  Eros.   The gods withhold me!
Shall I do that which all the Parthian darts,
Though enemy, lost aim, and could not?
  Ant.   Eros,

Wouldst thou be windowed in great Rome, and see
Thy master thus with pleached arms, bending down
His corrigible neck, his face subdued
To penetrative shame, whilst the wheeled seat
Of fortunate Cæsar, drawn before him, branded
His baseness that ensued.

  Eros.   I would not see't.
  Ant. Come then; for with a wound I must be cured.
Draw that thy honest sword, which thou hast worn
Most useful for thy country.

  Eros.   O, sir, pardon me.
  Ant. When I did make thee free, swor'st thou not then
To do this when I bade thee? Do it at once,
Or thy precedent services are all
But accidents unpurposed. Draw, and come.

  Eros. Turn from me then that noble countenance,
Wherein the worship of the whole world lies.

  Ant. Lo thee!   *[Turning from him*
  Eros. My sword is drawn.
  Ant.   Then let it do at once
The thing why thou hast drawn it.

  Eros.   My dear master,
My captain, and my emperor, let me say,
Before I strike this bloody stroke, farewell.

  Ant. 'T is said man; and farewell.
  Eros. Farewell, great chief. Shall I strike now?
  Ant.   Now, Eros.
  Eros. Why, there then:—*[falls on his sword]*—thus
     do I escape the sorrow
Of Antony's death.

  Ant.   Thrice-nobler than myself!
Thou teachest me, O valiant Eros, what
I should, and thou couldst not. My queen and Eros
Have, by their brave instruction, got upon me
A nobleness in record: but I will be
A bridegroom in my death, and run into't
As to the lover's bed. Come then; and, Eros,
Thy master dies thy scholar: to do thus
        [Falling on his sword
I learned of thee.—How! not dead? not dead?—
The guard, ho!—O, despatch me!

     Enter DERCETAS *and Guard*

  First Guard.   What's the noise?
  Ant. I have done my work ill, friends: O, make an end
Of what I have begun.

  Sec. Guard.   The star is fallen.
  First Guard. And time is at his period.
  All.   Alas, and woe!

Ant.   Let him that loves me strike me dead.
First Guard.   Not I.
Sec Guard.   Nor I.
Third Guard.   Nor any one.   [*Exeunt Guard*
Der.   Thy death and fortunes bid thy followers fly.
This sword but shown to Cæsar, with this tidings,
Shall enter me with him.

Enter DIOMEDES

Dio.   Where's Antony.
Der.   There, Diomed, there.
Dio.   Lives he?
Wilt thou not answer, man?   [*Exit Dercetas*
Ant.   Art thou there, Diomed?   Draw thy sword, and
          give me
Sufficient strokes for death.
Dio.   Most absolute lord,
My mistress Cleopatra sent me to thee.
Ant.   When did she send thee?
Dio.   Now, my lord.
Ant.   Where is she?
Dio.   Locked in her monument.   She had a prophesying
          fear
Of what hath come to pass; for when she saw—
Which never shall be found—you did suspect
She had disposed with Cæsar, and that your rage
Would not be purged, she sent you word she was dead;
But, fearing since how it might work, hath sent
Me to proclaim the truth; and I am come,
I dread, too late.
Ant.   Too late, good Diomed.   Call my guard, I pr'ythee.
Dio.   What, ho! the emperor's guard! The guard,
          what ho!
Come; your lord calls.

Enter some of the Guard

Ant.   Bear me, good friends, where Cleopatra bides:
'T is the last service that I shall command you.
First Guard.   Woe, woe are we, sir, you may not live to
          wear
All your true followers out.
All.   Most heavy day!
Ant.   Nay, good my fellows, do not please sharp fate
To grace it with your sorrows: bid that welcome
Which comes to punish us, and we punish it
Seeming to bear it lightly.   Take me up:
I have led you oft; carry me now, good friends,
And have my thanks for all.   [*Exeunt, bearing Antony*

SCENE XIII.—The Same.   A Monument

Enter, above, CLEOPATRA, CHARMIAN, *and* IRAS

Cleo.   O Charmian!   I will never go from hence.
Char.   Be comforted, dear madam.
Cleo.   No, I will not.
All strange and terrible events are welcome,
But comforts we despise: our size of sorrow,
Proportioned to our cause, must be as great
As that which makes it.

Enter, below, DIOMEDES

                                   How now? is he dead?
Dio.   His death's upon him, but not dead.
Look out o' the other side your monument;
His guard have brought him thither.

Enter, below, ANTONY, *borne by the Guard*

Cleo.   O sun,
Burn the great sphere thou mov'st in!—darkling stand
The varying shore o' the world.   O Antony,
Antony, Antony!   Help, Charmian, help, Iras, help:
Help, friends below; let's draw him hither.
Ant.   Peace!
Not Cæsar's valour hath o'erthrown Antony,
But Antony's hath triumphed on itself.
Cleo.   So it should be, that none but Antony
Should conquer Antony; but woe 't is so!
Ant.   I am dying, Egypt, dying; only
I here importune death awhile, until
Of many thousand kisses the poor last
I lay upon thy lips.
Cleo.   I dare not, dear,—
Dear, my lord, pardon,—I dare not,
Lest I be taken: not the imperious show
Of the full-fortuned Cæsar ever shall
Be brooched with me; if knife, drugs, serpents, have
Edge, sting, or operation, I am safe:
Your wife, Octavia, with her modest eyes
And still conclusion, shall acquire no honour
Demuring upon me.—But come, come, Antony,—
Help me, my women,—we must draw thee up,—
Assist, good friends.
Ant.   O, quick, or I am gone.
Cleo.   Here's sport, indeed!—How heavy weighs my
              lord!
Our strength is all gone into heaviness,

That makes the weight.   Had I great Juno's power,
The strong-winged Mercury should fetch thee up,
And set thee by Jove's side.   Yet come a little,—
Wishers were ever fools.—O! come, come, come;

                        [They draw Antony up
And welcome, welcome! die, where thou hast lived:
Quicken with kissing: had my lips that power,
Thus would I wear them out.
   All.   A heavy sight!
   Ant.   I am dying, Egypt, dying.
Give me some wine, and let me speak a little.
   Cleo.   No, let me speak; and let me rail so high,
That the false housewife Fortune break her wheel,
Provoked by my offence.
   Ant.   One word, sweet queen.
Of Cæsar seek your honour with your safety.—O!
   Cleo.   They do not go together.
   Ant.   Gentle, hear me;
None about Cæsar trust, but Proculeius.
   Cleo.   My resolution, and my hands, I'll trust;
None about Cæsar.
   Ant.   The miserable change now at my end
Lament nor sorrow at; but please your thoughts
In feeding them with those my former fortunes
Wherein I lived, the greatest prince o' the world,
The noblest; and do now not basely die,
Not cowardly put off my helmet to
My countryman, a Roman by a Roman
Valiantly vanquished.   Now, my spirit is going;
I can no more.
   Cleo.   Noblest of men, woo't die?
Hast thou no care of me? shall I abide
In this dull world, which in thy absence is
No better than a sty?—O! see, my women,

                              [Antony dies
The crown o' the earth doth melt.—My lord!—
O, withered is the garland of the war,
The soldier's pole is fallen: young boys and girls
Are level now with men; the odds is gone,
And there is nothing left remarkable
Beneath the visiting moon.
   Char.   O, quietness, lady!
   Iras.   She is dead too, our sovereign.
   Char.   Lady!—
   Iras.   Madam!
   Char.   O madam, madam, madam!
   Iras.   Royal Egypt!
Empress!
   Char.   Peace, peace, Iras!
   Cleo.   No more, but e'en a woman; and commanded

By such poor passion as the maid that milks,.
And does the meanest chares.   It were for me
To throw my sceptre at the injurious gods;
To tell them, that this world did equal theirs,
Till they had stolen our jewel.   All 's but naught;
Patience is sottish, and impatience does
Become a dog that 's mad: then is it sin,
To rush into the secret house of death,
Ere death dare come to us?—How do you, women?
What, what! good cheer! Why, how now, Charmian?
My noble girls!—Ah, women, women! look,
Our lamp is spent, it's out.—Good sirs, take heart:
We'll bury him; and then, what's brave, what's noble,
Let's do it after the high Roman fashion,
And make death proud to take us. Come, away:
This case of that huge spirit now is cold.
Ah, women, women! Come; we have no friend
But resolution, and the briefest end.

> [*Exeunt; those above bearing off Antony's body*

ACT FIVE

Scene I.—Cæsar's Camp before Alexandria

Enter Cæsar, Agrippa, Dolabella, Mecænas, Gallus,
Proculeius, *and others*

Cæs.   Go to him, Dolabella, bid him yield;
Being so frustrate, tell him he mocks
The pauses that he makes.
Dol.   Cæsar, I shall.   [*Exit*

Enter Dercetas, *with the sword of* Antony

Cæs.   Wherefore is that? and what art thou, that
          dar'st
Appear thus to us?
Der.   I am called Dercetas.
Mark Antony I served, who best was worthy
Best to be served: whilst he stood up, and spoke,
He was my master; and I wore my life,
To spend upon his haters.   If thou please
To take me to thee, as I was to him
I'll be to Cæsar; if thou pleasest not,
I yield thee up my life.
Cæs   What is't thou say'st?
Der.   I say, O Cæsar, Antony is dead.
Cæs.   The breaking of so great a thing should make

ANTONY AND CLEOPATRA   Act V Sc i

A greater crack: the round world should have shook
Lions into civil streets, and citizens
Into their dens. The death of Antony
Is not a single doom; in the name lay
A moiety of the world.
    Der.   He is dead, Cæsar,
Not by a public minister of justice,
Nor by a hiréd knife; but that self hand,
Which writ his honour in the acts it did,
Hath, with the courage which the heart did lend it,
Splitted the heart. This is his sword;
I robbed his wound of it: behold it stained
With his most noble blood.
    Cæs.   Look you sad, friends?
The gods rebuke me, but it is a tidings
To wash the eyes of kings.
    Agr.   And strange it is,
That nature must compel us to lament
Our most persisted deeds.
    Mec.   His taints and honours
Waged equal with him.
    Agr.   A rarer spirit never
Did steer humanity; but you, gods, will give us
Some faults to make us men. Cæsar is touched.
    Mec.   When such a spacious mirror's set before him,
He needs must see himself.
    Cæs.   O Antony!
I have followed thee to this:—but we do lance
Diseases in our bodies: I must perforce
Have shown to thee such a declining day,
Or look on thine: we could not stall together
In the whole world. But yet let me lament
With tears as sovereign as the blood of hearts,
That thou, my brother, my competitor
In top of all design, my mate in empire,
Friend and companion in the front of war,
The arm of mine own body, and the heart
Where mine his thoughts did kindle, that our stars,
Unreconciliable, should divide
Our equalness to this.—Hear me, good friends,—

Enter a Messenger

But I will tell you at some meeter season:
The business of this man looks out of him;
We'll hear him what he says.—Whence are you?
    Mess. A poor Egyptian yet. The queen my mistress
Confined in all she has, her monument,
Of thy intents desires instruction,
That she preparedly may frame herself

To the way she's forced to.
   Cæs.   Bid her have good heart:
She soon shall know of us, by some of ours,
How honourable and how kindly we
Determine for her; Cæsar cannot learn
To be ungentle.
   Mess. So the gods preserve thee.   [*Exit*
   Cæs. Come hither, Proculeius. Go, and say,
We purpose her no shame: give her what comforts
The quality of her passion shall require,
Lest in her greatness by some mortal stroke
She do defeat us; for her life in Rome
Would be eternal in our triumph. Go,
And with your speediest bring us what she says,
And how you find of her.
   Pro.   Cæsar, I shall.   [*Exit*
   Cæs. Gallus, go you along. [*Exit Gallus*]—Where's
          Dolabella,
To second Proculeius!
   Agr., Mec.   Dolabella!
   Cæs. Let him alone, for I remember now
How he's employed: he shall in time be ready.
Go with me to my tent: where you shall see
How hardly I was drawn into this war;
How calm and gentle I proceeded still
In all my writings. Go with me and see
What I can show in this.   [*Exeunt*

SCENE II.—Alexandria. The Monument

Enter CLEOPATRA, CHARMIAN, *and* IRAS

   Cleo. My desolation does begin to make
A better life. 'T is paltry to be Cæsar:
Not being Fortune, he's but Fortune's knave,
A minister of her will; and it is great
To do that thing that ends all other deeds,
Which shackles accidents, and bolts up change;
Which sleeps, and never palates more the dung,
The beggar's nurse and Cæsar's.

Enter PROCULEIUS, GALLAS, *and Soldiers*

   Pro. Cæsar sends greeting to the Queen of Egypt:
And bids thee study on what fair demands
Thou mean'st to have him grant thee.
   Cleo.   What's thy name?
   Pro. My name is Proculeius.
   Cleo.   Antony
Did tell me of you, bade me trust you; but

I do not greatly care to be deceived,
That have no use for trusting. If your master
Would have a queen his beggar, you must tell him,
That majesty, to keep decorum, must
No less beg than a kingdom: if he please
To give me conquered Egypt for my son,
He gives me so much of mine own as I
Will kneel to him with thanks.
  Pro.   Be of good cheer;
You are fallen into a princely hand, fear nothing,
Make your full reference freely to my lord,
Who is so full of grace that it flows over
On all that need. Let me report to him
Your sweet dependency, and you shall find
A conqueror that will pray in aid for kindness
Where he for grace is kneeled to.
  Cleo.   Pray you, tell him
I am his fortune's vassal, and I send him
The greatness he has got. I hourly learn
A doctrine of obedience, and would gladly
Look him i' the face.
  Pro.   This I'll report, dear lady.
Have comfort; for I know your plight is pitied
Of him that caused it.
  Gal. You see how easily she may be surprised.

[*Proculeius, and two of the Guard, ascend the monument
  by a ladder, and come behind Cleopatra. Some of
  the Guard unbar and open the gates*

[*To Proculeius and the Guard*] Guard her till Cæsar
  come.   [*Exit*
 Iras. Royal queen!
 Char. O Cleopatra, thou art taken, queen!—
 Cleo. Quick, quick, good hands.
          [*Drawing a dagger*
 Pro.   Hold, worthy lady, hold!
        [*Seizes and disarms her*
Do not yourself such wrong, who are in this
Relieved, but not betrayed.
  Cleo.   What, of death too,
That rids our dogs of languish?
  Pro.   Cleopatra,
Do not abuse my master's bounty by
The undoing of yourself: let the world see
His nobleness well acted, which your death
Will never let come forth.
  Cleo.   Where art thou, death?
Come hither, come! come, come, and take a queen
Worth many babes and beggars!
  Pro.   O, temperance, lady!

   Cleo. Sir, I will eat no meat, I'll not drink, sir;
If idle talk will once be necessary,
I'll not sleep, neither. This mortal house I'll ruin,
Do Cæsar what he can. Know, sir, that I
Will not wait pinioned at your master's court,
Nor once be chastised with the sober eye
Of dull Octavia. Shall they hoist me up,
And show me to the shouting varletry
Of censuring Rome? Rather a ditch in Egypt
Be gentle grave to me! rather on Nilus' mud
Lay me stark nak'd, and let the water-flies
Blow me into abhorring! rather make
My country's high pyramides my gibbet,
And hang me up in chains!
   Pro.   You do extend
These thoughts of horror further than you shall
Find cause in Cæsar.

Enter DOLABELLA

   Dol.   Proculeius,
What thou hast done thy master Cæsar knows,
And he hath sent me for thee: for the queen,
I'll take her to my guard.
   Pro.   So, Dolabella,
It shall content me best: be gentle to her.
[*To Cleopatra*] To Cæsar I will speak what you shall please,
If you'll employ me to him.
   Cleo.   Say I would die.
                 [*Exeunt Proculeius and Soldiers*
   Dol. Most noble empress, you have heard of me?
   Cleo. I cannot tell.
   Dol.   Assuredly, you know me.
   Cleo. No matter, sir, what I have heard or known.
You laugh when boys or women tell their dreams;
Is't not your trick?
   Dol.   I understand not, madam.
   Cleo. I dreamt, there was an emperor Antony:
O, such another sleep, that I might see
But such another man!
   Dol.   If it might please ye,—
   Cleo. His face was as the heavens, and therein stuck
A sun and moon, which kept their course, and lighted
The little O, the earth.
   Dol.   Most sovereign creature,—
   Cleo. His legs bestrid the ocean; his reared arm
Crested the world; his voice was propertied
As all the tuned spheres, and that to friends;
But when he meant to quail and shake the orb,
He was as rattling thunder. For his bounty,

There was no winter in 't; an autumn 't was,
That grew the more by reaping: his delights
Were dolphin-like; they showed his back above
The element they lived in: in his livery
Walked crowns and crownets; realms and islands were
As plates dropped from his pocket.
  Dol.   Cleopatra,—
  Cleo. Think you there was, or might be, such a man
As this I dreamt of?
  Dol.   Gentle madam, no.
  Cleo. You lie, up to the hearing of the gods.
But, if there be, or ever were, one such,
It's past the size of dreaming: nature wants stuff
To vie strange forms with fancy; yet, to imagine
An Antony, were nature's piece 'gainst fancy,
Condemning shadows quite.
  Dol.   Hear me, good madam.
Your loss is as yourself, great; and you bear it
As answering to the weight: would I might never
O'ertake pursued success, but I do feel,
By the rebound of yours, a grief that smites
My very heart at root.
  Cleo.   I thank you, sir.
Know you what Cæsar means to do with me?
  Dol. I am loath to tell you what I would you knew.
  Cleo. Nay, pray you, sir,—
  Dol.   Though he be honourable,—
  Cleo. He'll lead me then in triumph?
  Dol. Madam, he will; I know 't.
[*Within*]   Make way there!—Cæsar!

   Enter CÆSAR, GALLUS, PROCULEIUS, MECÆNAS,
    SELEUCUS, *and Attendants*

  Cæs. Which is the Queen of Egypt?
  Dol. It is the emperor, madam. [*Cleopatra kneels*
  Cæs. Arise, you shall not kneel:
I pray you, rise; rise, Egypt.
  Cleo.   Sir, the gods
Will have it thus: my master and my lord
I must obey.
  Cæs.   Take to you no hard thoughts:
The record of what injuries you did us,
Though written in our flesh, we shall remember
As things but done by chance.
  Cleo.   Sole sir o' the world
I cannot project mine own cause so well
To make it clear; but do confess, I have
Been laden with like frailties which before
Have often shamed our sex.

Cæs.   Cleopatra, know,
We will extenuate rather than enforce:
If you apply yourself to our intents—
Which towards you are most gentle—you shall find
A benefit in this change; but if you seek
To lay on me a cruelty, by taking
Antony's course, you shall bereave yourself
Of my good purposes, and put your children
To that destruction which I'll guard them from,
If thereon you rely. I'll take my leave.

Cleo. And may through all the world: 't is yours;
        and we,
Your scutcheons, and your signs of conquest, shall
Hang in what place you please. Here, my good lord.

Cæs. You shall advise me in all for Cleopatra.

Cleo. This is the brief of money, plate, and jewels,
I am possessed of: 't is exactly valued;
Not petty things admitted.—Where's Seleucus?

Sel. Here, madam.

Cleo. This is my treasurer: let him speak, my lord,
Upon his peril, that I have reserved
To myself nothing. Speak the truth, Seleucus.

Sel. Madam,
I had rather seal my lips, than, to my peril,
Speak that which is not.

Cleo.   What have I kept back?

Sel. Enough to purchase what you have made known.

Cæs. Nay, blush not, Cleopatra; I approve
Your wisdom in the deed.

Cleo.   See, Cæsar, O, behold,
How pomp is followed! mine will now be yours;
And, should we shift estates, yours would be mine.
The ingratitude of this Seleucus does
Even make me wild.—O slave, of no more trust
Than love that's hired!—What, goest thou back? thou
        shalt
Go back, I warrant thee; but I'll catch thine eyes,
Though they had wings. Slave, soulless villain dog!
O rarely base!

Cæs.   Good queen, let us entreat you.

Cleo. O Cæsar, what a wounding shame is this,
That thou, vouchsafing here to visit me,
Doing the honour of thy lordliness
To one so meek, that mine own servant should
Parcel the sum of my disgraces by
Addition of his envy! Say, good Cæsar,
That I some lady trifles have reserved,
Immoment toys, things of such dignity
As we greet modern friends withal; and say,
Some nobler tokens I have kept apart

For Livia, and Octavia, to induce
Their mediation; must I be unfolded
With one that I have bred?   The gods! it smites me
Beneath the fall I have.   [*To Seleucus*]   Pr'ythee, go
    hence;
Or I shall show the cinders of my spirits
Through the ashes of my chance.—Wert thou a man,
Thou wouldst have mercy on me.
    Cæs.   Forbear, Seleucus.
                                  [*Exit Seleucus*
    Cleo.   Be it known that we, the greatest, are misthought
For things that others do; and, when we fall,
We answer others' merits in our name,
Are therefore to be pitied.
    Cæs.   Cleopatra,
Not what you have reserved, nor what acknowledged,
Put we i' the roll of conquest: still be it yours,
Bestow it at your pleasure; and believe,
Cæsar's no merchant, to make prize with you
Of things that merchants sold.   Therefore be cheered;
Make not your thoughts your prisons: no, dear queen;
For we intend so to dispose you, as
Yourself shall give us counsel.   Feed, and sleep:
Our care and pity is so much upon you,
That we remain your friend; and so, adieu.
    Cleo.   My master, and my lord!
    Cæs.   Not so.   Adieu.
           [*Flourish. Exeunt Cæsar and his Train*
    Cleo.   He words me, girls, he words me, that I should not
Be noble to myself: but hark thee, Charmian.
                       [*Whispers Charmian*
    Iras.   Finish, good lady; the bright day is done,
And we are for the dark.
    Cleo.   Hie thee again:
I have spoke already, and it is provided;
Go, put it to the haste.
    Char.   Madam, I will.

Re-enter DOLABELLA

    Dol.   Where is the queen?
    Char.   Behold, sir.   [*Exit*
    Cleo.   Dolabella!
    Dol.   Madam, as thereto sworn by your command,
Which my love makes religion to obey,
I tell you this:—Cæsar through Syria
Intends his journey, and within three days
You with your children will he send before.
Make your best use of this; I have performed
Your pleasure, and my promise.

Cleo.   Dolabella,
I shall remain your debtor.
   Dol.   I your servant.
Adieu, good queen; I must attend on Cæsar.
   Cleo.   Farewell, and thanks,   [*Exit Dolabella*
                        Now, Iras, what think'st thou?
Thou, an Egyptian puppet, shalt be shown
In Rome, as well as I: mechanic slaves
With greasy aprons, rules, and hammers, shall
Uplift us to the view: in their thick breaths,
Rank of gross diet, shall we be enclouded,
And forced to drink their vapour.
   Iras.   The gods forbid!
   Cleo.   Nay, 't is most certain, Iras.   Saucy lictors
Will catch at us, like strumpets; and scald rhymers
Ballad us out o' tune: the quick comedians
Extemporally will stage us, and present
Our Alexandrian revels.   Antony
Shall be brought drunken forth, and I shall see
Some squeaking Cleopatra boy my greatness
I' the posture of a whore.
   Iras.   O, the good gods!
   Cleo.   Nay, that is certain.
   Iras.   I'll never see it; for, I am sure, my nails
Are stronger than mine eyes.
   Cleo.   Why, that's the way
To fool their preparation, and to conquer
Their most absurd intents.

                    Re-enter CHARMIAN

                        Now, Charmian?—
Show me, my women, like a queen:—go fetch
My best attires;—I am again for Cydnus,
To meet Mark Antony.—Sirrah, Iras, go.—
Now, noble Charmian, we'll despatch indeed;
And, when thou hast done this chare, I'll give thee leave
To play till doomsday.—Bring our crown and all.
                        [*Exit Iras.   A noise within*
Wherefore's this noise?

                    Enter one of the Guard

   Guard.   Here is a rural fellow,
That will not be denied your highness' presence:
He brings you figs.
   Cleo.   Let him come in   [*Exit Guard*]   What poor an
         instrument
May do a noble deed! he brings me liberty.
My resolution's placed, and I have nothing
Of woman in me: now from head to foot

I am marble-constant; now the fleeting moon
No planet is of mine.

Re-enter Guard, with a Clown bringing in a basket

Guard.   This is the man.
Cleo.   Avoid, and leave him.   [*Exit Guard*
Hast thou the pretty worm of Nilus there,
That kills and pains not?
   Clown.   Truly I have him; but I would not be the
party that should desire you to touch him, for his biting
is immortal: those that do die of it do seldom or never
recover.
   Cleo.   Remember'st thou any that have died on't
   Clown.   Very many, men and women too.   I heard of
one of them no longer than yesterday: a very honest
woman, but something given to lie, as a woman should
not do but in the way of honesty: how she died of the
biting of it, what pain she felt.—Truly, she makes a very
good report o' the worm; but he that will believe all that
they say, shall never be saved by half that they do.   But
this is most fallible, the worm's an odd worm.
   Cleo.   Get thee hence: farewell.
   Clown.   I wish you all joy of the worm.
                         [*Sets down the basket*
   Cleo.   Farewell.
   Clown.   You must think this, look you, that the worm
will do his kind.
   Cleo.   Ay, ay; farewell.
   Clown.   Look you, the worm is not to be trusted but in
the keeping of wise people; for, indeed, there is no good-
ness in the worm.
   Cleo.   Take thou no care: it shall be heeded.
   Clown. . Very good.   Give it nothing, I pray you, for
it is not worth the feeding.
   Cleo.   Will it eat me?
   Clown.   You must not think I am so simple, but I know
the devil himself will not eat a woman: I know that a
woman is a dish for the gods, if the devil dress her not.
But, truly, these same whoreson devils do the gods great
harm in their women, for in every ten that they make, the
devils mar five.
   Cleo.   Well, get thee gone: farewell.
   Clown.   Yes, forsooth; I wish you joy of the worm.
                         [*Exit*
      Re-enter IRAS, *with a robe, crown, etc.*

   Cleo.   Give me my robe, put on my crown; I have
Immortal longings in me.   Now, no more
The juice of Egypt's grape shall moist this lip.—
Yare, yare, good Iras! quick.—Methinks, I hear

Antony call: I see him rouse himself
To praise my noble act; I hear him mock
The luck of Cæsar, which the gods give men
To excuse their after-wrath.   Husband, I come:
Now to that name my courage prove my title!
I am fire and air; my other elements
I give to baser life.—So,—have you done?
Come then, and take the last warmth of my lips.
Farewell, kind Charmian:—Iras, long farewell.
                    [*Kisses them.   Iras falls and dies*
Have I the aspic in my lips?   Dost fall?
If thou and nature can so gently part,
The stroke of death is as a lover's pinch,
Which hurts, and is desired.   Dost thou lie still?
If thus thou vanishest, thou tell'st the world
It is not worth leave-taking.
    Char.   Dissolve, thick cloud, and rain, that I may say,
The gods themselves do weep.
    Cleo.   This proves me base:
If she first meet the curléd Antony,
He'll make demand of her, and spend that kiss,
Which is my heaven to have.   Come, thou mortal wretch.
                    [*To the asp, which she applies to her breast*
With thy sharp teeth this knot intrinsicate
Of life at once untie: poor venomous fool,
Be angry, and despatch.   O, couldst thou speak,
That I might hear thee call great Cæsar, ass
Unpolicied!
    Char.   O eastern star!
    Cleo.   Peace, peace!
Dost thou not see my baby at my breast,
That sucks the nurse asleep?
    Char.   O, break! O, break!
    Cleo.   As sweet as balm, as soft as air, as gentle,—
O Antony!—Nay, I will take thee too.
                    [*Applying another asp to her arm*
What should I stay—   [*Falls on a bed and dies*
    Char.   In this vile world?—So, fare thee well.—
Now boast thee, death, in thy possession lies
A lass unparalleled.—Downy windows, close;
And golden Phœbus never be beheld
Of eyes again so royal!   Your crown's awry;
I'll mend it, and then play.

            Enter the Guard, rushing in

    First Guard.   Where is the queen?
    Char.   Speak softly; wake her not.
    First Guard.   Cæsar hath sent—
    Char.   Too slow a messenger
                    [*Applies the asp*

159

O! come; apace; despatch: I partly feel thee.
   First Guard. Approach, ho! All's not well: Cæsar's
     beguiled.
   Sec. Guard. There's Dolabella sent from Cæsar: call
     him.
   First Guard. What work is here?—Charmian, is this
     well done?
   Char. It is well done, and fitting for a princess
Descended of so many royal kings.
Ah, soldier!   *[Dies*

Re-enter DOLABELLA

   Dol. How goes it here?
   Sec. Guard.   All dead.
   Dol.   Cæsar, thy thoughts
Touch their effects in this: thyself art coming
To see performed the dreaded act, which thou
So sought'st to hinder.
[Within]   A way there! a way for Cæsar!

Re-enter CÆSAR *and all his Train*

   Dol. O, sir, you are too sure an augurer:
That you did fear, is done.
   Cæs.   Bravest at the last:
She levelled at our purposes, and, being royal,
Took her own way.—The manner of their deaths?
I do not see them bleed.
   Dol.   Who was last with them?
   First Guard. A simple countryman that brought her
     figs:
This was his basket.
   Cæs.   Poisoned then.
   First Guard.   O Cæsar!
This Charmian lived but now; she stood, and spake:
I found her trimming up the diadem
On her dead mistress; tremblingly she stood,
And on the sudden dropped.
   Cæs.   O noble weakness!—
If they had swallowed poison, 't would appear
By external swelling; but she looks like sleep,
As she would catch another Antony
In her strong toil of grace.
   Dol.   Here, on her breast,
There is a vent of blood, and something blown:
The like is on her arm.
   First Guard. This is an aspic's trail; and these fig-
     leaves
Have slime upon them, such as the aspic leaves
Upon the caves of Nile.
   Cæs.   Most probable,

That so she died; for her physician tells me,
She hath pursued conclusions infinite
Of easy ways to die.—Take up her bed,
And bear her women from the monument.
She shall be buried by her Antony:
No grave upon the earth shall clip in it
A pair so famous.   High events as these
Strike those that make them; and their story is
No less in pity than his glory which
Brought them to be lamented.   Our army shall
In solemn show attend this funeral,
And then to Rome.—Come, Dolabella, see
High order in this great solemnity.   [*Exeunt*

AS YOU LIKE IT

DRAMATIS PERSONÆ

DUKE, *living in banishment*
FREDERICK, *his brother, and usurper of his dominions*
AMIENS }
JAQUES } *lords attending on the banished Duke*
LE BEAU, *a courtier*
CHARLES, *a wrestler*
OLIVER   }
JAQUES   } *sons of Sir Rowland de Bois*
ORLANDO }
ADAM   }
DENNIS } *servants to Oliver*
TOUCHSTONE, *a clown*
SIR OLIVER MAR-TEXT, *a vicar*
CORIN   }
SILVIUS } *shepherds*
WILLIAM, *a country fellow, in love with Audrey*
HYMEN

ROSALIND, *daughter to the banished Duke*
CELIA, *daughter to Frederick*
PHEBE, *a shepherdess*
AUDREY, *a country wench*

Lords, Pages, Foresters, and other Attendants

SCENE—*Near Oliver's House; Duke Frederick's Court; and the Forest of Arden.*

164

AS YOU LIKE IT

ACT ONE

Scene I.—Oliver's Orchard

Enter Orlando *and* Adam

Orl. As I remember, Adam, it was upon this fashion. He bequeathed me by will but poor a thousand crowns, and, as thou say'st, charged my brother on his blessing to breed me well: and there begins my sadness. My brother Jaques he keeps at school, and report speaks goldenly of his profit: for my part, he keeps me rustically at home, or to speak more properly, stays me here at home unkept, for call you that keeping for a gentleman of my birth, that differs not from the stalling of an ox? His horses are bred better; for, besides that they are fair with their feeding, they are taught their manage, and to that end riders dearly hired: but I, his brother, gain nothing under him but growth, for the which his animals on his dunghills are as much bound to him as I. Besides this nothing that he so plentifully gives me, the something that Nature gave me his countenance seems to take from me: he lets me feed with his hinds, bars me the place of a brother, and, as much as in him lies, mines my gentility with my education. This is it, Adam, that grieves me; and the spirit of my father, which I think is within me, begins to mutiny against this servitude. I will no longer endure it, though yet I know no wise remedy how to avoid it.

Adam. Yonder comes my master, your brother.

Orl. Go apart, Adam, and thou shalt hear how he will shake me up.

Enter Oliver

Oli. Now, sir! what make you here?

Orl. Nothing: I am not taught to make anything.

Oli. What mar you then, sir?

Orl. Marry, sir, I am helping you to mar that which God made, a poor unworthy brother of yours, with idleness.

Oli. Marry, sir, be better employed, and be naught awhile.

Orl. Shall I keep your hogs, and eat husks with them? What prodigal portion have I spent, that I should come to such penury?

Oli. Know you where you are, sir?

Orl. O, sir, very well: here, in your orchard.

Oli. Know you before whom, sir?

Orl. Ay, better than him I am before know me. I know you are my eldest brother; and, in the gentle condition of blood, you should so know me. The courtesy of nations allows you my better, in that you are the first-born; but the same tradition takes not away my blood, were there twenty brothers betwixt us. I have as much of my father in me, as you; albeit, I confess, your coming before me is nearer to his reverence.

Oli. What, boy!

Orl. Come, come, elder brother, you are too young in this.

Oli. Wilt thou lay hands on me, villain?

Orl. I am no villain: I am the youngest son of Sir Rowland de Bois; he was my father, and he is thrice a villain that says such a father begot villains. Wert thou not my brother, I would not take this hand from thy throat till this other had pulled out thy tongue for saying so; thou hast railed on thyself.

Adam. [*Coming forward*] Sweet masters, be patient: for your father's remembrance, be at accord.

Oli. Let me go, I say.

Orl. I will not, till I please; you shall hear me. My father charged you in his will to give me good education: you have trained me like a peasant, obscuring and hiding from me all gentleman-like qualities. The spirit of my father grows strong in me, and I will no longer endure it; therefore, allow me such exercises as may become a gentleman, or give me the poor allottery my father left me by testament: with that I will go buy my fortunes.

Oli. And what will thou do? beg, when that is spent? Well, sir, get you in: I will not long be troubled with you; you shall have some part of your will. I pray you, leave me.

Orl. I will no further offend you than becomes me for my good.

Oli. Get you with him, you old dog.

Adam. Is old dog my reward? Most true, I have lost my teeth in your service.—God be with my old master! he would not have spoke such a word.

[*Exeunt Orlando and Adam*

Oli. Is it even so? begin you to grow upon me? I will physic your rankness, and yet give no thousand crowns neither. Holla, Dennis!

Enter DENNIS

Den. Calls your worship?
Oli. Was not Charles, the duke's wrestler, here to speak with me?
Den. So please you, he is here at the door, and importunes access to you.
Oli. Call him in. [*Exit Dennis*]—'T will be a good way; and to-morrow the wrestling is.

Enter CHARLES

Cha. Good morrow to your worship.
Oli. Good Monsieur Charles: what's the new news at the new court.
Cha. There's no news at the court, sir, but the old news: that is, the old duke is banished by his younger brother the new duke, and three or four loving lords have put themselves into voluntary exile with him, whose lands and revenues enrich the new duke; therefore, he gives them good leave to wander.
Oli. Can you tell, if Rosalind, the duke's daughter, be banished with her father?
Cha. O, no; for the duke's daughter, her cousin, so loves her, being ever from their cradles bred together, that she would have followed her exile, or have died to stay behind her. She is at the court, and no less beloved of her uncle than his own daughter; and never two ladies loved as they do.
Oli. Where will the old duke live?
Cha. They say, he is already in the forest of Arden, and a many merry men with him; and there they live like the old Robin Hood of England. They say, many young gentlemen flock to him every day, and fleet the time carelessly, as they did in the golden world.
Oli. What, you wrestle to-morrow before the new duke?
Cha. Marry, do I, sir; and I came to acquaint you with a matter. I am given, sir, secretly to understand, that your younger brother Orlando hath a disposition to come in disguised against me to try a fall. To-morrow, sir, I wrestle for my credit, and he that escapes me without some broken limb shall acquit him well. Your brother is but young, and tender, and, for your love, I would be loath to foil him, as I must for my own honour if he come in: therefore, out of my love to you, I came hither to acquaint you withal, that either you might stay him from his intendment, or brook such disgrace well as he shall run into, in that it is a thing of his own search, and altogether against my will.

167

Oli. Charles, I thank thee for thy love of me, which thou shalt find I will most kindly requite. I had myself notice of my brother's purpose herein, and have by under-hand means laboured to dissuade him from it; but he is resolute. I'll tell thee, Charles, it is the stubbornest young fellow of France, full of ambition, an envious emulator of every man's good parts, a secret and villainous contriver against me his natural brother: therefore, use thy discretion, I had as lief thou didst break his neck as his finger. And thou wert best look to't; for if thou dost him any slight disgrace, or if he do not mightily grace himself on thee, he will practise against thee by poison, entrap thee by some treacherous device, and never leave thee till he hath ta'en thy life by some indirect means or other; for, I assure thee (and almost with tears I speak it), there is not one so young and so villainous this day living. I speak but brotherly of him, but should I anato-mise him to thee as he is, I must blush and weep, and thou must look pale and wonder.

Cha. I am heartily glad I came hither to you. If he come to-morrow, I'll give him his payment: if ever he go alone again, I'll never wrestle for prize more; and so, God keep your worship!   [*Exit*

Oli. Farewell, good Charles.—Now will I stir this gamester. I hope I shall see an end of him; for my soul, yet I know not why, hates nothing more than he: yet he's gentle; never schooled, and yet learned; full of noble device; of all sorts enchantingly beloved, and indeed, so much in the heart of the world, and, especially of my own people, who best know him, that I am altogether misprised. But it shall not be so long; this wrestler shall clear all: nothing remains but that I kindle the boy thither, which now I'll go about.   [*Exit*

SCENE II.—A Lawn before the DUKE'S Palace

Enter ROSALIND *and* CELIA

Cel. I pray thee, Rosalind, sweet my coz, be merry.

Ros. Dear Celia, I show more mirth than I am mistress of, and would you yet were merrier? Unless you could teach me to forget a banished father, you must not learn me how to remember any extraordinary pleasure.

Cel. Herein I see, thou lovest me not with the full weight that I love thee. If my uncle, thy banished father, had banished thy uncle, the duke, my father, so thou hadst been still with me, I could have taught my love to take thy father for mine: so wouldst thou, if the truth of thy love to me were so righteously tempered, as mine is to thee.

Ros. Well, I will forget the condition of my estate to rejoice in yours.

Cel. You know, my father hath no child but I, nor none is like to have; and, truly, when he dies, thou shalt be his heir: for what he hath taken away from thy father perforce, I will render thee again in affection: by mine honour I will; and when I break that oath, let me turn monster. Therefore, my sweet Rose, my dear Rose, be merry.

Ros. From henceforth I will, coz, and devise sports. Let me see; what think you of falling in love?

Cel. Marry, I pr'ythee do, to make sport withal: but love no man in good earnest; nor no further in sport neither, than with safety of a pure blush thou may'st in honour come off again.

Ros. What shall be our sport then?

Cel. Let us sit, and mock the good housewife, Fortune, from her wheel, that her gifts may henceforth be bestowed equally.

Ros. I would we could do so; for her benefits are mightily misplaced, and the bountiful blind woman doth most mistake in her gifts to women.

Cel. 'T is true, for those that she makes fair she scarce makes honest; and those that she makes honest she makes very ill-favourably.

Ros. Nay, now thou goest from Fortune's office to Nature's: Fortune reigns in gifts of the world, not in the lineaments of Nature.

Enter TOUCHSTONE

Cel. No: when Nature hath made a fair creature, may she not by Fortune fall into the fire?—Though Nature hath given us wit to flout at Fortune, hath not Fortune sent in this fool to cut off the argument?

Ros. Indeed, there is Fortune too hard for Nature, when Fortune makes Nature's natural the cutter-off of Nature's wit.

Cel. Peradventure this is not Fortune's work neither, but Nature's, who, perceiving our natural wits too dull to reason of such goddesses, hath sent this natural for our whetstone, for always the dulness of the fool is the whetstone of the wits.—How now, wit? whither wander you?

Touch. Mistress, you must come away to your father.

Cel. Were you made the messenger?

Touch. No, by mine honour, but I was bid to come for you.

Ros. Where learned you that oath, fool?

Touch. Of a certain knight, that swore by his honour they were good pancakes, and swore by his honour the

169

mustard was naught: now I'll stand to it the pancakes were naught and the mustard was good, and yet was not the knight forsworn.

Cel. How prove you that, in the great heap of your knowledge?

Ros. Ay, marry, now unmuzzle your wisdom.

Touch. Stand you both forth now: stroke your chins, and swear by your beards that I am a knave.

Cel. By our beards, if we had them, thou art.

Touch. By my knavery, if I had it, then I were. But if you swear by that that is not, you are not forsworn: no more was this knight, swearing by his honour, for he never had any; or, if he had, he had sworn it away before ever he saw those pancakes, or that mustard.

Cel. Pr'ythee, who is't that thou mean'st?

Touch. One that old Frederick, your father, loves.

Cel. My father's love is enough to honour him enough. Speak no more of him; you'll be whipped for taxation one of these days.

Touch. The more pity, that fools may not speak wisely, what wise men do foolishly.

Cel. By my troth thou say'st true; for since the little wit that fools have was silenced, the little foolery that wise men have makes a great show. Here comes Monsieur Le Beau.

Enter LE BEAU

Ros. With his mouth full of news.

Cel. Which he will put on us, as pigeons feed their young.

Ros. Then shall we be news-crammed.

Cel. All the better; we shall be the more marketable. *Bon jour, Monsieur Le Beau:* what's the news?

Le Beau. Fair princess, you have lost much good sport.

Cel. Sport? Of what colour?

Le Beau. What colour, madam? How shall I answer you?

Ros. As wit and fortune will.

Touch. Or as the Destinies decree.

Cel. Well said, that was laid on with a trowel.

Touch. Nay, if I keep not my rank,—

Ros. Thou losest thy old smell.

Le Beau. You amaze me, ladies! I would have told you of good wrestling which you have lost the sight of.

Ros. Yet tell us the manner of the wrestling.

Le Beau. I will tell you the beginning, and, if it please your ladyships, you may see the end, for the best is yet to do, and here, where you are, they are coming to perform it.

Cel. Well, the beginning that is dead and buried.

Le Beau. There comes an old man and his three sons,—

Cel. I could match this beginning with an old tale.

Le Beau. Three proper young men, of excellent growth and presence;—

Ros. With bills on their necks: Be it known unto all men by these presents.

Le Beau. The eldest of the three wrestled with Charles, the duke's wrestler; which Charles in a moment threw him, and broke three of his ribs, that there is little hope of life in him; so he served the second, and so the third. Yonder they lie, the poor old man, their father, making such pitiful dole over them, that all the beholders take his part with weeping.

Ros. Alas!

Touch. But what is the sport, monsieur, that the ladies have lost?

Le Beau. Why, this that I speak of.

Touch. Thus men may grow wiser every day. It is the first time that ever I heard breaking of ribs was sport for ladies.

Cel. Or I, I promise thee.

Ros. But is there any else longs to see this broken music in his sides? is there yet another dotes upon rib-breaking? Shall we see this wrestling, cousin?

Le Beau. You must if you stay here, for here is the place appointed for the wrestling, and they are ready to perform it.

Cel. Yonder, sure, they are coming; let us now stay and see it.

Flourish. Enter Duke Frederick, *Lords,* Orlando, Charles, *and Attendants*

Duke F. Come on, since the youth will not be entreated, his own peril on his forwardness.

Ros. Is yonder the man?

Le Beau. Even he, madam.

Cel. Alas! he is too young: yet he looks successfully.

Duke F. How now, daughter and cousin: are you crept hither to see the wrestling?

Ros. Ay, my liege, so please you give us leave.

Duke F. You will take little delight in it, I can tell you, there is such odds in the man. In pity of the challenger's youth I would fain dissuade him, but he will not be entreated. Speak to him, ladies, see if you can move him.

Cel. Call him hither, good Monsieur Le Beau.

Duke F. Do so; I'll not be by.

[*Duke goes apart*

Le Beau. Monsieur the challenger, the princesses call for you.

Orl. I attend them, with all respect and duty.

Ros. Young man, have you challenged Charles the wrestler?

Orl. No, fair princess; he is the general challenger: I come but in, as others do, to try with him the strength of my youth.

Cel. Young gentleman, your spirits are too bold for your years. You have seen cruel proof of this man's strength: if you saw yourself with your eyes, or knew yourself with your judgment, the fear of your adventure would counsel you to a more equal enterprise. We pray you, for your own sake, to embrace your own safety, and give over this attempt.

Ros. Do, young sir, your reputation shall not therefore be misprised: we will make it our suit to the duke, that the wrestling might not go forward.

Orl. I beseech you, punish me not with your hard thoughts, wherein I confess me much guilty to deny so fair and excellent ladies anything. But let your fair eyes and gentle wishes go with me to my trial; wherein if I be foiled, there is but one shamed that was never gracious; if killed, but one dead that is willing to be so. I shall do my friends no wrong, for I have none to lament me; the world no injury, for in it I have nothing; only in the world I fill up a place, which may be better supplied when I have made it empty.

Ros. The little strength that I have, I would it were with you.

Cel. And mine, to eke out hers.

Ros. Fare you well. Pray Heaven, I be deceived in you!

Cel. Your heart's desires be with you.

Cha. Come, where is this young gallant, that is so desirous to lie with his mother earth?

Orl. Ready, sir; but his will hath in it a more modest working.

Duke F. You shall try but one fall.

Cha. No, I warrant your grace, you shall not entreat him to a second, that have so mightily persuaded him from a first.

Orl. You mean to mock me after: you should not have mocked me before: but come your ways.

Ros. Now, Hercules be thy speed, young man!

Cel. I would I were invisible, to catch the strong fellow by the leg.

[*Charles and Orlando wrestle*

Ros. O excellent young man!

Cel. If I had a thunderbolt in mine eye, I can tell who should down.

[*Charles is thrown. Shout*

Duke F. No more, no more.

172

Orl. Yes, I beseech your grace, I am not yet well
breathed.
Duke F. How dost thou, Charles?
Le Beau. He cannot speak, my lord.
Duke. Bear him away.

[Charles is borne out
What is thy name, young man?
Orl. Orlando, my liege, the youngest son of Sir Rowland
de Bois.
Duke F. I would thou hadst been son to some man else.
The world esteemed thy father honourable,
But I did find him still mine enemy:
Thou shouldst have better pleased me with this deed,
Hadst thou descended from another house.
But fare thee well, thou art a gallant youth.
I would thou hadst told me of another father.

[Exeunt Duke Frederick, Train, and Le Beau
Cel. Were I my father, coz, would I do this?
Orl. I am more proud to be Sir Rowland's son,
His youngest son—and would not change that calling,
To be adopted heir to Frederick.
Ros. My father loved Sir Rowland as his soul,
And all the world was of my father's mind:
Had I before known this young man his son,
I should have given him tears unto entreaties,
Ere he should thus have ventured.
Cel.   Gentle cousin,
Let us go thank him, and encourage him:
My father's rough and envious disposition
Sticks me at heart.—Sir, you have well deserved:
If you do keep your promises in love
But justly, as you have exceeded all promise,
Your mistress shall be happy.
Ros.   Gentleman,

[Giving him a chain from her neck
Wear this for me; one out of suits with fortune,
That could give more, but that her hand lacks means.
Shall we go, coz?
Cel. Ay. Fare you well, fair gentleman.
Orl. Can I not say, I thank you? My better parts
Are all thrown down, and that which here stands up
Is but a quintain, a mere lifeless block.
Ros. He calls us back. My pride fell with my fortunes;
I'll ask him what he would.—Did you call, sir?—
Sir, you have wrestled well, and overthrown
More than your enemies.
Cel.   Will you go, coz?
Ros. Have with you.—Fare you well.

[Exeunt Rosalind and Celia
Orl. What passion hangs these weights upon my tongue?

173

I cannot speak to her, yet she urged conference.
O poor Orlando! thou art overthrown.
Or Charles, or something weaker, masters thee.

Re-enter LE BEAU

Le Beau. Good sir, I do in friendship counsel you
To leave this place.   Albeit you have deserved
High commendation, true applause, and love,
Yet such is now the duke's condition,
That he misconstrues all that you have done.
The duke is humorous: what he is, indeed,
More suits you to conceive, than I to speak of.
Orl. I thank you, sir; and, pray you, tell me this:
Which of the two was daughter of the duke,
That here was at the wrestling?
Le Beau. Neither his daughter, if we judge by manners:
But yet, indeed, the smaller is his daughter:
The other is daughter to the banished duke,
And here detained by her usurping uncle,
To keep his daughter company; whose loves
Are dearer than the natural bond of sisters.
But I can tell you, that of late this duke
Hath ta'en displeasure 'gainst his gentle niece.
Grounded upon no other argument
But that the people praise her for her virtues
And pity her for her good father's sake;
And, on my life, his malice 'gainst the lady
Will suddenly break forth.—Sir, fare you well:
Hereafter, in a better world than this,
I shall desire more love and knowledge of you.
Orl. I rest much bounden to you: fare you well.
                                        [*Exit Le Beau*
Thus must I from the smoke into the smother,
From tyrant duke unto a tyrant brother.—
But heavenly Rosalind!   [*Exit*

SCENE III.—A Room in the Palace

Enter CELIA *and* ROSALIND

Cel. Why, cousin, why, Rosalind!—Cupid have mercy!
Not a word?
Ros. Not one to throw at a dog.
Cel. No, thy words are too precious to be cast away
upon curs, throw some of them at me: come, lame me with
reasons.
Ros. Then there were two cousins laid up, when the
one should be lamed with reasons, and the other mad
without any.

Cel. But is all this for your father?

Ros. No, some of it is for my father's child: O, how full of briars is this working-day world!

Cel. They were but burs, cousin, thrown upon thee in holiday foolery: if we walk not in the trodden paths, our very petticoats will catch them.

Ros. I could shake them off my coat: these burs are in my heart.

Cel. Hem them away.

Ros. I would try, if I could cry hem, and have him.

Cel. Come, come; wrestle with thy affections.

Ros. O, they take the part of a better wrestler than myself.

Cel. O, a good wish upon you: you will try in time, in despite of a fall. But, turning these jests out of service, let us talk in good earnest. Is it possible, on such a sudden, you should fall into so strong a liking with old Sir Rowland's youngest son?

Ros. The duke my father loved his father dearly.

Cel. Doth it therefore ensue, that you should love his son dearly? By this kind of chase, I should hate him, for my father hated his father dearly; yet I hate not Orlando.

Ros. No, 'faith, hate him not, for my sake.

Cel. Why should I not? doth he not deserve well?

Ros. Let me love him for that; and do you love him, because I do.—Look, here comes the duke.

Cel. With his eyes full of anger.

Enter DUKE FREDERICK, *with Lords*

Duke F. Mistress, despatch you with your safest haste, And get you from our court.

Ros.   Me, uncle?

Duke F.   You, cousin:
Within these ten days if that thou be'st found
So near our public court as twenty miles,
Thou diest for it.

Ros.   I do beseech your grace,
Let me the knowledge of my fault bear with me.
If with myself I hold intelligence,
Or have acquaintance with mine own desires,
If that I do not dream, or be not frantic
(As I do trust I am not) then, dear uncle,
Never so much as in a thought unborn
Did I offend your highness.

Duke F.   Thus do all traitors.
If their purgation did consist in words,
They are as innocent as grace itself.
Let it suffice thee, that I trust thee not.

Ros. Yet your mistrust cannot make me a traitor.

Tell me whereon the likelihood depends.
    Duke F. Thou art thy father's daughter; there's
      enough.
    Ros. So was I when your highness took his dukedom;
So was I when your highness banished him.
Treason is not inherited, my lord;
Or, if we did derive it from our friends,
What's that to me? my father was no traitor.
Then, good my liege, mistake me not so much,
To think my poverty is treacherous.
    Cel. Dear sovereign, hear me speak.
    Duke F. Ay, Celia, we stayed her for your sake;
Else had she with her father ranged along.
    Cel. I did not then entreat to have her stay,
It was your pleasure, and your own remorse.
I was too young that time to value her,
But now I know her: if she be a traitor,
Why, so am I: we still have slept together,
Rose at an instant, learned, played, eat together;
And wheresoe'er we went, like Juno's swans,
Still we went coupled and inseparable.
    Duke F. She is too subtle for thee, and her smoothness,
Her very silence, and her patience,
Speak to the people, and they pity her.
Thou art a fool: she robs thee of thy name,
And thou wilt show more bright, and seem more virtuous,
When she is gone. Then, open not thy lips:
Firm and irrevocable is my doom
Which I have passed upon her. She is banished.
    Cel. Pronounce that sentence, then, on me, my liege:
I cannot live out of her company.
    Duke F. You are a fool:—You, niece, provide yourself:
If you outstay the time, upon mine honour,
And in the greatness of my word, you die.
                  [Exeunt Duke Frederick and Lords
    Cel. O my poor Rosalind! whither wilt thou go?
Wilt thou change fathers? I will give thee mine.
I charge thee, be not thou more grieved than I am.
    Ros. I have more cause.
    Cel.   Thou hast not, cousin.
Pr'ythee, be cheerful: know'st thou not, the duke
Hath banished me, his daughter?
    Ros.   That he hath not.
    Cel. No? hath not? Rosalind lacks then the love
Which teacheth thee that thou and I am one.
Shall we be sundered? shall we part, sweet girl?
No: let my father seek another heir.
Therefore, devise with me how we may fly,
Whither to go, and what to bear with us:
And do not seek to take your change upon you,

To bear your griefs yourself and leave me out;
For, by heaven, now at our sorrows pale.
Say what thou canst, I'll go along with thee.
    Ros. Why, whither shall we go?
    Cel. To seek my uncle in the forest of Arden.
    Ros. Alas, what danger will it be to us,
Maids as we are, to travel forth so far!
Beauty provoketh thieves sooner than gold.
    Cel. I'll put myself in poor and mean attire,
And with a kind of umber smirch my face.
The like do you: so shall we pass along,
And never stir assailants.
    Ros.   Were it not better,
Because that I am more than common tall,
That I did suit me all points like a man?
A gallant curtle-axe upon my thigh,
A boar-spear in my hand, and, in my heart
Lie there what hidden woman's fear there will,
We'll have a swashing and a martial outside,
As many other mannish cowards have
That do outface it with their semblances.
    Cel. What shall I call thee when thou art a man?
    Ros. I'll have no worse a name than Jove's own page,
And therefore look you call me Ganymede.
But what will you be called?
    Cel. Something that hath a reference to my state:
No longer Celia, but Aliena.
    Ros. But, cousin, what if we essayed to steal
The clownish fool out of your father's court?
Would he not be a comfort to our travel?
    Cel. He'll go along o'er the wide world with me,
Leave me alone to woo him.   Let's away,
And get our jewels and our wealth together,
Devise the fittest time and safest way
To hide us from pursuit that will be made
After my flight.   Now go we in content
To liberty, and not to banishment.

                                        [*Exeunt*

ACT TWO

SCENE I.—The Forest of Arden

Enter DUKE *Senior,* AMIENS, *and two or three
Lords, like foresters*

    Duke S. Now, my co-mates, and brothers in exile,
Hath not old custom made his life more sweet
Than that of painted pomp?   Are not these woods

More free from peril than the envious court?
Here feel we but the penalty of Adam,
The seasons' difference; as the icy fang,
And churlish chiding of the winter's wind,
Which when it bites and blows upon my body,
Even till I shrink with cold, I smile, and say,
This is no flattery: these are counsellors
That feelingly persuade me what I am.
Sweet are the uses of adversity,
Which, like the toad, ugly and venomous,
Wears yet a precious jewel in his head;
And this our life, exempt from public haunt,
Finds tongues in trees, books in the running brooks,
Sermons in stones, and good in everything.
   Ami. I would not change it.   Happy is your grace,
That can translate the stubbornness of fortune
Into so quiet and so sweet a style.
   Duke S. Come, shall we go and kill us venison?
And yet it irks me the poor dappled fools,
Being native burghers of this desert city,
Should, in their own confines, with forked heads
Have their round haunches gored.
   First Lord.   Indeed, my lord,
The melancholy Jaques grieves at that;
And in that kind swears you do more usurp
Than doth your brother that hath banished you.
To-day my Lord of Amiens and myself
Did steal behind him as he lay along
Under an oak, whose antique root peeps out
Upon the brook that brawls along this wood,
To the which place a poor sequestered stag,
That from the hunter's aim had ta'en a hurt,
Did come to languish: and, indeed, my lord,
The wretched animal heaved forth such groans,
That their discharge did stretch his leathern coat
Almost to bursting; and the big round tears
Coursed one another down his innocent nose
In piteous chase: and thus the hairy fool,
Much markéd of the melancholy Jaques,
Stood on the extremest verge of the swift brook,
Augmenting it with tears.
   Duke S.   But what said Jaques?
Did he not moralise this spectacle?
   First Lord. O yes, into a thousand similes.
First, for his weeping into the needless stream;
'Poor deer,'' quoth he, 'thou mak'st a testament
As worldlings do, giving thy sum of more
To that which had too much.'   Then, being there alone,
Left and abandoned of his velvet friends;
' 'T is right,' quoth he; 'thus misery doth part

The flux of company.' Anon, a careless herd,
Full of the pasture, jumps along by him,
And never stays to greet him: 'Ay,' quoth Jaques.
'Sweep on, you fat and greasy citizens;
'Tis just the fashion: wherefore do you look
Upon the poor and broken bankrupt there?'
Thus most invectively he pierceth through
The body of the country, city, court,
Yea, and of this our life; swearing, that we
Are mere usurpers, tyrants, and what's worse,
To fright the animals, and to kill them up
In their assigned and native dwelling-place.
 Duke S. And did you leave him in this contemplation?
 Sec. Lord. We did, my lord, weeping and commenting
Upon the sobbing deer.
 Duke S.   Show me the place.
I love to cope him in these sullen fits,
For then he's full of matter.
 Sec. Lord. I'll bring you to him straight.   [*Exeunt*

SCENE II.—A Room in the Palace

Enter DUKE FREDERICK, *Lords, and Attendants*

 Duke F. Can it be possible that no man saw them?
It cannot be: some villains of my court
Are of consent and sufferance in this.
 First Lord. I cannot hear of any that did see her.
The ladies, her attendants of her chamber,
Saw her a-bed; and, in the morning early,
They found the bed untreasured of their mistress.
 Sec. Lord. My lord, the roynish clown, at whom so oft
Your grace was wont to laugh, is also missing.
Hesperia, the princess' gentlewoman,
Confesses that she secretly o'erheard
Your daughter and her cousin much commend
The parts and graces of the wrestler
That did but lately foil the sinewy Charles;
And she believes, wherever they are gone,
That youth is surely in their company.
 Duke F. Send to his brother, fetch that gallant hither;
If he be absent, bring his brother to me,
I'll make him find him. Do this suddenly,
And let not search and inquisition quail
To bring again these foolish runaways.   [*Exeunt*

SCENE III.—Before OLIVER'S House

Enter ORLANDO *and* ADAM, *meeting*

Orl. Who's there?
Adam. What, my young master?—O my gentle master,
O my sweet master, O you memory
Of old Sir Rowland; why, what make you here?
Why are you virtuous? why do people love you?
And wherefore are you gentle, strong, and valiant?
Why would you be so fond to overcome
The bony priser of the humorous duke?
Your praise is come too swiftly home before you.
Know you not, master, to some kind of men
Their graces serve them but as enemies?
No more do yours: your virtues, gentle master,
Are sanctified and holy traitors to you.
O, what a world is this, when what is comely
Envenoms him that bears it!
   Orl. Why, what's the matter?
   Adam.   O unhappy youth,
Come not within these doors: within this roof
The enemy of all your graces lives.
Your brother—(no, no brother: yet the son—
Yet not the son—I will not call him son
Of him I was about to call his father)—
Hath heard your praises, and this night he means
To burn the lodging where you use to lie,
And you within it: if he fail of that,
He will have other means to cut you off.
I overheard him, and his practices.
This is no place, this house is but a butchery;
Abhor it, fear it, do not enter it.
   Orl. Why, whither, Adam, wouldst thou have me go?
   Adam. No matter whither, so you come not here.
   Orl. What, wouldst thou have me go and beg my food,
Or with a base and boisterous sword enforce
A thievish living on the common road?
This I must do, or know not what to do;
Yet this I will not do, do how I can.
I rather will subject me to the malice
Of a diverted blood, and bloody brother.
   Adam. But do not so. I have five hundred crowns,
The thrifty hire I saved under your father,
Which I did store to be my foster-nurse
When service should in my old limbs lie lame,
And unregarded age in corners thrown:
Take that; and He that doth the ravens feed,
Yea, providently caters for the sparrow,

Be comfort to my age!   Here is the gold;
All this I give you.   Let me be your servant:
Though I look old, yet I am strong and lusty;
For in my youth I never did apply
Hot and rebellious liquors in my blood;
Nor did not with unbashful forehead woo
The means of weakness and debility;
Therefore my age is as a lusty winter,
Frosty, but kindly.   Let me go with you:
I'll do the service of a younger man
In all your business and necessities.
    Orl.   O good old man, how well in thee appears
The constant service of the antique world,
When service sweat for duty, not for meed!
Thou art not for the fashion of these times,
Where none will sweat but for promotion;
And having that, do choke their service up
Even with the having: it is not so with thee.
But, poor old man, thou prun'st a rotten tree
That cannot so much as a blossom yield
In lieu of all thy pains and husbandry.
But come thy ways; we'll go along together;
And ere we have thy youthful wages spent,
We'll light upon some settled low content.
    Adam.   Master, go on, and I will follow thee
To the last gasp with truth and loyalty,
From seventeen years till now almost fourscore,
Here livéd I, but now live here no more.
At seventeen years many their fortunes seek;
But at fourscore it is too late a week:
Yet Fortune cannot recompense me better
Than to die well, and not my master's debtor.   [*Exeunt*

SCENE IV.—The Forest of Arden

Enter ROSALIND *in boy's clothes,* CELIA *dressed like a shepherdess, and* TOUCHSTONE

    Ros.   O Jupiter, how weary are my spirits!
    Touch.   I care not for my spirits, if my legs were not weary.
    Ros.   I could find in my heart to disgrace my man's apparel, and to cry like a woman; but I must comfort the weaker vessel, as doublet and hose ought to show itself courageous to petticoat: therefore, courage, good Aliena.
    Cel.   I pray you, bear with me; I can go no further.
    Touch.   For my part, I had rather bear with you than bear you: yet I should bear no cross, if I did bear you; for I think you have no money in your purse.

Ros. Well, this is the forest of Arden.

Touch. Ay, now am I in Arden; the more fool I; when I was at home, I was in a better place: but travellers must be content.

Ros. Ay, be so, good Touchstone.—Look you, who comes here; a young man, and an old, in solemn talk.

Enter CORIN *and* SILVIUS

Cor. That is the way to make her scorn you still.

Sil. O Corin, that thou knew'st how I do love her!

Cor. I partly guess, for I have loved ere now.

Sil. No, Corin; being old, thou canst not guess.
Though in thy youth thou wast as true a lover
As ever sighed upon a midnight pillow:
But if thy love were ever like to mine,
As sure I think did never man love so,
How many actions most ridiculous
Hast thou been drawn to by thy fantasy?

Cor. Into a thousand that I have forgotten.

Sil. O, thou didst then ne'er love so heartily:
If thou remember'st not the slightest folly
That ever love did make thee run into,
Thou hast not loved:
Or if thou hast not sat, as I do now,
Wearing thy hearer in thy mistress' praise,
Thou hast not loved:
Or if thou hast not broke from company
Abruptly, as my passion now makes me,
Thou has not loved.—O Phebe, Phebe, Phebe!   [*Exit*

Ros. Alas, poor shepherd! searching of thy wound, I have by hard adventure found mine own.

Touch. And I mine. I remember, when I was in love I broke my sword upon a stone, and bid him take that for coming a-night to Jane Smile; and I remember the kissing of her batlet, and the cow's dugs that her pretty chopped hands had milked; and I remember the wooing of a peascod instead of her, from whom I took two cods, and, giving her them again, said with weeping tears, 'Wear these for my sake.' We that are true lovers run into strange capers; but as all is mortal in nature, so is all nature in love mortal in folly.

Ros. Thou speakest wiser than thou art ware of.

Touch. Nay, I shall ne'er be ware of mine own wit till I break my shins against it.

Ros. Jove, Jove! this shepherd's passion
       Is much upon my fashion.

Touch. And mine; but it grows something stale with me.

Cel. I pray you, one of you question yond man,

If he for gold will give us any food:
I faint almost to death.
   Touch. Holla, you clown!
   Ros. Peace, fool: he's not thy kinsman.
   Cor. Who calls?
   Touch. Your betters, sir.
   Cor. Else are they very wretched.
   Ros.   Peace, I say.—
Good even to you, friend.
   Cor. And to you, gentle sir, and to you all.
   Ros. I pr'ythee, shepherd, if that love or gold
Can in this desert place buy entertainment,
Bring us where we may rest ourselves and feed.
Here's a young maid with travel much oppressed,
And faints for succour.
   Cor.   Fair sir, I pity her,
And wish, for her sake more than for mine own,
My fortunes were more able to relieve her;
But I am shepherd to another man,
And do not shear the fleeces that I graze;
My master is of churlish disposition,
And little recks to find the way to heaven
By doing deeds of hospitality:
Besides, his cote, his flocks, and bounds of feed,
Are now on sale; and at our sheepcote now,
By reason of his absence, there is nothing
That you will feed on; but what is, come see,
And in my voice most welcome shall you be.
   Ros. What is he that shall buy his flock and pasture?
   Cor. That young swain that you saw here but erewhile,
That little cares for buying anything.
   Ros. I pray thee, if it stand with honesty,
Buy thou the cottage, pasture, and the flock,
And thou shalt have to pay for it of us.
   Cel. And we will mend thy wages. I like this place,
And willingly could waste my time in it.
   Cor. Assuredly, the thing is to be sold:
Go with me: if you like, upon report,
The soil, the profit, and this kind of life,
I will your very faithful feeder be,
And buy it with your gold right suddenly.   *[Exeunt*

SCENE V.—Another Part of the Forest

Enter AMIENS, JAQUES, *and others*

SONG

Ami.   *Under the greenwood tree*
               Who loves to lie with me,

> *And tune his merry note*
> *Unto the sweet bird's throat,*
> *Come hither, come hither, come hither :*
> *Here shall he see*
> *No enemy*
> *But winter and rough weather.*

Jaq.   More, more, I pr'ythee, more.

Ami.   It will make you melancholy, Monsieur Jaques.

Jaq.   I thank it. More, I pr'ythee, more. I can suck melancholy out of a song, as a weasel sucks eggs. More, I pr'ythee, more.

Ami.   My voice is ragged; I know I cannot please you.

Jaq.   I do not desire you to please me; I do desire you to sing. Come, more; another stanza. Call you 'em stanzas?

Ami.   What you will, Monsieur Jaques.

Jaq.   Nay, I care not for their names; they owe me nothing. Will you sing?

Ami.   More at your request than to please myself.

Jaq.   Well then, if ever I thank any man, I'll thank you: but that they call compliment is like the encounter of two dog-apes; and when a man thanks me heartily, methinks I have given him a penny, and he renders me the beggarly thanks. Come, sing; and you that will not, hold your tongues.

Ami.   Well, I'll end the song.—Sirs, cover the while; the duke will drink under this tree.—He hath been all this day to look you.

Jaq.   And I have been all this day to avoid him. He is too disputable for my company: I think of as many matters as he; but I give Heaven thanks, and make no boast of them. Come, warble, come.

Song

[*All together here*

> *Who doth ambition shun,*
> *And loves to live i' the sun,*
> *Seeking the food he eats,*
> *And pleased with what he gets,*
> *Come hither, come hither, come hither :*
> *Here shall he see*
> *No enemy*
> *But winter and rough weather.*

Jaq.   I'll give you a verse to this note, that I made yesterday in despite of my invention.

Ami.   And I'll sing it.

Jaq.   Thus it goes—

> *If it do come to pass*
> *That any man turn ass,*
> *Leaving his wealth and ease*
> *A stubborn will to please,*
> *Ducdame, ducdame, ducdame :*
> *Here shall he see*
> *Gross fools as he,*
> *An if he will come to me.*

Ami. What 's that *ducdame?*

Jaq. 'T is a Greek invocation to call fools into a circle. I'll go sleep if I can; if I cannot, I'll rail against all the first-born of Egypt.

Ami. And I'll go seek the duke: his banquet is prepared.

[Exeunt severally

SCENE VI.—Another Part of the Forest

Enter ORLANDO *and* ADAM

Adam. Dear master, I can go no further: O, I die for food! Here lie I down, and measure out my grave. Farewell, kind master.

Orl. Why, how now, Adam! no greater heart in thee? Live a little; comfort a little; cheer thyself a little. If this uncouth forest yield anything savage, I will either be food for it, or bring it for food to thee. Thy conceit is nearer death than thy powers. For my sake be comfortable, hold death awhile at the arm's end: I will here be with thee presently, and if I bring thee not something to eat, I will give thee leave to die: but if thou diest before I come, thou art a mocker of my labour. Well said, thou look'st cheerily; and I'll be with thee quickly.—Yet thou liest in the bleak air: come, I will bear thee to some shelter, and thou shalt not die for lack of a dinner, if there live anything in this desert. Cheerly, good Adam!   *[Exeunt*

SCENE VII.—Another Part of the Forest

A table set out. Enter DUKE *Senior,* AMIENS, *and others*

Duke S. I think he be transformed into a beast,
For I can nowhere find him like a man.

First Lord. My lord, he is but even now gone hence:
Here was he merry, hearing of a song.

Duke S. If he, compact of jars, grow musical,
We shall have shortly discord in the spheres.
Go, seek him: tell him, I would speak with him.

First Lord. He saves my labour by his own approach.

Enter JAQUES

   Duke S. Why, how now, monsieur, what a life is this,
That your poor friends must woo your company?
What, you look merrily.
   Jaq. A fool, a fool!—I met a fool i' the forest,
A motley fool;—a miserable world!—
As I do live by food, I met a fool,
Who laid him down and basked him in the sun,
And railed on Lady Fortune in good terms,
In good set terms,—and yet a motley fool!
'Good morrow, fool,' quoth I:—'No sir,' quoth he,
'Call me not fool, till Heaven hath sent me fortune.'
And then he drew a dial from his poke,
And looking on it with lack-lustre eye,
Says very wisely, 'It is ten o'clock:
Thus may we see,' quoth he, 'how the world wags.
'T is but an hour ago since it was nine,
And after one hour more 't will be eleven:
And so from hour to hour we ripe and ripe,
And then from hour to hour we rot and rot,
And thereby hangs a tale.' When I did hear
The motley fool thus moral on the time,
My lungs began to crow like chanticleer,
That fools should be so deep-contemplative;
And I did laugh, sans intermission,
An hour by his dial.—O noble fool!
A worthy fool! Motley's the only wear.
   Duke S. What fool is this?
   Jaq. O worthy fool!—One that hath been a courtier,
And says, if ladies be but young and fair,
They have the gift to know it; and in his brain,
Which is as dry as the remainder biscuit
After a voyage, he hath strange places crammed
With observation, the which he vents
In mangled forms.—O, that I were a fool!
I am ambitious for a motley coat.
   Duke S. Thou shalt have one.
   Jaq.   It is my only suit;
Provided that you weed your better judgments
Of all opinion that grows rank in them
That I am wise. I must have liberty
Withal, as large a charter as the wind,
To blow on whom I please; for so fools have:
And they that are most gallèd with my folly
They most must laugh. And why, sir, must they so?
The way is plain as way to parish church:
He, that a fool doth very wisely hit
Doth very foolishly, although he smart,
Not to seem senseless of the bob; if not,

The wise man's folly is anatomised
Even by the squandering glances of the fool.
Invest me in my motley; give me leave
To speak my mind, and I will through and through
Cleanse the foul body of the infected world,
If they will patiently receive my medicine.
  Duke S.   Fie on thee!   I can tell what thou wouldst do.
  Jaq.   What, for a counter, would I do but good?
  Duke S.   Most mischievous foul sin, in chiding sin:
For thou thyself hast been a libertine,
As sensual as the brutish sting itself;
And all the embosséd sores, and headed evils
That thou with license of free foot hast caught,
Wouldst thou disgorge into the general world.
  Jaq.   Why, who cries out on pride,
That can therein tax any private party?
Doth it not flow as hugely as the sea,
Till that the customary means do ebb?
What woman in the city do I name,
When that I say the city-woman bears
The cost of princes on unworthy shoulders?
Who can come in, and say that I mean her,
When such a one as she, such is her neighbour?
Or what is he of basest function,
That says his bravery is not on my cost,—
Thinking that I mean him,—but therein suits
His folly to the mettle of my speech?
There then; how.then? what then?   Let me see wherein
My tongue hath wronged him: if it do him right,
Then he hath wronged himself; if he be free,
Why, then my taxing like a wild-goose flies,
Unclaimed of any man.—But who comes here?

Enter ORLANDO, *with his sword drawn*

  Orl.   Forbear, and eat no more.
  Jaq.   Why, I have eat none yet.
  Orl.   Nor shalt not, till necessity be served.
  Jaq.   Of what kind should this cock come of?
  Duke S.   Art thou thus boldened, man, by thy distress,
Or else a rude despiser of good manners,
That in civility thou seem'st so empty?
  Orl.   You touched my vein at first: the thorny point
Of bare distress hath ta'en from me the show
Of smooth civility; yet am I inland bred,
And know some nurture.   But forbear, I say:
He dies that touches any of this fruit,
Till I and my affairs are answeréd.
  Jaq.   An you will not be answered with reason, I must
die.

187

Duke S.   What would you have?   Your gentleness shall
        force,
More than your force move us to gentleness.
Orl.   I almost die for food, and let me have it.
Duke S.   Sit down and feed, and welcome to our table.
Orl.   Speak you so gently?   Pardon me, I pray you:
I thought that all things had been savage here,
And therefore put I on the countenance
Of stern commandment.   But whate'er you are
That in this desert inaccessible,
Under the shade of melancholy boughs,
Lose and neglect the creeping hours of time:
If ever you have looked on better days,
If ever been where bells have knolled to church,
If ever sat at any good man's feast,
If ever from your eyelids wiped a tear,
And know what 't is to pity, and be pitied,
Let gentleness my strong enforcement be:
In the which hope, I blush, and hide my sword.
Duke S.   True is it that we have seen better days,
And have with holy bell been knolled to church,
And sat at good men's feasts, and wiped our eyes
Of drops that sacred pity hath engendered:
And therefore sit you down in gentleness,
And take upon command what help we have
That to your wanting may be ministered.
Orl.   Then, but forbear your food a little while
Whiles, like a doe, I go to find my fawn,
And give it food.   There is an old poor man,
Who after me hath many a weary step
Limped in pure love: till he be first sufficed,—
Oppressed with two weak evils, age and hunger,—
I will not touch a bit.
Duke S.   Go find him out,
And we will nothing waste till you return.
Orl.   I thank ye, and be blessed for your good comfort!
                                        [*Exit*
Duke S.   Thou seest, we are not all alone unhappy:
This wide and universal theatre
Presents more woeful pageants than the scene
Wherein we play in.
Jaq.   All the world's a stage,
And all the men and women merely players:
They have their exits and their entrances;
And one man in his time plays many parts,
His acts being seven ages.   At first, the infant,
Mewling and puking in the nurse's arms.
And then, the whining school-boy, with his satchel,
And shining morning face, creeping like snail
Unwillingly to school.   And then, the lover,

Sighing like furnace, with a woeful ballad
Made to his mistress' eyebrow.   Then, a soldier,
Full of strange oaths, and bearded like the pard,
Jealous in honour, sudden and quick in quarrel,
Seeking the bubble reputation
Even in the cannon's mouth.   And then, the justice,
In fair round belly with good capon lined,
With eyes severe and beard of formal cut,
Full of wise saws and modern instances;
And so he plays his part.   The sixth age shifts
Into the lean and slippered pantaloon,
With spectacles on nose and pouch on side;
His youthful hose well saved, a world too wide
For his shrunk shank; and his big manly voice,
Turning again toward childish treble, pipes
And whistles in his sound.   Last scene of all,
That ends this strange eventful history,
Is second childishness and mere oblivion,
Sans teeth, sans eyes, sans taste, sans everything.

Re-enter ORLANDO, *with* ADAM

   Duke S.   Welcome.   Set down your venerable burden,
And let him feed.
   Orl.   I thank you most for him.
   Adam.   So had you need:
I scarce can speak to thank you for myself.
   Duke S.   Welcome; fall to: I will not trouble you
As yet to question you about your fortunes.
Give us some music; and, good cousin, sing.

SONG

Ami.   *Blow, blow, thou winter wind,*
                Thou art not so unkind
                    As man's ingratitude ;
                Thy tooth is not so keen,
                Because thou art not seen,
                    Although thy breath be rude.
Heigh, ho! sing, heigh, ho! unto the green holly:
Most friendship is feigning, most loving mere folly :
                Then, heigh, ho ! the holly !
                This life is most jolly.

                Freeze, freeze, thou bitter sky,
                That dost not bite so nigh
                    As benefits forgot :
                Though thou the waters warp,
                Thy sting is not so sharp
                    As friend remembered not.
Heigh, ho ! sing, etc.

Duke S. If that you were the good Sir Rowland's son,
As you have whispered faithfully you were,
And as mine eye doth his effigies witness
Most truly limned and living in your face,
Be truly welcome hither. I'm the duke,
That loved your father. The residue of your fortune,
Go to my cave and tell me.—Good old man,
Thou art right welcome as thy master is.
Support him by the arm.—Give me your hand,—
And let me all your fortunes understand.   [*Exeunt*

ACT THREE

Scene I.—A Room in the Palace

Enter Duke Frederick, Oliver, *and attendants*

Duke F. Not see him since? Sir, sir, that cannot be:
But were I not the better part made mercy,
I should not seek an absent argument
Of my revenge, thou present. But look to it:
Find out thy brother, wheresoe'er he is;
Seek him with candle; bring him, dead or living,
Within this twelvemonth, or turn thou no more
To seek a living in our territory.
Thy lands, and all things that thou dost call thine,
Worth seizure, do we seize into our hands,
Till thou canst quit thee by thy brother's mouth
Of what we think against thee.
Oli. O, that your highness knew my heart in this!
I never loved my brother in my life.
Duke F. More villain thou.—Well, push him out of
          doors;
And let my officers of such a nature
Make an extent upon his house and lands.
Do this expediently, and turn him going.   [*Exeunt*

Scene II.—The Forest of Arden

Enter Orlando, *with a paper*

Orl. Hang there, my verse, in witness of my love:
And thou, thrice-crownéd queen of night, survey
With thy chaste eye, from thy pale sphere above,
Thy huntress' name, that my full life doth sway.
O Rosalind! these trees shall be my books,
And in their barks my thoughts I'll character,

That every eye, which in this forest looks,
Shall see thy virtue witnessed everywhere.
Run, run, Orlando: carve on every tree
The fair, the chaste, and unexpressive she.   [*Exit*

Enter CORIN *and* TOUCHSTONE

    Cor. And how like you this shepherd's life, Master
Touchstone?
    Touch. Truly, shepherd, in respect of itself, it is a good
life, but in respect that it is a shepherd's life, it is naught.
In respect that it is solitary, I like it very well; but in
respect that it is private, it is a very vile life. Now, in
respect it is in the fields, it pleaseth me well; but in respect
it is not in the court, it is tedious. As it is a spare life,
look you, it fits my humour well; but as there is no more
plenty in it, it goes much against my stomach. Hast any
philosophy in thee, shepherd?
    Cor. No more but that I know the more one sickens
the worse at ease he is; and that he that wants money,
means, and content, is without three good friends; that
the property of rain is to wet, and fire to burn; that good
pasture makes fat sheep, and that a great cause of the
night is lack of the sun; that he hath learned no wit by
Nature nor Art may complain of good breeding, or comes
of a very dull kindred.
    Touch. Such a one is a natural philosopher. Wast
ever in court, shepherd?
    Cor. No, truly.
    Touch. Then thou art damned.
    Cor. Nay, I hope,—
    Touch. Truly, thou art damned; like an ill-roasted
egg, all on one side.
    Cor. For not being at court? Your reason.
    Touch. Why, if thou never wast at court, thou never
saw'st good manners; if thou never saw'st good manners,
then thy manners must be wicked; and wickedness is sin,
and sin is damnation. Thou art in a parlous state, shepherd.
    Cor. Not a whit, Touchstone: those that are good
manners at the court, are as ridiculous in the country
as the behaviour of the country is most mockable at the
court. You told me you salute not at the court, but
you kiss your hands: that courtesy would be uncleanly,
if courtiers were shepherds.
    Touch. Instance, briefly; come, instance.
    Cor. Why, we are still handling our ewes; and their
fells, you know, are greasy.
    Touch. Why, do not your courtier's hands sweat? and
is not the grease of a mutton as wholesome as the sweat of a
man? Shallow, shallow. A better instance, I say; come.

Cor.   Besides, our hands are hard.

Touch.   Your lips will feel them the sooner: shallow again.   A more sounder instance, come.

Cor.   And they are often tarred over with the surgery of our sheep; and would you have us kiss tar?   The courtier's hands are perfumed with civit.

Touch.   Most shallow man!   Thou wormsmeat in respect of a good piece of flesh indeed!—Learn of the wise, and perpend: civet is of a baser birth than tar; the very uncleanly flux of a cat.   Mend the instance, shepherd.

Cor.   You have too courtly a wit for me: I'll rest.

Touch.   Wilt thou rest damned?   God help thee, shallow man: God make incision in thee, thou art raw.

Cor.   Sir, I am a true labourer: I earn that I eat, get that I wear; owe no man hate, envy no man's happiness; glad of other men's good, content with my harm; and the greatest of my pride is, to see my ewes graze and my lambs suck.

Touch.   That is another simple sin in you, to bring the ewes and the rams together, and to offer to get your living by the copulation of cattle; to be bawd to a bell-wether, and to betray a she-lamb of a twelvemonth, to a crooked-pated, old cuckoldly ram, out of all reasonable match.   If thou be'st not damned for this, the devil himself will have no shepherds: I cannot see how thou should'st scape.

Cor.   Here comes young Master Ganymede, my new mistress's brother.

Enter ROSALIND, *reading a paper*

Ros.　　　　　*From the east to western Ind*
　　　　　　　No jewel is like Rosalind.
　　　　　　　Her worth, being mounted on the wind,
　　　　　　　Through all the world bears Rosalind.
　　　　　　　All the pictures fairest lined
　　　　　　　Are but black to Rosalind.
　　　　　　　Let no face be kept in mind
　　　　　　　But the face of Rosalind.

Touch.   I'll rhyme you so eight years together, dinners, and suppers, and sleeping hours excepted: it is the right butter-women's rank to market.

Ros.   Out, fool!

Touch.   For a taste:—

　　　　　　　If a hart do lack a hind,
　　　　　　　Let him seek out Rosalind.
　　　　　　　If the cat will after kind,
　　　　　　　So, be sure, will Rosalind.

Winter garments must be lined,
So must slender Rosalind.
They that reap must sheaf and bind,
Then to cart with Rosalind.
Sweetest nut hath sourest rind,
Such a nut is Rosalind.
He that sweetest rose will find,
Must find love's prick and Rosalind.

This is the very false gallop of verses: why do you infect
yourself with them?

Ros.   Peace, you dull fool: I found them on a tree.

Touch.   Truly, the tree yields bad fruit.

Ros.   I'll graff it with you, and then I shall graff it
with a medlar: then it will be the earliest fruit i' the
country; for you'll be rotten ere you be half ripe, and
that's the right virtue of the medlar.

Touch.   You have said; but whether wisely or no, let
the forest judge.

Ros.   Peace!

Here comes my sister, reading: stand aside

Enter CELIA, *reading a paper*

Cel.   *Why should this a desert be?*
   For it is unpeopled?   No;
Tongues I'll hang on every tree,
   That shall civil sayings show.
Some, how brief the life of man
   Runs his erring pilgrimage,
That the stretching of a span
   Buckles in his sum of age.
Some, of violated vows
   'Twixt the souls of friend and friend:
But upon the fairest boughs,
   Or at every sentence' end,
Will I Rosalinda write;
   Teaching all that read, to know
The quintessence of every sprite
   Heaven would in little show.
Therefore Heaven Nature charged
   That one body should be filled
With all graces wide enlarged;
   Nature presently distilled
Helen's cheek, but not her heart,
   Cleopatra's majesty,
Atalanta's better part,
   Sad Lucretia's modesty.
Thus Rosalind of many parts
   By heavenly synod was devised,

193

> *Of many faces, eyes, and hearts*
> *To have the touches dearest prized.*
> *Heaven would that she these gifts should have,*
> *And I to live and die her slave.*

Ros. O most gentle Jupiter, what tedious homily of love have you wearied your parishioners withal and never cried, 'Have patience, good people!'

Cel. How now? back friends: shepherd, go off a little —go with him, sirrah.

Touch. Come, shepherd, let us make an honourable retreat; though not with bag-and baggage, yet with scrip and scrippage.   [*Exeunt Corin and Touchstone*

Cel. Didst thou hear these verses?

Ros. O, yes, I heard them all, and more too; for some of them had in them more feet than the verses would bear.

Cel. That's no matter: the feet might bear the verses.

Ros. Ay, but the feet were lame, and could not bear themselves without the verse, and therefore stood lamely in the verse.

Cel. But didst thou hear without wondering how thy name should be hanged and carved upon these trees?

Ros. I was seven of the nine days out of the wonder before you came; for look here what I found on a palm-tree: I was never so be-rhymed since Pythagoras' time, that I was an Irish rat, which I can hardly remember.

Cel. Trow you, who hath done this?

Ros. Is it a man?

Cel. And a chain, that you once wore, about his neck. Change you colour?

Ros. I pr'ythee, who?

Cel. O Lord, Lord! it is a hard matter for friends to meet; but mountains may be removed with earthquakes and so encounter.

Ros. Nay, but who is it?

Cel. Is it possible?

Ros. Nay, I pr'ythee, now, with most petitionary vehemence, tell me who it is.

Cel. O, wonderful, wonderful, and most wonderful wonderful! and yet again wonderful! and after that, out of all whooping!

Ros. Good my complexion! dost thou think, though I am caparisoned like a man, I have a doublet and hose in my disposition? One inch of delay more is a South Sea of discovery; I pr'ythee, tell me, who is it, quickly, and speak apace. I would thou couldst stammer, that thou mightst pour this concealed man out of thy mouth, as wine comes out of a narrow-mouthed bottle; either

too much at once, or none at all. I pr'ythee, take the
cork out of thy mouth, that I may drink thy tidings.

Cel. So you may put a man in your belly.

Ros. Is he of God's making? What manner of man?
Is his head worth a hat, or his chin worth a beard?

Cel. Nay, he hath but a little beard.

Ros. Why, God will send more, if the man will be thankful. Let me stay the growth of his beard, if thou delay
me not the knowledge of his chin.

Cel. It is young Orlando, that tripped up the wrestler's
heels and your heart, both in an instant.

Ros. Nay, but the devil take mocking: speak, sad
brow and true maid.

Cel. I' faith, coz, 't is he.

Ros. Orlando?

Cel. Orlando.

Ros. Alas the day! what shall I do with my doublet
and hose?—What did he when thou saw'st him? What
said he? How look'd he? Wherein went he? What
makes he here? Did he ask for me? Where remains he?
How parted he with thee, and when shalt thou see him
again? Answer me in one word.

Cel. You must borrow me Gargantua's mouth first:
't is a word too great for any mouth of this age's size. To
say ay and no to these particulars is more than to answer
in a catechism.

Ros. But doth he know that I am in this forest, and
in man's apparel? Looks he as freshly as he did the
day he wrestled?

Cel. It is as easy to count atomies, as to resolve the
propositions of a lover: but take a taste of my finding
him, and relish it with good observance. I found him
under a tree, like a dropped acorn.

Ros. It may well be called Jove's tree, when it drops
forth such fruit.

Cel. Give me audience, good madam.

Ros. Proceed.

Cel. There lay he, stretched along like a wounded knight.

Ros. Though it be pity to see such a sight, it well
becomes the ground.

Cel. Cry holla to thy tongue, I pr'ythee: it curvets
unseasonably. He was furnished like a hunter.

Ros. O, ominous! he comes to kill my heart.

Cel. I would sing my song without a burden: thou
bringest me out of tune.

Ros. Do you not know I am a woman? when I think,
I must speak. Sweet, say on.

Cel. You bring me out.—Soft! comes he not here?

Ros. 'T is he: slink by, and note him.

[Rosalind and Celia retire

Enter ORLANDO *and* JAQUES

Jaq. I thank you for your company; but, good faith, I had as lief have been myself alone.

Orl. And so had I; but yet, for fashion's sake, I thank you too for your society.

Jaq. God buy you: let's meet as little as we can.

Orl. I do desire we may be better strangers.

Jaq. I pray you, mar no more trees with writing love-songs in their barks.

Orl. I pray you, mar no more of my verses with reading them ill-favouredly.

Jaq. Rosalind is your love's name?

Orl. Yes, just.

Jaq. I do not like her name.

Orl. There was no thought of pleasing you when she was christened.

Jaq. What stature is she of?

Orl. Just as high as my heart.

Jaq. You are full of pretty answers. Have you not been acquainted with goldsmiths' wives, and conned them out of rings?

Orl. Not so; but I answer you right painted cloth, from whence you have studied your questions.

Jaq. You have a nimble wit: I think 'twas made of Atalanta's heels. Will you sit down with me? and we too will rail against our mistress the world, and all our misery.

Orl. I will chide no breather in the world but myself, against whom I know most faults.

Jaq. The worst fault you have is to be in love.

Orl. 'T is a fault I will not change for your best virtue. I am weary of you.

Jaq. By my troth, I was seeking for a fool when I found you.

Orl. He is drowned in the brook: look but in, and you shall see him.

Jaq. There I shall see mine own figure.

Orl. Which I take to be either a fool or a cypher.

Jaq. I'll tarry no longer with you: farewell, good Signior Love.

Orl. I am glad of your departure: adieu, good Monsieur Melancholy.

[*Exit Jaques.—Rosalind and Celia come forward*

Ros. [*Aside to Celia*] I will speak to him like a saucy lackey, and under that habit play the knave with him.—Do you hear, forester?

Orl. Very well: what would you?

Ros. I pray you, what is't o'clock?

Orl. You should ask me, what time o' day: there's no clock in the forest.

Ros. Then, there is no true lover in the forest; else sighing every minute, and groaning every hour, would detect the lazy foot of Time as well as a clock.

Orl. And why not the swift foot of Time? had not that been as proper?

Ros. By no means, sir. Time travels in divers paces with divers persons. I'll tell you, who Time ambles withal, who Time trots withal, who Time gallops withal, and who he stands still withal.

Orl. I pr'ythee, who doth he trot withal?

Ros. Marry, he trots hard with a young maid, between the contract of her marriage and the day it is solemnised; if the interim be but a se'nnight, Time's pace is so hard that it seems the length of seven years.

Orl. Who ambles Time withal?

Ros. With a priest that lacks Latin, and a rich man that hath not the gout; for the one sleeps easily, because he cannot study; and the other lives merrily because he feels no pain: the one lacking the burden of lean and wasteful learning; the other knowing no burden of heavy tedious penury. These Time ambles withal.

Orl. Who doth he gallop withal?

Ros. With a thief to the gallows; for though he go as softly as foot can fall, he thinks himself too soon there.

Orl. Who stays it still withal?

Ros. With lawyers in the vacation; for they sleep between term and term, and then they perceive not how Time moves.

Orl. Where dwell you, pretty youth?

Ros. With this shepherdess, my sister; here in the skirts of the forest, like fringe upon a petticoat.

Orl. Are you native of this place?

Ros. As the cony, that you see dwell where she is kindled.

Orl. Your accent is something finer than you could purchase in so removed a dwelling.

Ros. I have been told so of many: but, indeed, an old religious uncle of mine taught me to speak, who was in his youth an inland man; one that knew courtship too well, for there he fell in love. I have heard him read many lectures against it; and I thank God, I am not a woman, to be touched with so many giddy offences as he hath generally taxed their whole sex withal.

Orl. Can you remember any of the principal evils that he laid to the charge of women?

Ros. There were none principal: they were all like one another, as half-pence are; every one fault seeming monstrous till its fellow fault came to match it.

Orl. I pr'ythee, recount some of them.

Ros. No; I will not cast away my physic but on

those that are sick. There is a man haunts the forest, that abuses our young plants with carving Rosalind on their barks; hangs odes upon hawthorns, and elegies on brambles; all, forsooth, deifying the name of Rosalind: if I could meet that fancy-monger, I would give him some good counsel, for he seems to have the quotidian of love upon him.

Orl. I am he that is so love-shaked: I pray you, tell me your remedy.

Ros. There is none of my uncle's marks upon you: he taught me how to know a man in love; in which cage of rushes, I am sure, you are not prisoner.

Orl. What were his marks?

Ros. A lean cheek, which you have not; a blue eye, and sunken, which you have not; an unquestionable spirit, which you have not; a beard neglected, which you have not:—but I pardon you for that, for simply, your having in beard is a younger brother's revenue.— Then your hose should be ungartered, your bonnet un- banded, your sleeve unbuttoned, your shoe untied, and everything about you demonstrating a careless desolation. But you are no such man: you are rather point-device in your accoutrements, as loving yourself, than seeming the lover of any other.

Orl. Fair youth, I would I could make thee believe I love.

Ros. Me believe it? you may as soon make her that you love believe it; which, I warrant, she is apter to do than to confess she does; that is one of the points in the which women still give the lie to their consciences. But, in good sooth, are you he that hangs the verses on the trees, wherein Rosalind is so admired?

Orl. I swear to thee, youth, by the white hand of Rosalind, I am that he, that unfortunate he.

Ros. But are you so much in love as your rhymes speak?

Orl. Neither rhyme nor reason can express how much.

Ros. Love is merely a madness; and, I tell you, deserves as well a dark house and a whip as madmen do; and the reason why they are not so punished and cured is, that the lunacy is so ordinary that the whippers are in love too. Yet I profess curing it by counsel.

Orl. Did you ever cure any so?

Ros. Yes, one; and in this manner. He was to imagine me his love, his mistress, and I set him every day to woo me: at which time would I, being but a moonish youth, grieve, be effeminate, changeable, longing, and liking; proud, fantastical, apish, shallow, inconstant, full of tears, full of smiles; for every passion something, and for no passion truly anything, as boys and women are, for the most part, cattle of this colour: would now like him, now loathe him; then entertain him, then forswear him; now weep for him, then spit at him; that I drave my suitor from his mad humour of love, to a living humour of madness, which was, to forswear the full stream of the world and to live in a nook merely monastic. And thus I cured him; and in this way will I take upon me to wash your liver as clean as a sound sheep's heart, that there shall not be one spot of love in't.

Orl. I would not be cured, youth.

Ros. I would cure you, if you would but call me Rosalind, and come every day to my cote, and woo me.

Orl. Now, by the faith of my love, I will. Tell me where it is.

Ros. Go with me to it, and I'll show it you; and, by the way, you shall tell me where in the forest you live. Will you go?

Orl. With all my heart, good youth.

Ros. Nay, you must call me Rosalind.—Come, sister, will you go?   *[Exeunt*

SCENE III.—Another Part of the Forest

Enter TOUCHSTONE *and* AUDREY; JAQUES *behind*

Touch. Come apace, good Audrey: I will fetch up your goats, Audrey. And how, Audrey? am I the man yet? doth my simple feature content you?

Aud. Your features? Lord warrant us! what features?

Touch. I am here with thee and thy goats, as the most capricious poet, honest Ovid, was among the Goths.

Jaq. [*Aside*] O knowledge, ill-inhabited, worse than Jove in a thatched house!

Touch. When a man's verses cannot be understood, nor a man's good wit seconded with the forward child understanding, it strikes a man more dead than a great reckoning in a little room.—Truly, I would the gods had made thee poetical.

Aud. I do not know what poetical is. Is it honest in deed and word? Is it a true thing?

Touch. No, truly, for the truest poetry is the most feigning; and lovers are given to poetry, and what they swear in poetry, may be said, as lovers they do feign.

Aud. Do you wish, then, that the gods had made me poetical?

Touch. I do, truly; for thou swear'st to me thou art honest: now, if thou wert a poet, I might have some hope thou didst feign.

Aud. Would you not have me honest?

Touch. No, truly, unless thou wert hard-favoured, for honesty coupled to beauty, is to have honey a sauce to sugar.

Jaq. [*Aside*] A material fool.

Aud. Well, I am not fair; and therefore I pray the gods make me honest.

Touch. Truly, and to cast away honesty upon a foul slut were to put good meat into an unclean dish.

Aud. I am not a slut, though I thank the gods I am foul.

Touch. Well, praised be the gods for thy foulness: sluttishness may come hereafter. But be it as it may be, I will marry thee; and to that end, I have been with Sir Oliver Mar-text, the vicar of the next village, who hath promised to meet me in this place of the forest, and to couple us.

Jaq. [*Aside*] I would fain see this meeting.

Aud. Well, the gods give us joy!

Touch. Amen. A man may, if he were of a fearful heart, stagger in this attempt; for here we have no temple but the wood, no assembly but horn-beasts. But what though? Courage! As horns are odious, they are necessary. It is said, 'Many a man knows no end of his goods': right; many a man has good horns, and knows no end of them. Well, that is the dowry of his wife; 't is none of his own getting. Horns, even so. Poor men alone?—No, no; the noblest deer hath them as huge as the rascal. Is the single man therefore blessed? No: as a walled town is more worthier than a village, so is the forehead of a married man more honourable than the bare brow of a bachelor; and by how much defence is better than no skill, by so much is a horn more precious than to want. Here comes Sir Oliver.

Enter SIR OLIVER MAR-TEXT

Sir Oliver Mar-text, you are well met: will you despatch us here under this tree, or shall we go with you to your chapel?

Sir Oli. Is there none here to give the woman?

Touch. I will not take her on gift of any man.

Sir Oli. Truly, she must be given, or the marriage is not lawful.

Jaq. [*Coming forward*] Proceed, proceed: I'll give her.

Touch. Good even, good Master What-ye-call't: how do you, sir? You are very well met: God ild you for your last company: I am very glad to see you.—Even a toy in hand here, sir.—Nay; pray, be covered.

Jaq. Will you be married, motley?

Touch. As the ox hath his bow, sir, the horse his curb,

and the falcon her bells, so man hath his desires; and as
pigeons bill, so wedlock would be nibbling.

Jaq.   And will you, being a man of your breeding, be
married under a bush, like a beggar? Get you to church,
and have a good priest that can tell you what marriage is:
this fellow will but join you together as they join wainscot;
then one of you will prove a shrunk panel, and, like green
timber, warp, warp.

Touch.   [*Aside*] I am not in the mind but I were better
to be married of him than of another; for he is not like
to marry me well; and not being well married, it will be
a good excuse for me hereafter to leave my wife.

Jaq.   Go thou with me, and let me counsel thee.

Touch.   Come, sweet Audrey:
We must be married, or we must live in bawdry.
Farewell, good Master Oliver!—Not,

O sweet Oliver!
O brave Oliver!
Leave me not behind thee:

but,—

Wind away,
Begone, I say,
I will not to wedding with thee.

[*Exeunt Jaques, Touchstone, and Audrey*

Sir Oli.   'T is no matter: ne'er a fantastical knave of
them all shall flout me out of my calling.   [*Exit*

SCENE IV.—Another Part of the Forest
Before a Cottage

Enter ROSALIND *and* CELIA

Ros.   Never talk to me; I will weep.

Cel.   Do, I pr'ythee; but yet have the grace to consider
that tears do not become a man.

Ros.   But have I not cause to weep?

Cel.   As good cause as one would desire; therefore
weep.

Ros.   His hair is of the dissembling colour.

Cel.   Something browner than Judas's. Marry, his
kisses are Judas's own children.

Ros.   I'faith, his hair is of a good colour.

Cel.   An excellent colour: your chestnut was ever the
only colour.

Ros.   And his kissing is as full of sanctity as the touch
of holy bread.

Cel.   He hath bought a pair of cast lips of Diana: a
nun of winter's sisterhood kisses not more religiously; the
very ice of chastity is in them.

201

Ros. But why did he swear he would come this morning, and comes not?

Cel. Nay, certainly, there is no truth in him.

Ros. Do you think so?

Cel. Yes: I think he is not a pick-purse, nor a horse-stealer; but for his verity in love, I do think him as concave as a covered goblet or a worm-eaten nut.

Ros. Not true in love?

Cel. Yes, when he is in; but I think he is not in.

Ros. You have heard him swear downright he was.

Cel. *Was* is not *is*: besides, the oath of a lover is no stronger than the word of a tapster; they are both the confirmers of false reckonings. He attends here in the forest on the duke your father.

Ros. I met the duke yesterday, and had much question with him. He asked me, of what parentage I was: I told him, of as good as he; so he laughed and let me go. But what talk we of fathers, when there is such a man as Orlando?

Cel. O, that's a brave man! he writes brave verses, speaks brave words, swears brave oaths, and breaks them bravely, quite traverse, athwart the heart of his lover; as a puny tilter that spurs his horse but on one side breaks his staff like a noble goose. But all's brave that youth mounts and folly guides.—Who comes here?

Enter CORIN

Cor. Mistress and master, you have oft inquired
After the shepherd that complained of love,
Who you saw sitting by me on the turf
Praising the proud disdainful shepherdess
That was his mistress.

Cel.   Well, and what of him?

Cor. If you will see a pageant truly played
Between the pale complexion of true love
And the red glow of scorn and proud disdain,
Go hence a little, and I shall conduct you,
If you will mark it.

Ros.   O, come, let us remove:
The sight of lovers feedeth those in love.—
Bring us to see this sight, and you shall say
I'll prove a busy actor in their play.   [*Exeunt*

SCENE V.—Another Part of the Forest

Enter SILVIUS *and* PHEBE

Sil. Sweet Phebe, do not scorn me; do not, Phebe:
Say that you love me not; but say not so

In bitterness. The common executioner,
Whose heart the accustomed sight of death makes hard,
Falls not the axe upon the humbled neck
But first begs pardon: will you sterner be
Than he that dies and lives by bloody drops?

Enter ROSALIND, CELIA, *and* CORIN, *behind*

   Phe. I would not be thy executioner:
I fly thee, for I would not injure thee.
Thou tell'st me, there is murder in mine eye:
'T is pretty, sure, and very probable,
That eyes—that are the frail'st and softest things,
Who shut their coward gates on atomies,—
Should be called tyrants, butchers, murderers!
Now I do frown on thee with all my heart;
And if mine eyes can wound, now let them kill thee;
Now counterfeit to swoon, why, now fall down;
Or, if thou canst not, O, for shame, for shame,
Lie not, to say mine eyes are murderers.
Now show the wound mine eye hath made in thee;
Scratch thee but with a pin, and there remains
Some scar of it; lean but upon a rush,
The cicatrice and capable impressure
Thy palm some moment keeps, but now mine eyes
Which I have darted at thee, hurt thee not,
Nor, I am sure, there is no force in eyes
That can do hurt.
   Sil.   O dear Phebe,
If ever (as that ever may be near)
You meet in some fresh cheek the power of fancy,
Then shall you know the wounds invisible
That love's keen arrows make.
   Phe.   But till that time
Come not thou near me: and when that time comes,
Afflict me with thy mocks, pity me not,
As till that time I shall not pity thee.
   Ros. [*Coming forward*] And why, I pray you?
          Who might be your mother,
That you insult, exult, and all at once,
Over the wretched? What though you have no beauty
(As, by my faith, I see no more in you
Than without candle may go dark to bed)
Must you be therefore proud and pitiless?
Why, what means this? Why do you look on me?
I see no more in you, than in the ordinary
Of nature's sale-work—Od's my little life!
I think she means to tangle my eyes too.
No, 'faith, proud mistress, hope not after it:
'T is not your inky brows, your black silk hair,

Your bugle eye-balls, nor your cheek of cream,
That can entame my spirits to your worship.—
You foolish shepherd, wherefore do you follow her,
Like foggy south, puffing with wind and rain?
You are a thousand times a properer man,
Than she a woman: 't is such fools as you
That make the world full of ill-favoured children.
'T is not her glass, but you, that flatters her;
And out of you she sees herself more proper
Than any of her lineaments can show her.
But, mistress, know yourself: down on your knees,
And thank Heaven, fasting, for a good man's love;
For I must tell you friendly in your ear,—
Sell when you can: you are not for all markets.
Cry the man mercy; love him; take his offer:
Foul is most foul, being foul to be a scoffer.—
So, take her to thee, shepherd.—Fare you well.
    Phe. Sweet youth, I pray you, chide a year together.
I had rather hear you chide than this man woo.
    Ros. He's fallen in love with your foulness, and she'll
fall in love with my anger. If it be so, as fast as she
answers thee with frowning looks, I'll sauce her with bitter
words.—Why look you so upon me?
    Phe. For no ill will I bear you.
    Ros. I pray you, do not fall in love with me,
For I am falser than vows made in wine:
Besides, I like you not.—If you will know my house,
'T is at the tuft of olives, here hard by.—
Will you go, sister?—Shepherd, ply her hard.—
Come, sister.—Shepherdess, look on him better,
And be not proud: though all the world could see,
None could be so abused in sight as he.
Come, to our flock.   [*Exeunt Rosalind, Celia, and Corin*
    Phe. Dead shepherd, now I find thy saw of might.
'Who ever loved, that loved not at first sight?'
    Sil. Sweet Phebe,—
    Phe.   Ha, what say'st thou, Silvius?
    Sil. Sweet Phebe, pity me.
    Phe. Why, I am sorry for thee, gentle Silvius.
    Sil. Wherever sorrow is, relief would be:
If you do sorrow at my grief in love,
By giving love, your sorrow and my grief
Were both extermined.
    Phe. Thou hast my love: is not that neighbourly?
    Sil. I would have you.
    Phe.   Why, that were covetousness.
Silvius, the time was that I hated thee,
And yet it is not that I bear thee love;
But since that thou canst talk of love so well,
Thy company, which erst was irksome to me,

I will endure, and I'll employ thee too;
But do not look for further recompense
Than thine own gladness that thou art employed.
   Sil. So holy, and so perfect is my love,
And I in such a poverty of grace,
That I shall think it a most plenteous crop
To glean the broken ears after the man
That the main harvest rcaps: loose now and then
A scattered smile, and that I'll live upon.
   Phe. Know'st thou the youth that spoke to me ere-
      while?
   Sil. Not very well; but I have met him oft;
And he hath bought the cottage and the bounds
That the old Carlot once was master of.
   Phe. Think not I love him, though I ask for him.
'T is but a peevish boy:—yet he talks well:—
But what care I for words? yet words do well,
When he that speaks them pleases those that hear.
It is a pretty youth:—not very pretty:—
But, sure, he's proud; and yet his pride becomes him.
He'll make a proper man: the best thing in him
Is his complexion: and faster than his tongue
Did make offence, his eye did heal it up.
He is not very tall; yet for his years he's tall.
His leg is but so so; and yet 't is well.
There was a pretty redness in his lip;
A little riper, and more lusty red
Than that mixed in his cheek: 't was just the difference
Betwixt the constant red and mingled damask.
There be some women, Silvius, had they marked him
In parcels, as I did, would have gone near
To fall in love with him; but, for my part,
I love him not, nor hate him not; and yet
I have more cause to hate him than to love him:
For what had he to do to chide at me?
He said, mine eyes were black, and my hair black;
And, now I am remembered, scorned at me.
I marvel why I answered not again:
But that's all one; omittance is no quittance.
I'll write to him a very taunting letter,
And thou shalt bear it; wilt thou, Silvius?
   Sil. Phebe, with all my heart.
   Phe.   I'll write it straight;
The matter's in my head, and in my heart:
I will be bitter with him and passing short.
Go with me, Silvius.   *[Exeunt*

ACT FOUR

SCENE I.—The Forest of Arden

Enter ROSALIND, CELIA, *and* JAQUES

Jaq. I pr'ythee, pretty youth, let me be better acquainted with thee.

Ros. They say you are a melancholy fellow.

Jaq. I am so: I do love it better than laughing.

Ros. Those that are in extremity of either are abominable fellows, and betray themselves to every modern censure worse than drunkards.

Jaq. Why, 't is good to be sad and say nothing.

Ros. Why, then, 't is good to be a post.

Jaq. I have neither the scholar's melancholy, which is emulation; nor the musician's, which is fantastical; nor the courtier's, which is proud; nor the soldier's, which is ambitious; nor the lawyer's, which is politic; nor the lady's, which is nice; nor the lover's, which is all these; but it is a melancholy of mine own, compounded of many simples, extracted from many objects, and, indeed, the sundry contemplation of my travels; which, by often rumination, wraps me in a most humorous sadness.

Ros. A traveller! By my faith, you have great reason to be sad. I fear, you have sold your own lands, to see other men's; then, to have seen much, and to have nothing, is to have rich eyes and poor hands.

Jaq. Yes, I have gained my experience.

Ros. And your experience makes you sad. I had rather have a fool to make me merry, than experience to make me sad; and to travel for it, too!

Enter ORLANDO

Orl. Good day, and happiness, dear Rosalind.

Jaq. Nay then, God be wi' you, an you talk in blank verse.

Ros. Farewell, Monsieur Traveller. Look you lisp, and wear strange suits; disable all the benefits of your own country; be out of love with your nativity; and almost chide God for making you that countenance you are: or I will scarce think you have swam in a gondola. [*Exit Jaques*] Why, how now, Orlando! where have you been all this while? You a lover?—An you serve me such another trick, never come in my sight more.

Orl. My fair Rosalind, I come within an hour of my promise.

Ros. Break an hour's promise in love! He that will

divide a minute into a thousand parts, and break but a
part of the thousandth part of a minute in the affairs of
love, it may be said of him that Cupid hath clapped him o'
the shoulder, but I'll warrant him heart-whole.

Orl. Pardon me, dear Rosalind.

Ros. Nay, an you be so tardy, come no more in my
sight: I had as lief be woo'd of a snail.

Orl. Of a snail?

Ros. Ay, of a snail; for though he comes slowly, he
carries his house on his head; a better jointure, I think,
than you make a woman. Besides, he brings his destiny
with him.

Orl. What's that?

Ros. Why, horns; which such as you are fain to be
beholding to your wives for: but he comes armed in his
fortune, and prevents the slander of his wife.

Orl. Virtue is no horn-maker, and my Rosalind is
virtuous.

Ros. And I am your Rosalind.

Cel. It pleases him to call you so; but he hath a Rosalind
of a better leer than you.

Ros. Come, woo me, woo me; for now I am in a holiday
humour, and like enough to consent.—What would you say
to me now, an I were your very very Rosalind?

Orl. I would kiss before I spoke.

Ros. Nay, you were better speak first; and when you
were gravelled for lack of matter, you might take occasion
to kiss. Very good orators, when they are out, they will
spit; and for lovers, lacking (God warn us) matter, the
cleanliest shift is to kiss.

Orl. How if the kiss be denied?

Ros. Then she puts you to entreaty, and there begins
new matter.

Orl. Who could be out, being before his beloved
mistress?

Ros. Marry, that should you, if I were your mistress,
or I should think my honesty ranker than my wit.

Orl. What, of my suit?

Ros. Not out of your apparel, and yet out of your suit.
Am not I your Rosalind?

Orl. I take some joy to say you are, because I would
be talking of her.

Ros. Well, in her person, I say—I will not have you.

Orl. Then, in mine own person, I die.

Ros. No, 'faith, die by attorney. The poor world is
almost six thousand years old, and in all this time there
was not any man died in his own person, *videlicet*, in a love-
cause. Troilus had his brains dashed out with a Grecian
club; yet he did what he could to die before, and he is one
of the patterns of love. Leander, he would have lived

many a fair year though Hero had turned nun, if it had
not been for a hot mid-summer-night; for, good youth,
he went but forth to wash him in the Hellespont, and,
being taken with the cramp, was drowned, and the foolish
chroniclers of that age found it was—Hero of Sestos But
these are all lies: men have died from time to time, and
worms have eaten them, but not for love.

Orl. I would not have my right Rosalind of this mind,
for, I protest, her frown might kill me.

Ros. By this hand, it will not kill a fly. But come, now
I will be your Rosalind in a more coming-on disposition;
and ask me what you will, I will grant it.

Orl. Then love me, Rosalind.

Ros. Yes, 'faith will I; Fridays, and Saturdays, and all.

Orl. And wilt thou have me?

Ros. Ay, and twenty such.

Orl. What say'st thou?

Ros. Are you not good?

Orl. I hope so.

Ros. Why then, can one desire too much of a good
thing?—Come, sister, you shall be the priest, and marry
us.—Give me your hand, Orlando.—What do you say,
sister?

Orl. Pray thee, marry us.

Cel. I cannot say the words.

Ros. You must begin,—'Will you, Orlando,'—

Cel. Go to.—Will you, Orlando, have to wife this
Rosalind?

Orl. I will.

Ros. Ay, but when?

Orl. Why now, as fast as she can marry us.

Ros. Then you must say,—'I take thee, Rosalind, for
wife.'

Orl. I take thee, Rosalind, for wife.

Ros. I might ask you for your commission; but,—I
do take thee, Orlando, for my husband:—there's a girl
goes before the priest; and certainly, a woman's thought
runs before her actions.

Orl. So do all thoughts: they are winged.

Ros. Now tell me how long you would have her, after
you have possessed her.

Orl. For ever, and a day.

Ros. Say a day, without the ever. No, no, Orlando:
men are April when they woo, December when they wed;
maids are May when they are maids, but the sky changes
when they are wives. I will be more jealous of thee than a
Barbary cock-pigeon over his hen; more clamorous than a
parrot against rain; more new-fangled than an ape; more
giddy in my desires than a monkey: I will weep for nothing,
like Diana in the fountain, and I will do that when you are

disposed to be merry; I will laugh like a hyen, and that
when thou art inclined to sleep.

Orl. But will my Rosalind do so?

Ros. By my life, she will do as I do.

Orl. O, but she is wise.

Ros. Or else she could not have the wit to do this:
the wiser, the waywarder. Make the doors upon a woman's
wit, and it will out at the casement; shut that, and 't
will out at the key-hole; stop that, and 't will fly with the
smoke out of the chimney.

Orl. A man that had a wife with such a wit, he might
say,—'Wit, whither wilt?'

Ros. Nay, you might keep that check for it, till you
met your wife's wit going to your neighbour's bed.

Orl. And what wit would wit have to excuse that?

Ros. Marry, to say,—she came to seek you there. You
shall never take her without her answer, unless you take
her without her tongue: O, that woman that cannot make
her fault her husband's occasion, let her never nurse her
child herself, for she will breed it like a fool.

Orl. For these two hours, Rosalind, I will leave thee.

Ros. Alas, dear love, I cannot lack thee two hours.

Orl. I must attend the duke at dinner: by two o'clock
I will be with thee again.

Ros. Ay, go your ways, go your ways.—I knew what
you would prove; my friends told me as much, and I
thought no less:—that flattering tongue of yours won me:
't is but one cast away, and so,—come, death!—Two
o'clock is your hour?

Orl. Ay, sweet Rosalind.

Ros. By my troth, and in good earnest, and so God
mend me, and by all pretty oaths that are not dangerous,
if you break one jot of your promise, or come one minute
behind your hour, I will think you the most pathetical
break-promise, and the most hollow lover, and the most
unworthy of her you call Rosalind, that may be chosen
out of the gross band of the unfaithful. Therefore, beware
my censure, and keep your promise

Orl. With no less religion, than if thou wert indeed
my Rosalind: so, adieu.

Ros. Well, Time is the old justice that examines all
such offenders, and let Time try. Adieu. [*Exit Orlando*

Cel. You have simply misused our sex in your love-
prate. We must have your doublet and hose plucked over
your head, and show the world what the bird hath done
to her own nest.

Ros. O, coz, coz, coz, my pretty little coz, that thou
didst know how many fathom deep I am in love! But
I cannot be sounded: my affection hath an unknown
bottom, like the bay of Portugal.

Cel. Or, rather, bottomless; that as fast as you pour your affection in, it runs out.

Ros. No; that same wicked bastard of Venus, that was begot of thought, conceived of spleen, and born of madness, that blind rascally boy that abuses every one's eyes because his own are out, let him be judge how deep I am in love.—I'll tell thee, Aliena, I cannot be out of the sight of Orlando. I'll go find a shadow, and sigh till he come.

Cel. And I'll sleep.   [*Exeunt*

SCENE II.—Another Part of the Forest

Enter JAQUES *and Lords, like foresters*

Jaq. Which is he that killed the deer?

First Lord. Sir, it was I.

Jaq. Let's present him to the duke, like a Roman conqueror; and it would do well to set the deer's horns upon his head for a branch of victory. Have you no song, forester, for this purpose?

Sec. Lord. Yes, sir.

Jaq. Sing it: 't is no matter how it be in tune, so it make noise enough.

SONG

What shall he have, that killed the deer :
His leather skin and horns to wear.
   Then sing him home.
           [*The rest shall bear this burden :*]
Take thou no scorn to wear the horn.
It was a crest ere thou wast born.
   Thy father's father wore it,
    And thy father bore it :
The horn, the horn, the lusty horn,
Is not a thing to laugh to scorn.   [*Exeunt*

SCENE III.—Another Part of the Forest

Enter ROSALIND *and* CELIA

Ros. How say you now? Is it not past two o'clock? and here much Orlando!

Cel. I warrant you, with pure love and troubled brain, he hath ta'en his bow and arrows, and is gone forth—to sleep. Look, who comes here?

Enter SILVIUS

Sil. My errand is to you, fair youth.—

My gentle Phebe bid me give you this: [*Giving a letter*
I know not the contents; but, as I guess
By the stern brow and waspish action
Which she did use as she was writing of it,
It bears an angry tenor.   Pardon me,
I am but as a guiltless messenger.
   Ros. Patience herself would startle at this letter,
And play the swaggerer: bear this, bear all.
She says, I am not fair; that I lack manners:
She calls me proud, and that she could not love me,
Were man as rare as phœnix.   Od's my will!
Her love is not the hare that I do hunt:
Why writes she so to me?—Well, shepherd, well;
This is a letter of your own device.
   Sil. No, I protest; I know not the contents:
Phebe did write it.
   Ros.   Come, come, you are a fool,
And turned into the extremity of love.
I saw her hand; she has a leathern hand,
A freestone-coloured hand; I verily did think
That her old gloves were on, but't was her hands;
She has a housewife's hand; but that's no matter.
I say, she never did invent this letter;
This is a man's invention, and his hand.
   Sil. Sure, it is hers.
   Ros. Why, 't is a boisterous and a cruel style,
A style for challengers: why, she defies me,
Like Turk to Christian.   Woman's gentle brain
Could not drop forth such giant-rude invention,
Such Ethiop words, blacker in their effect
Than in their countenance.—Will you hear the letter?
   Sil. So please you; for I never heard it yet,
Yet heard too much of Phebe's cruelty.
   Ros. She Phebes me.   Mark how the tyrant writes.
     'Art thou god to shepherd turned,
      That a maiden's heart hath burned?'—
Can a woman rail thus?
   Sil. Call you this railing?
   Ros.   'Why, thy godhead laid apart,
      Warr'st thou with a woman's heart?'
Did you ever hear such railing?—
     'Whiles the eye of man did woo me,
      That could do no vengeance to me.'
Meaning me a beast.—
      'If the scorn of your bright eyne
      Have power to raise such love in mine,
      Alack, in me what strange effect
      Would they work in mild aspect?
      Whiles you chid me, I did love;
      How then might your prayers move?

He that brings this love to thee
Little knows this love in me:
And by him seal up thy mind,
Whether that thy youth and kind
Will the faithful offer take
Of me, and all that I can make;
Or else by him my love deny,
And then I'll study how to die.'

Sil. Call you this chiding?

Cel. Alas, poor shepherd!

Ros. Do you pity him? no; he deserves no pity.
Wilt thou love such a woman?—What, to make thee an
instrument, and play false strains upon thee? not to be
endured! Well, go your way to her, (for, I see, love hath
made thee a tame snake,) and say this to her:—that if she
love me, I charge her to love thee; if she will not, I will
never have her, unless thou entreat for her.—If you be a
true lover, hence, and not a word, for here comes more
company.   [*Exit Silvius*

Enter OLIVER

Oli. Good morrow, fair ones. Pray you, if you know,
Where in the purlieus of this forest stands
A sheepcote fenced about with olive-trees?

Cel. West of this place, down in the neighbour bottom:
The rank of osiers by the murmuring stream,
Left on your right hand, brings you to the place.
But at this hour the house doth keep itself;
There's none within.

Oli. If that an eye may profit by a tongue,
Then should I know you by description;
Such garments, and such years:—'The boy is fair,
Of female favour, and bestows himself
Like a ripe sister: but the woman low,
And browner than her brother.' Are not you
The owners of the house I did inquire for?

Cel. It is no boast, being asked, to say, we are.

Oli. Orlando doth commend him to you both;
And to that youth he calls his Rosalind,
He sends this bloody napkin. Are you he?

Ros. I am. What must we understand by this?

Oli. Some of my shame; if you will know of me
What man I am, and how, and why, and where
This handkercher was stained.

Cel.   I pray you, tell it.

Oli. When last the young Orlando parted from you,
He left a promise to return again
Within an hour; and, pacing through the forest,
Chewing the food of sweet and bitter fancy,
Lo, what befell! he threw his eye aside,

212

And, mark, what object did present itself:
Under an oak, whose boughs were mossed with age,
And high top bald with dry antiquity,
A wretched, ragged man, o'ergrown with hair,
Lay sleeping on his back: about his neck
A green and gilded snake had wreathed itself,
Who with her head, nimble in threats, approached
The opening of his mouth; but suddenly,
Seeing Orlando, it unlinked itself,
And with indented glides did slip away
Into a bush; under which bush's shade
A lioness, with udders all drawn dry,
Lay couching, head on ground, with catlike watch,
When that the sleeping man should stir; for 't is
The royal disposition of that beast
To prey on nothing that doth seem as dead.
This seen, Orlando did approach the man,
And found it was his brother, his elder brother.
    Cel. O, I have heard him speak of that same brother;
And he did render him the most unnatural
That lived 'mongst men.
    Oli.   And well he might so do,
For well I know he was unnatural.
    Ros. But, to Orlando.—Did he leave him there,
Food to the sucked and hungry lioness?
    Oli. Twice did he turn his back, and purposed so;
But kindness, nobler ever than revenge,
And nature, stronger than his just occasion,
Made him give battle to the lioness,
Who quickly fell before him: in which hurtling
From miserable slumber I awaked.
    Cel. Are you his brother?
    Ros.   Was it you he reached?
    Cel. Was 't you that did so oft contrive to kill him?
    Oli. 'T was I; but 't is not I. I do not shame
To tell you what I was, since my conversion
So sweetly tastes, being the thing I am.
    Ros. But, for the bloody napkin?
    Oli.   By-and-by.
When from the first to last, betwixt us two,
Tears our recountments had most kindly bathed,
As, how I came into that desert place:—
In brief, he led me to the gentle duke,
Who gave me fresh array, and entertainment,
Committing me unto my brother's love;
Who led me instantly unto his cave,
There stripped himself; and here, upon his arm,
The lioness had torn some flesh away,
Which all this while has bled; and now he fainted,
And cried, in fainting, upon Rosalind.

Brief, I recovered him, bound up his wound;
And, after some small space, being strong at heart,
He sent me hither, stranger as I am,
To tell this story, that you might excuse
His broken promise; and to give this napkin,
Dyed in his blood, unto the shepherd youth
That he in sport doth call his Rosalind.

[Rosalind swoons

Cel. Why, how now, Ganymede? sweet Ganymede!
Oli. Many will swoon when they do look on blood.
Cel. There is more in it.—Cousin!—Ganymede!
Oli. Look, he recovers.
Ros. I would I were at home.
Cel.   We'll lead you thither.—
I pray you, will you take him by the arm?
Oli. Be of good cheer, youth.—You a man? You lack
a man's heart.
Ros. I do so, I confess it. Ah, sirrah, a body would
think this was well counterfeited. I pray you, tell your
brother how well I counterfeited.—Heigh-ho!—
Oli. This was not counterfeit: there is too great
testimony in your complexion, that it was a passion of
earnest.
Ros. Counterfeit, I assure you.
Oli. Well then, take a good heart, and counterfeit to
be a man.
Ros. So I do; but, i' faith, I should have been a woman
by right.
Cel. Come; you look paler and paler: pray you, draw
homewards.—Good sir, go with us.
Oli. That will I, for I must bear answer back,
How you excuse my brother, Rosalind.
Ros. I shall devise something. But, I pray you, com-
mend my counterfeiting to him.—Will you go? *[Exeunt*

ACT FIVE

SCENE I.—The Forest of Arden

Enter TOUCHSTONE *and* AUDREY

Touch. We shall find a time, Audrey: patience, gentle
Audrey.
Aud. 'Faith, the priest was good enough, for all the old
gentleman's saying.
Touch. A most wicked Sir Oliver, Audrey; a most vile
Mar-text. But, Audrey, there is a youth here in the forest
ways claim to you.

214

Aud. Ay, I know who't is: he hath no interest in me in the world. Here comes the man you mean.

Enter WILLIAM

Touch. It is meat and drink to me to see a clown. By my troth, we that have good wits have much to answer for: we shall be flouting; we cannot hold.

Will. Good even, Audrey.

Aud. God ye good even, William.

Will. And good even to you, sir.

Touch. Good even, gentle friend. Cover thy head, cover thy head, nay, pr'ythee, be covered. How old are you, friend?

Will. Five-and-twenty, sir.

Touch. A ripe age. Is thy name William?

Will. William, sir.

Touch. A fair name. Wast born i' the forest here?

Will. Ay, sir, I thank God.

Touch. Thank God;—a good answer. Art rich?

Will. 'Faith, sir, so, so.

Touch. So, so, is good, very good, very excellent good: and yet it is not; it is but so, so. Art thou wise?

Will. Ay, sir, I have a pretty wit.

Touch. Why, thou say'st well. I do now remember a saying, 'The fool doth think he is wise, but the wise man knows himself to be a fool.' The heathen philosopher, when he had a desire to eat a grape, would open his lips when he put it into his mouth, meaning thereby, that grapes were made to eat, and lips to open. You do love this maid?

Will. I do, sir.

Touch. Give me your hand. Art thou learned?

Will. No, sir.

Touch. Then learn this of me. To have, is to have; for it is a figure in rhetoric, that drink, being poured out of a cup into a glass, by filling the one doth empty the other; for all your writers do consent, that *ipse* is he: now, you are not *ipse*, for I am he.

Will. Which he, sir?

Touch. He, sir, that must marry this woman. Therefore, you clown, abandon—which is in the vulgar, leave—the society—which in the boorish is, company,—of this female, which in the common is, woman; which together is, abandon the society of this female, or, clown, thou perishest; or, to thy better understanding, diest; or, to wit, I kill thee, make thee away, translate thy life into death, thy liberty into bondage. I will deal in poison with thee, or in bastinado, or in steel: I will bandy with thee in faction; I will o'errun thee with policy; I will kill thee a hundred and fifty ways: therefore tremble, and depart.

Aud. Do, good William.
Will. God rest you merry, sir.   [*Exit*

Enter CORIN

Cor. Our master and mistress seek you: come, away,
away!
Touch. Trip, Audrey, trip, Audrey.—I attend, I attend.
                                                    [*Exeunt*

SCENE II.—Another Part of the Forest

Enter ORLANDO *and* OLIVER

Orl. Is't possible, that on so little acquaintance you
should like her? that, but seeing, you should love her?
and, loving, woo? and, wooing, she should grant? and
will you persevere to enjoy her?
Oli. Neither call the giddiness of it in question, the
poverty of her, the small acquaintance, my sudden wooing,
nor her sudden consenting; but say with me, I love Aliena;
say with her, that she loves me; consent with both, that
we may enjoy each other: it shall be to your good; for
my father's house, and all the revenue that was old Sir
Rowland's, will I estate upon you, and here live and die
a shepherd.
Orl. You have my consent. Let your wedding be to-
morrow: thither will I invite the duke, and all his contented
followers. Go you, and prepare Aliena; for, look you,
here comes my Rosalind.

Enter ROSALIND

Ros. God save you, brother.
Oli. And you, fair sister.   [*Exit*
Ros. O, my dear Orlando, how it grieves me to see thee
wear thy heart in a scarf.
Orl. It is my arm.
Ros. I thought thy heart had been wounded with the
claws of a lion.
Orl. Wounded it is, but with the eyes of a lady.
Ros. Did your brother tell you how I counterfeited to
swoon, when he showed me your handkercher?
Orl. Ay, and greater wonders than that.
Ros. O, I know where you are.—Nay, 't is true: there
was never anything so sudden, but the fight of two rams,
and Cæsar's thrasonical brag of—'I came, saw, and over-
came:' for your brother and my sister no sooner met but
they looked; no sooner looked, but they loved; no sooner
loved, but they sighed; no sooner sighed, but they asked

one another the reason; no sooner knew the reason, but
they sought the remedy: and in these degrees have they
made a pair of stairs to marriage, which they will climb
incontinent, or else be incontinent before marriage. They
are in the very wrath of love, and they will together:
clubs cannot part them.

Orl. They shall be married to-morrow, and I will bid
the duke to the nuptial. But, O, how bitter a thing it is
to look into happiness through another man's eyes! By
so much the more shall I to-morrow be at the height of
heart-heaviness, by how much I shall think my brother
happy in having what he wishes for.

Ros. Why then, to-morrow I cannot serve your turn for
Rosalind?

Orl. I can live no longer by thinking.

Ros. I will weary you then no longer with idle talking.
Know of me then (for now I speak to some purpose), that
I know you are a gentleman of good conceit. I speak not
this, that you should bear a good opinion of my knowledge,
insomuch I say, I know you are; neither do I labour for a
greater esteem than may in some little measure draw a
belief from you, to do yourself good, and not to grace me.
Believe then, if you please, that I can do strange things.
I have, since I was three years old, conversed with a
magician, most profound in his art, and yet not damnable.
If you do love Rosalind so near the heart as your gesture
cries it out, when your brother marries Aliena, shall you
marry her. I know into what straits of fortune she is
driven; and it is not impossible to me, if it appears not
inconvenient to you, to set her before your eyes to-morrow,
human as she is, and without any danger.

Orl. Speak'st thou in sober meaning?

Ros. By my life, I do; which I tender dearly, though
I say I am a magician. Therefore, put you in your best
array, bid your friends, for if you will be married to-
morrow, you shall; and to Rosalind, if you will. Look,
here comes a lover of mine, and a lover of hers.

Enter Silvius *and* Phebe

Phe. Youth, you have done me much ungentleness,
To show the letter that I writ to you.

Ros. I care not, if I have: it is my study
To seem despiteful and ungentle to you.
You are there followed by a faithful shepherd:
Look upon him, love him; he worships you.

Phe. Good shepherd, tell this youth what 't is to love.

Sil. It is to be all made of sighs and tears;—
And so am I for Phebe.

Phe. And I for Ganymede.

217

Orl. And I for Rosalind.
Ros. And I for no woman.
Sil. It is to be all made of faith and service;—
And so am I for Phebe.
Phe. And I for Ganymede.
Orl. And I for Rosalind.
Ros. And I for no woman.
Sil. It is to be all made of fantasy,
All made of passion, and all made of wishes;
All adoration, duty, and observance;
All humbleness, all patience, and impatience;
All purity, all trial, all observance;—
And so am I for Phebe.
Phe. And so am I for Ganymede.
Orl. And so am I for Rosalind.
Ros. And so am I for no woman.
Phe. [*To Rosalind*] If this be so, why blame you me
     to love you?
Sil. [*To Phebe*] If this be so, why blame you me to
     love you?
Orl. If this be so, why blame you me to love you?
Ros. Who do you speak to, 'Why blame you me to
love you?'
Orl. To her, that is not here, nor doth not hear.
Ros. Pray you, no more of this: 't is like the howling
of Irish wolves against the moon.—[*To Silvius*] I will
help you, if I can:—[*To Phebe*] I would love you, if I
could.—To-morrow meet me all together.—[*To Phebe*]
I will marry you, if ever I marry woman, and I'll be
married to-morrow:—[*To Orlando*] I will satisfy you, if
ever I satisfied man, and you shall be married to-morrow:—
[*To Silvius*] I will content you, if what pleases you con-
tents you, and you shall be married to-morrow.—[*To
Orlando*] As you love Rosalind, meet:—[*To Silvius*]
As you love Phebe, meet: and as I love no woman, I'll
meet.—So, fare you well: I have left you commands.
Sil. I'll not fail, if I live.
Phe. Nor I.
Orl. Nor I.
                                                    [*Exeunt*

SCENE III.—Another Part of the Forest

Enter TOUCHSTONE *and* AUDREY

Touch. To-morrow is the joyful day, Audrey: to-
morrow will we be married.
Aud. I do desire it with all my heart, and I hope it is
no dishonest desire, to desire to be a woman of the world.
Here come two of the banished duke's pages.

Enter Two Pages

First Page. Well met, honest gentleman.
Touch. By my troth, well met. Come, sit, sit, and a song.
Sec. Page. We are for you : sit i' the middle.
First Page. Shall we clap into't roundly, without hawking, or spitting, or saying we are hoarse, which are the only prologues to a bad voice?
Sec. Page. I' faith, i' faith; and both in a tune, like two gipsies on a horse.

SONG

It was a lover and his lass,
With a hey, and a ho, and a hey nonino,
That o'er the green corn-field did pass,
In the spring time, the only pretty ring time,
When birds do sing, hey ding a ding, ding;
Sweet lovers love the spring.

Between the acres of the rye,
With a hey, and a ho, and a hey nonino,
These pretty country folks would lie,
In the spring time, etc.

This carol they began that hour,
With a hey, and a ho, and a hey nonino,
How that a life was but a flower
In the spring time, etc.

And therefore take the present time,
With a hey, and a ho, and a hey nonino
For love is crownèd with the prime
In the spring time, etc.

Touch. Truly, young gentlemen, though there was no great matter in the ditty, yet the note was very untuneable.
First Page. You are deceived, sir: we kept time; we lost not our time.
Touch. By my troth, yes; I count it but time lost to hear such a foolish song. God be wi' you; and God mend your voices. Come, Audrey.   [*Exeunt*

SCENE IV.—Another Part of the Forest

Enter DUKE *Senior,* AMIENS, JAQUES, ORLANDO, OLIVER, *and* CELIA

Duke S. Dost thou believe, Orlando, that the boy
Can do all this that he hath promiséd?

Orl. I sometimes do believe, and sometimes do not;
As those that fear they hope, and know they fear.

Enter ROSALIND, SILVIUS, *and* PHEBE

Ros. Patience once more, whiles our compact is urged.—
[*To the Duke*] You say, if I bring in your Rosalind,
You will bestow her on Orlando here?
> *Duke S.* That would I, had I kingdoms to give with her.
> *Ros.* [*To Orlando*] And you say, you will have her,
> when I bring her?
> *Orl.* That would I, were I of all kingdoms king.
> *Ros.* [*To Phebe*] You say, you'll marry me, if I be
> willing?
> *Phe.* That will I, should I die the hour after.
> *Ros.* But if you do refuse to marry me,
You'll give yourself to this most faithful shepherd?
> *Phe.* So is the bargain.
> *Ros.* [*To Silvius*] You say that you'll have Phebe,
> if she will?
> *Sil.* Though to have her and death were both one thing.
> *Ros.* I have promised to make all this matter even.
Keep you your word, O duke, to give your daughter;—
You yours, Orlando, to receive his daughter;—
Keep you your word, Phebe, that you'll marry me,
Or else, refusing me, to wed this shepherd;—
Keep your word, Silvius, that you'll marry her,
If she refuse me:—and from hence I go,
To make these doubts all even.

[Exeunt Rosalind and Celia
Duke S. I do remember in this shepherd boy
Some lively touches of my daughter's favour.
Orl. My lord, the first time that I ever saw him,
Methought he was a brother to your daughter;
But, my good lord, this boy is forest-born,
And hath been tutored in the rudiments
Of many desperate studies by his uncle,
Whom he reports to be a great magician,
Obscuréd in the circle of this forest.
Jaq. There is, sure, another flood toward, and these
couples are coming to the ark. Here comes a pair of very
strange beasts, which in all tongues are called fools.

Enter TOUCHSTONE *and* AUDREY

Touch. Salutation and greeting to you all.
Jaq. Good my lord, bid him welcome. This is the
motley-minded gentleman, that I have so often met in the
forest: he hath been a courtier, he swears.
Touch. If any man doubt that, let him put me to my
purgation. I have trod a measure; I have flattered a

lady; I have been politic with my friend, smooth with mine enemy; I have undone three tailors; I have had four quarrels, and like to have fought one.

Jaq. And how was that ta'en up?

Touch. 'Faith, we met, and found the quarrel was upon the seventh cause.

Jaq. How seventh cause? Good my lord, like this fellow.

Duke S. I like him very well.

Touch. God ild you, sir; I desire you of the like. I press in here, sir, amongst the rest of the country copulatives, to swear, and to forswear, according as marriage binds, and blood breaks.—A poor virgin, sir, an ill-favoured thing, sir, but mine own: a poor humour of mine, sir, to take that no man else will. Rich honesty dwells like a miser, sir, in a poor house, as your pearl in your foul oyster.

Duke S. By my faith, he is very swift and sententious.

Touch. According to the fool's bolt, sir, and such dulcet diseases.

Jaq. But, for the seventh cause, how did you find the quarrel on the seventh cause?

Touch. Upon a lie seven times removed.—Bear your body more seeming, Audrey.—As thus, Sir. I did dislike the cut of a certain courtier's beard: he sent me word, if I said his beard was not cut well, he was in the mind it was: this is called the 'Retort Courteous.' If I sent him word again It was not well cut, he would send me word he cut it to please himself: this is called the 'Quip Modest.' If again It was not well cut, he disabled my judgment: this is called the 'Reply Churlish.' If again It was not well cut, he would answer, I spake not true: this is called the 'Reproof Valiant.' If again It was not well cut, he would say, I lie: this is called the 'Countercheck Quarrelsome:' and so to the 'Lie Circumstantial,' and the 'Lie Direct.'

Jaq. And how oft did you say, his beard was not well cut?

Touch. I durst go no further than the 'Lie Circumstantial,' nor he durst not give me the 'Lie Direct;' and so we measured swords, and parted.

Jaq. Can you nominate in order now the degrees of the lie?

Touch. O sir, we quarrel in print, by the book; as you have books for good manners: I will name you the degrees. The first, the retort courteous; the second, the quip modest; the third, the reply churlish; the fourth, the reproof valiant; the fifth, the countercheck quarrelsome; the sixth, the lie with circumstance; the seventh, the lie direct. All these you may avoid, but the lie direct. and you may avoid that too, with an *if*. I knew when seven justices could not take up a quarrel; but when the parties were met themselves, one of them thought but of an *if*, as *if you said so, then I said so;* and they shook hands and swore brothers. Your *if* is the only peace-maker: much virtue in *if*.

Jaq. Is not this a rare fellow, my lord? he's as good at anything, and yet a fool.

Duke S. He uses his folly like a stalking-horse, and under the presentation of that, he shoots his wit.

Enter HYMEN *leading* ROSALIND *in woman's clothes, and* CELIA

Still Music

Hym. *Then is there mirth in heaven,*
   When earthly things made even
    Atone together.
   Good duke, receive thy daughter,
   Hymen from heaven brought her,
    Yea, brought her hither,
   That thou mightst join her hand with his
   Whose heart within her bosom is.

Ros. [*To Duke S.*] To you I give myself, for I am yours.
[*To Orlando*] To you I give myself, for I am yours.
Duke S. If there be truth in sight, you are my daughter.
Orl. If there be truth in sight, you are my Rosalind.
Phe. If sight and shape be true,
  Why then, my love adieu!
Ros. [*To Duke S.*] I'll have no father, if you be not he:—
[*To Orlando*] I'll have no husband, if you be not he:—
[*To Phebe*] Nor ne'er wed woman, if you be not she.
Hym. Peace, ho! I bar confusion.
  'T is I must make conclusion
   Of these most strange events:
  Here's eight that must take hands,
  To join in Hymen's bands,
   If truth holds true contents.
  [*To Orlando and Rosalind*] You and you no
   cross shall part:
  [*To Oliver and Celia*] You and you are heart
   in heart:
  [*To Phebe*] You to his love must accord,
  Or have a woman to your lord:
  [*To Touchstone and Audrey*] You and you are
   sure together,
  As the winter to foul weather.

Whiles a wedlock-hymn we sing
Feed yourselves with questioning,
That reason wonder may diminish
How thus we met, and these things finish.

Song

Wedding is great Juno's crown :
O blessed bond of board and bed !
'T is Hymen peoples every town;
High wedlock then be honourèd.
Honour, high honour, and renown,
To Hymen, god of every town !

Duke S.   O my dear niece, welcome thou art to me:
Even daughter welcome in no less degree.
   Phe.   [*To Silvius*]   I will not eat my word, now thou
      art mine;
Thy faith my fancy to thee doth combine.

Enter JAQUES DE BOIS

Jaq. de B.   Let me have audience for a word or two.
I am the second son of old Sir Rowland,
That bring these tidings to this fair assembly.—
Duke Frederick, hearing how that every day
Men of great worth resorted to this forest,
Addressed a mighty power, which were on foot
In his own conduct, purposely to take
His brother here, and put him to the sword.
And to the skirts of this wild wood he came,
Where, meeting with an old religious man,
After some question with him, was converted
Both from his enterprise and from the world;
His crown bequeathing to his banished brother,
And all their lands restored to them again
That were with him exiled.   This to be true
I do engage my life.
   Duke S.   Welcome, young man;
Thou offer'st fairly to thy brothers' wedding:
To one, his lands withheld; and to the other,
A land itself at large, a potent dukedom.
First, in this forest, let us do these ends
That here were well begun, and well begot:
And after, every of this happy number
That have endured shrewd days and nights with us
Shall share the good of our returnèd fortune,
According to the measure of their states.
Meantime, forget this new-fall'n dignity,
And fall into our rustic revelry.—
Play, music! and you brides and bridegrooms all,
With measure heaped in joy, to the measures fall.

Jaq. Sir, by your patience.—If I heard you rightly,
The duke hath put on a religious life.
And thrown into neglect the pompous court!
Jaq. de B. He hath.
Jaq. To him will I: out of these convertites
There is much matter to be heard and learned.—
[*To Duke S.*] You to your former honour I bequeath;
Your patience, and your virtue, well deserves it:—
[*To Orlando*] You to a love, that your true faith doth
          merit:—
[*To Oliver*] You to your land, and love, and great
          allies:—
[*To Silvius*] You to a long and well-deservéd bed:—
[*To Touchstone*] And you to wrangling; for thy loving
          voyage
Is but for two months victualled.—So, to your pleasures:
I am for other than for dancing measures.
Duke S. Stay, Jaques, stay.
Jaq. To see no pastime, I:—what you would have
I'll stay to know at your abandoned cave.   [*Exit*
Duke S. Proceed, proceed: we will begin these rites,
As we do trust they'll end, in true delights.   [*A dance*

EPILOGUE

Ros. It is not the fashion to see the lady the epilogue;
but it is no more unhandsome than to see the lord the
prologue. If it be true that good wine needs no bush, 't
is true that a good play needs no epilogue; yet to good
wine they do use good bushes, and good plays prove the
better by the help of good epilogues. What a case am I
in then, that am neither a good epilogue, nor cannot
insinuate with you in the behalf of a good play? I am
not furnished like a beggar, therefore to beg will not become
me: my way is, to conjure you; and I'll begin with the
women. I charge you, O women, for the love you bear
to men, to like as much of this play as please you: and I
charge you, O men, for the love you bear to women (as I
perceive by your simpering, none of you hates them), that
between you and the women, the play may please. If I
were a woman, I would kiss as many of you as had beards
that pleased me, complexions that liked me, and breaths
that I defied not; and I am sure, as many as have good
beards, or good faces, or sweet breaths, will for my kind
offer, when I make curtsy, bid me farewell.   [*Exeunt*

224

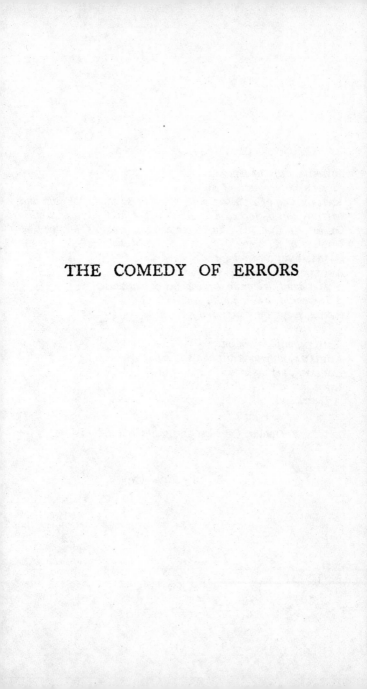

THE COMEDY OF ERRORS

DRAMATIS PERSONÆ

SOLINUS, *duke of Ephesus*
ÆGEON, *a merchant of Syracuse*
ANTIPHOLUS of Ephesus ⎫ *twin brothers, sons to Ægeon and*
ANTIPHOLUS of Syracuse ⎭ *Æmilia, but unknown to each other*
DROMIO OF Ephesus ⎫ *twin brothers, attendants on the two*
DROMIO of Syracuse ⎭ *Antipholuses*
BALTHAZAR, *a merchant*
ANGELO, *a goldsmith*
A Merchant, friend to Antipholus of Syracuse
A Merchant, trading with Angelo
PINCH, *a schoolmaster, and a conjurer*

ÆMILIA, *wife to Ægeon*
ADRIANA, *wife to Antipholus of Ephesus*
LUCIANA, *her sister*
LUCE, *servant to Adriana*
A Courtesan

Gaoler, Officers, and other Attendants

SCENE—*Ephesus*

THE COMEDY OF ERRORS

ACT ONE

Scene I.—A Hall in the Duke's Palace

Enter Duke, Ægeon, *Gaoler, Officers, and other Attendants*

Ægeon. Proceed, Solinus, to procure my fall,
And by the doom of death end woes and all.
    Duke. Merchant of Syracusa, plead no more.
I am not partial, to infringe our laws:
The enmity and discord which of late
Sprung from the rancorous outrage of your duke
To merchants, our well-dealing countrymen,—
Who, wanting gilders to redeem their lives,
Have sealed his rigorous statutes with their bloods,—
Excludes all pity from our threatening looks.
For, since the mortal and intestine jars
'Twixt thy seditious countrymen and us,
It hath in solemn synods been decreed,
Both by the Syracusans and ourselves,
To admit no traffic to our adverse towns:
Nay, more, if any, born at Ephesus,
Be seen at Syracusan marts and fairs;
Again, if any Syracusan born
Come to the bay of Ephesus, he dies,
His goods confiscate to the duke's dispose;
Unless a thousand marks be leviéd,
To quit the penalty, and to ransom him.
Thy substance, valued at the highest rate,
Cannot amount unto a hundred marks:
Therefore, by law thou art condemned to die.
    Æge. Yet this my comfort; when your words are done,
My woes end likewise with the evening sun.
    Duke. Well, Syracusan; say, in brief, the cause
Why thou departedst from thy native home,
And for what cause thou cam'st to Ephesus.
    Æge. A heavier task could not have been imposed
Than I to speak my griefs unspeakable;
Yet, that the world may witness that my end

Was wrought by nature not by vile offence,
I'll utter what my sorrow gives me leave.
In Syracusa was I born, and wed
Unto a woman happy but for me,
And by me too, had not our hap been bad.
With her I lived in joy: our wealth increased
By prosperous voyages I often made
To Epidamnum; till my factor's death,
And the great care of goods at random left,
Drew me from kind embracements of my spouse:
From whom my absence was not six months old,
Before herself—almost at fainting under
The pleasing punishment that women bear—
Had made provision for her following me,
And soon, and safe, arrivéd where I was.
There had she not been long, but she became
A joyful mother of two goodly sons;
And, which was strange, the one so like the other,
As could not be distinguished but by names.
That very hour, and in the self-same inn,
A meaner woman was deliveréd
Of such a burden, male twins, both alike.
Those, for their parents were exceeding poor,
I bought, and brought up to attend my sons.
My wife, not meanly proud of two such boys,
Made daily motions for our home return:
Unwilling I agreed; alas, too soon
We came aboard:
A league from Epidamnum had we sailed
Before the always-wind-obeying deep
Gave any tragic instance of our harm:
But longer did we not retain much hope;
For what obscuréd light the heavens did grant
Did but convey unto our fearful minds
A double warrant of immediate death,
Which, though myself would gladly have embraced,
Yet the incessant weepings of my wife,
Weeping before for what she saw must come,
And piteous plainings of the pretty babes,
That mourned for fashion ignorant what to fear,
Forced me to seek delays for them and me.
And this it was,—for other means was none,—
The sailors sought for safety by our boat,
And left the ship, then sinking-ripe, to us.
My wife, more careful for the latter-born,
Had fastened him unto a small spare mast,
Such as seafaring men provide for storms:
To him one of the other twins was bound,
Whilst I had been like heedful of the other.
The children thus disposed, my wife and I,

Fixing our eyes on whom our care was fixed,
Fastened ourselves at either end the mast;
And floating straight, obedient to the stream,
Were carried towards Corinth, as we thought.
At length the sun, gazing upon the earth,
Dispersed those vapours that offended us,
And by the benefit of his wished light
The seas waxed calm, and we discoveréd
Two ships from far making amain to us,—
Of Corinth that, of Epidaurus this:
But ere they came,—O, let me say no more!
Gather the sequel by that went before.
   Duke. Nay, forward, old man; do not break off so;
For we may pity, though not pardon thee.
   Æge. O, had the gods done so, I had not now
Worthily termed them merciless to us!
For, ere the ships could meet by twice five leagues,
We were encountered by a mighty rock;
Which being violently borne upon,
Our helpful ship was splitted in the midst;
So that in this unjust divorce of us
Fortune had left to both of us alike
What to delight in, what to sorrow for.
Her part, poor soul, seeming as burdenéd
With lesser weight, but not with lesser woe,
Was carried with more speed before the wind,
And in our sight they three were taken up
By fishermen of Corinth, as we thought.
At length another ship had seized on us;
And, knowing whom it was their hap to save,
Gave healthful welcome to their shipwrecked guests;
And would have reft the fishers of their prey,
Had not their bark been very slow of sail,
And therefore homeward did they bend their course.—
Thus have you heard me severed from my bliss,
That by misfortunes was my life prolonged,
To tell sad stories of my own mishaps.
   Duke. And, for the sake of them thou sorrowest for,
Do me the favour to dilate at full
What hath befallen of them and thee till now.
   Æge. My youngest boy, and yet my eldest care,
At eighteen years became inquisitive
After his brother; and importuned me,
That his attendant—so his case was like,
Reft of his brother, but retained his name—
Might bear him company in the quest of him;
Whom whilst I laboured of a love to see,
I hazarded the loss of whom I loved.
Five summers have I spent in farthest Greece,
Roaming clean through the bounds of Asia,

And, coasting homeward, came to Ephesus,
Hopeless to find, yet loath to leave unsought
Or that or any place that harbours men.
But there must end the story of my life;
And happy were I in my timely death,
Could all my travels warrant me they live.
   Duke. Hapless Ægeon, whom the fates have marked
To bear the extremity of dire mishap!
Now, trust me, were it not against our laws,
Against my crown, my oath, my dignity,
Which princes, would they, may not disannul,
My soul should sue as advocate for thee.
But though thou art adjudgéd to the death,
And passéd sentence may not be recalled
But to our honour's great disparagement,
Yet will I favour thee in what I can:
Therefore, merchant, I'll limit thee this day,
To seek thy help by beneficial hands:
Try all the friends thou hast in Ephesus;
Beg thou, or borrow, to make up the sum,
And live; if no, then thou art doomed to die.—
Gaoler, take him to thy custody.
   Gaol. I will, my lord.
   Æge. Hopeless, and helpless, doth Ægeon wend,
But to procrastinate his lifeless end.   [*Exeunt*

Scene II.—A Public Place

Enter Antipholus *of Syracuse,* Dromio *of Syracuse,*
and a Merchant

   Mer. Therefore, give out you are of Epidamnum,
Lest that your goods too soon be confiscate.
This very day, a Syracusan merchant
Is apprehended for arrival here,
And, not being able to buy out his life
According to the statute of the town,
Dies ere the weary sun set in the west.
There is your money that I had to keep.
   Ant. S. [*To Dromio S.*] Go bear it to the Centaur,
      where we host,
And stay there, Dromio, till I come to thee.
Within this hour it will be dinner-time:
Till that, I'll view the manners of the town,
Peruse the traders, gaze upon the buildings,
And then return and sleep within mine inn;
For with long travel I am stiff and weary.
Get thee away.
   Dro. S. Many a man would take you at your word,
And go indeed, having so good a mean.   [*Exit*

Ant. S. A trusty villain, sir, that very oft,
When I am dull with care and melancholy,
Lightens my humour with his merry jests.
What, will you walk with me about the town,
And then go to my inn, and dine with me?
    Mer. I am invited, sir, to certain merchants,
Of whom I hope to make much benefit;
I crave your pardon. Soon, at five o'clock,
Please you, I'll meet with you upon the mart,
And afterwards consort you till bed-time:
My present business calls me from you now.
    Ant. S. Farewell till then: I will go lose myself,
And wander up and down to view the city.
    Mer. Sir, I commend you to your own content.   [*Exit*
    Ant. S. He that commends me to mine own content,
Commends me to the thing I cannot get.
I to the world am like a drop of water
That in the ocean seeks another drop;
Who, falling there to find his fellow forth,
Unseen, inquisitive, confounds himself:
So I, to find a mother and a brother,
In quest of them, unhappy, lose myself.

Enter DROMIO *of Ephesus*

Here comes the almanac of my true date.
What now? How chance thou art returned so soon?
    Dro. E. Returned so soon! rather approached too late.
The capon burns, the pig falls from the spit,
The clock hath strucken twelve upon the bell;
My mistress made it one upon my cheek:
She is so hot, because the meat is cold;
The meat is cold, because you come not home;
You come not home, because you have no stomach;
You have no stomach, having broke your fast;
But we, that know what 't is to fast and pray,
Are penitent for your default to-day.
    Ant. S. Stop in your wind, sir. Tell me this, I pray:
Where have you left the money that I gave you?
    Dro. E. O,—sixpence, that I had o' Wednesday last
To pay the saddler for my mistress' crupper;
The saddler had it, sir; I kept it not.
    Ant. S. I am not in a sportive humour now.
Tell me, and dally not, where is the money?
We being strangers here, how dar'st thou trust
So great a charge from thine own custody?
    Dro. E. I pray you, jest, sir, as you sit at dinner.
I from my mistress come to you in post;
If I return, I shall be post indeed,
For she will score your fault upon my pate.

Methinks, your maw, like mine, should be your clock,
And strike you home without a messenger.

    Ant. S.   Come, Dromio, come; these jests are out of
        season:
Reserve them till a merrier hour than this.
Where is the gold I gave in charge to thee?

    Dro. E.   To me, sir? why, you gave no gold to me.

    Ant. S.   Come on, sir knave; have done your foolishness,
And tell me how thou hast disposed thy charge.

    Dro. E.   My charge was but to fetch you from the mart
Home to your house, the Phœnix, sir, to dinner.
My mistress and her sister stay for you.

    Ant. S.   Now, as I am a Christian, answer me,
In what safe place you have bestowed my money,
Or I shall break that merry sconce of yours
That stands on tricks when I am undisposed.
Where is the thousand marks thou hadst of me?

    Dro. E.   I have some marks of yours upon my pate;
Some of my mistress' marks upon my shoulders,
But not a thousand marks between you both.
If I should pay your worship those again,
Perchance, you will not bear them patiently.

    Ant. S.   Thy mistress' marks! what mistress, slave,
        hast thou?

    Dro. E.   Your worship's wife, my mistress at the
        Phœnix;
She that doth fast till you come home to dinner,
And prays that you will hie you home to dinner.

    Ant. S.   What, wilt thou flout me thus unto my face,
Being forbid?   There, take you that, sir knave.
                                  [Strikes him

    Dro. E.   What mean you, sir? for God's sake, hold
        your hands.
Nay, an you will not, sir, I'll take my heels.   *[Exit*

    Ant. S.   Upon my life, by some device or other
The villain is o'er-raught of all my money.
They say this town is full of cozenage;
As, nimble jugglers that deceive the eye,
Dark-working sorcerers that change the mind,
Soul-killing witches that deform the body,
Disguisèd cheaters, prating mountebanks,
And many such-like liberties of sin:
If it prove so, I will be gone the sooner.
I'll to the Centaur to go seek this slave:
I greatly fear my money is not safe.   *[Exit*

ACT TWO

Scene I.—House of Antipholus of Ephesus

Enter Adriana *and* Luciana

Adr. Neither my husband nor the slave returned,
That in such haste I sent to seek his master!
Sure, Luciana, it is two o'clock.
Luc. Perhaps, some merchant hath invited him,
And from the mart he's somewhere gone to dinner.
Good sister, let us dine, and never fret:
A man is master of his liberty:
Time is their master; and, when they see time,
They'll go or come: if so, be patient, sister.
Adr. Why should their liberty than ours be more?
Luc. Because their business still lies out o' door.
Adr. Look, when I serve him so he takes it ill.
Luc. O, know he is the bridle of your will.
Adr. There's none but asses will be bridled so.
Luc. Why, headstrong liberty is lashed with woe.
There's nothing situate under heaven's eye
But hath his bound, in earth, in sea, in sky:
The beasts, the fishes, and the wingéd fowls,
Are their males' subjects and at their controls.
Men, more divine, the masters of all these,
Lords of the wide world, and wild wat'ry seas,
Indued with intellectual sense and souls,
Of more pre-eminence than fish and fowls,
Are masters to their females, and their lords:
Then, let your will attend on their accords.
Adr. This servitude makes you keep unwed.
Luc. Not this, but troubles of the marriage-bed.
Adr. But, were you wedded, you would bear some sway
Luc. Ere I learn love I'll practise to obey.
Adr. How if your husband start some other where?
Luc. Till he come home again I would forbear.
Adr. Patience unmoved, no marvel though she pause;
They can be meek that have no other cause.
A wretched soul, bruised with adversity,
We bid be quiet, when we hear it cry;
But were we burdened with like weight of pain,
As much or more we should ourselves complain;
So thou, that hast no unkind mate to grieve thee,
With urging helpless patience wouldst relieve me:
But if thou live to see like right bereft,
This fool-begged patience in thee will be left.
Luc. Well, I will marry one day, but to try.—
Here comes your man: now is your husband nigh.

Enter DROMIO *of Ephesus*

Adr. Say, is your tardy master now at hand?
Dro. E. Nay, he is at two hands with me, and that my
two ears can witness.
Adr. Say, didst thou speak with him? Know'st thou
          his mind?
Dro. E. Ay, ay; he told his mind upon mine ear.
Beshrew his hand, I scarce could understand it.
Luc. Spake he so doubtfully thou couldst not feel his
meaning?
Dro. E. Nay, he struck so plainly I could too well feel
his blows; and withal so doubtfully, that I could scarce
understand them.
Adr. But say, I pr'ythee, is he coming home?
It seems he hath great care to please his wife.
Dro. E. Why, mistress, sure my master is horn-mad.
Adr. Horn-mad, thou villain!
Dro. E. I mean not cuckold-mad; but, sure, he is
          stark mad.
When I desired him to come home to dinner,
He asked me for a thousand marks in gold:
' 'T is dinner-time,' quoth I; 'My gold!' quoth he:
'Your meat doth burn,' quoth I; 'My gold!' quoth he:
'Will you come home?' quoth I; 'My gold!' quoth he:
'Where is the thousand marks I gave thee, villain?'
'The pig,' quoth I, 'is burned'; 'My gold!' quoth he:
'My mistress, sir,' quoth I; 'Hang up thy mistress!
I know not thy mistress: out on thy mistress!'
Luc. Quoth who?
Dro. E. Quoth my master:
'I know,' quoth he, 'no house, no wife, no mistress.'
So that my errand, due unto my tongue,
I thank him, I bear home upon my shoulders;
For, in conclusion, he did beat me there.
Adr. Go back again, thou slave, and fetch him home.
Dro. E. Go back again, and be new beaten home?
For God's sake, send some other messenger.
Adr. Back, slave, or I will break thy pate across.
Dro. E. And he will bless that cross with other beating.
Between you I shall have a holy head.
Adr. Hence, prating peasant! fetch thy master home.
Dro. E. Am I so round with you as you with me,
That like a football you do spurn me thus?
You spurn me hence, and he will spurn me hither:
If I last in this service, you must case me in leather. [*Exit*
Luc. Fie, how impatience lowereth in your face!
Adr. His company must do his minions grace
Whilst I at home starve for a merry look.
Hath homely age the alluring beauty took

234

From my poor cheek? then he hath wasted it:
Are my discourses dull? barren my wit?
If voluble and sharp discourse be marred,
Unkindness blunts it more than marble hard.
Do their gay vestments his affections bait?
That's not my fault; he's master of my state.
What ruins are in me that can be found
By him not ruined? then is he the ground
Of my defeatures.   My decayéd fair
A sunny look of his would soon repair;
But, too unruly deer, he breaks the pale
And feeds from home: poor I am but his stale.
   Luc.   Self-harming jealousy!—fie, beat it hence!
   Adr.   Unfeeling fools can with such wrongs dispense.
I know his eye doth homage otherwhere,
Or else what lets it but he would be here?
Sister, you know he promised me a chain:
'Would that alone alone he would detain,
So he would keep fair quarter with his bed!
I see, the jewel best enamelléd
Will lose his beauty: and though gold bides still
That others touch, yet often touching will
Wear gold; and so no man, that hath a name,
But falsehood and corruption doth it shame.
Since that my beauty cannot please his eye,
I'll weep what's left away, and weeping die.
   Luc.   How many fond fools serve mad jealousy

                                [Exeunt

SCENE II.—A Public Place

Enter ANTIPHOLUS *of Syracuse*

   Ant. S.   The gold I gave to Dromio is laid up
Safe at the Centaur; and the heedful slave
Is wandered forth, in care to seek me out.
By computation and mine host's report,
I could not speak with Dromio since at first
I sent him from the mart.   See, here he comes.

Enter DROMIO *of Syracuse*

How now, sir? is your merry humour altered?
As you love strokes, so jest with me again.
You know no Centaur?   You received no gold?
Your mistress sent to have me home to dinner?
My house was at the Phœnix?   Wast thou mad,
That thus so madly thou didst answer me?
   Dro. S.   What answer, sir? when spake I such a word?
   Ant. S.   Even now, even here, not half an hour since.

Dro. S.   I did not see you since you sent me hence
Home to the Centaur with the gold you gave me.

Ant. S.   Villain, thou didst deny the gold's receipt,
And toldst me of a mistress, and a dinner;
For which, I hope, thou feltst I was displeased.

Dro. S.   I am glad to see you in this merry vein,
What means this jest? I pray you, master, tell me.

Ant. S.   Yea, dost thou jeer, and flout me in the teeth?
Think'st thou, I jest? Hold, take thou that, and that.

                                [Beating him

Dro. S.   Hold, sir, for God's sake! now your jest is
    earnest:
Upon what bargain do you give it me?

Ant. S.   Because that I familiarly sometimes
Do use you for my fool and chat with you,
Your sauciness will jest upon my love
And make a common of my serious hours.
When the sun shines, let foolish gnats make sport,
But creep in crannies when he hides his beams.
If you will jest with me, know my aspect,
And fashion your demeanour to my looks,
Or I will beat this method in your sconce.

Dro. S.   Sconce, call you it? so you would leave
battering, I had rather have it a head: an you use these
blows long I must get a sconce for my head and ensconce
it too; or else I shall seek my wit in my shoulders. But,
I pray, sir, why am I beaten?

Ant. S.   Dost thou not know?

Dro. S.   Nothing, sir, but that I am beaten.

Ant. S.   Shall I tell you why?

Dro. S.   Ay, sir, and wherefore; for, they say, every
why hath a wherefore.

Ant. S.   Why, first—for flouting me, and then, wherefore,—
For urging it the second time to me.

Dro. S.   Was there ever any man thus beaten out of
    season,
When in the why and the wherefore is neither rhyme nor
    reason?—
Well, sir, I thank you.

Ant. S.   Thank me, sir? for what?

Dro. S.   Marry, sir, for this something that you gave
me for nothing.

Ant. S.   I'll make you amends next, to give you nothing
for something. But say, sir, is it dinner-time?

Dro. S.   No, sir: I think the meat wants that I have.

Ant. S.   In good time, sir,—what's that?

Dro. S.   Basting.

Ant. S.   Well, sir, then't will be dry.

Dro. S.   If it be, sir, I pray you eat none of it.

Ant. S.   Your reason?

Dro. S.   Lest it make you choleric, and purchase me another dry basting.

Ant. S.   Well, sir, learn to jest in good time: there's a time for all things.

Dro. S.   I durst have denied that, before you were so choleric.

Ant. S.   By what rule, sir?

Dro. S.   Marry, sir, by a rule as plain as the plain bald pate of Father Time himself.

Ant. S.   Let's hear it.

Dro. S.   There's no time for a man to recover his hair that grows bald by nature.

Ant. S.   May he not do it by fine and recovery?

Dro. S.   Yes, to pay a fine for a periwig, and recover the lost hair of another man.

Ant. S.   Why is Time such a niggard of hair, being, as it is, so plentiful an excrement?

Dro. S.   Because it is a blessing that he bestows on beasts: and what he hath scanted men in hair he hath given them in wit.

Ant. S.   Why, but there's many a man hath more hair than wit.

Dro. S.   Not a man of those but he hath the wit to lose his hair.

Ant. S.   Why, thou didst conclude hairy men plain dealers without wit.

Dro. S.   The plainer dealer, the sooner lost: yet he loseth it in a kind of jollity.

Ant. S.   For what reason?

Dro. S.   For two; and sound ones too.

Ant. S.   Nay, not sound, I pray you.

Dro. S.   Sure ones then.

Ant. S.   Nay, not sure, is a thing falsing.

Dro. S.   Certain ones then.

Ant. S.   Name them.

Dro. S.   The one, to save the money that he spends in tiring; the other, that at dinner they should not drop in his porridge.

Ant. S.   You would all this time have proved, there is no time for all things.

Dro. S.   Marry, and did, sir; namely, no time to recover hair lost by nature.

Ant. S.   But your reason was not substantial, why there is no time to recover.

Dro. S.   Thus I mend it: Time himself is bald, and therefore, to the world's end, will have bald followers.

Ant. S.   I knew't would be a bald conclusion. But soft! who wafts us yonder?

Enter ADRIANA *and* LUCIANA

  Adr. Ay, ay, Antipholus, look strange and frown:
Some other mistress hath thy sweet aspects,
I am not Adriana, nor thy wife.
The time was once, when thou unurged wouldst vow
That never words were music to thine ear,
That never object pleasing in thine eye,
That never touch well-welcome to thy hand,
That never meat sweet-savoured in thy taste,
Unless I spake, or looked, or touched, or carved to thee.
How comes it now, my husband, O, how comes it,
That thou art thus estrangéd from thyself?
Thyself I call it, being strange to me,
That, undividable, incorporate,
Am better than thy dear self's better part.
Ah, do not tear away thyself from me;
For know, my love, as easy may'st thou fall
A drop of water in the breaking gulf,
And take unmingled thence that drop again
Without addition or diminishing,
As take from me thyself and not me too.
How dearly would it touch thee to the quick,
Shouldst thou but hear I were licentious,
And that this body, consecrate to thee,
By ruffian lust should be contaminate!
Wouldst thou not spit at me and spurn at me
And hurl the name of husband in my face,
And tear the stained skin off my harlot-brow,
And from my false hand cut the wedding-ring,
And break it with a deep-divorcing vow?
I know thou canst; and therefore, see thou do it:
I am possessed with an adulterate blot;
My blood is mingled with the crime of lust:
For, if we two be one, and thou play false,
I do digest the poison of thy flesh.
Being strumpeted by thy contagion.
Keep then fair league and truce with thy true bed;
I live distained, thou undishonouréd.
  Ant. S. Plead you to me, fair dame?   I know you not.
In Ephesus I am but two hours old,
As strange unto your town as to your talk;
Who, every word by all my wit being scanned,
Want wit in all one word to understand.
  Luc. Fie, brother: how the world is changed with you!
When were you wont to use my sister thus?
She sent for you by Dromio home to dinner.
  Ant. S. By Dromio?
  Dro. S. By me?
  Adr. By thee; and this thou didst return from him,—

That he did buffet thee, and in his blows
Denied my house for his, me for his wife.
    Ant. S.   Did you converse, sir, with this gentlewoman?
What is the course and drift of your compact?
    Dro. S.   I, sir? I never saw her till this time.
    Ant. S.   Villain, thou liest; for even her very words
Didst thou deliver to me on the mart.
    Dro. S.   I never spake with her in all my life.
    Ant. S.   How can she thus then call us by our names,
Unless it be by inspiration?
    Adr.   How ill agrees it with your gravity
To counterfeit thus grossly with your slave,
Abetting him to thwart me in my mood!
Be it my wrong, you are from me exempt,
But wrong not that wrong with a more contempt.
Come, I will fasten on this sleeve of thine;
Thou art an elm, my husband, I a vine,
Whose weakness, married to thy stronger state,
Makes me with thy strength to communicate:
If aught possess thee from me, it is dross,
Usurping ivy, brier, or idle moss;
Who, all for want of pruning, with intrusion
Infect thy sap, and live on thy confusion.
    Ant. S.   To me she speaks; she moves me for her theme!
What, was I married to her in my dream,
Or sleep I now, and think I hear all this?
What error drives our eyes and ears amiss?
Until I know this sure uncertainty,
I'll entertain the offered fallacy.
    Luc.   Dromio, go bid the servants spread for dinner.
    Dro. S.   O, for my beads! I cross me for a sinner.
This is the fairy land: O, spite of spites!
We talk with goblins, owls, and elvish sprites.
If we obey them not, this will ensue,
They'll suck our breath, or pinch us black and blue.
    Luc.   Why prat'st thou to thyself, and answer'st not?
Dromio, thou drone, thou snail, thou slug, thou sot!
    Dro. S.   I am transforméd, am I not?
    Ant. S.   I think thou art, in mind, and so am I.
    Dro. S.   Nay, master, both in mind and in my shape.
    Ant. S.   Thou hast thine own form.
    Dro. S.   No, I am an ape.
    Luc.   If thou art changed to aught, 't is to an ass.
    Dro. S.   'T is true; she rides me, and I long for grass,
'T is so, I am an ass; else it could never be
But I should know her as well as she knows me.
    Adr.   Come, come; no longer will I be a fool,
To put the finger in the eye and weep,
Whilst man and master laugh my woes to scorn.
Come, sir, to dinner.—Dromio, keep the gate.—

Husband, I'll dine above with you to-day,
And shrive you of a thousand idle pranks.—
Sirrah, if any ask you for your master,
Say he dines forth, and let no creature enter.—
Come, sister.—Dromio, play the porter well.
    Ant. S.   Am I in earth, in heaven, or in hell?
Sleeping or waking? mad, or well advised?
Known unto these, and to myself disguised?
I'll say as they say, and perséver so,
And in this mist at all adventures go.
    Dro. S.   Master, shall I be porter at the gate?
    Adr.   Ay; and let none enter, lest I break your pate.
    Luc.   Come, come, Antipholus; we dine too late.
                               [Exeunt

ACT THREE

SCENE I.—Before the House of ANTIPHOLUS of Ephesus

Enter ANTIPHOLUS *of Ephesus*, DROMIO *of Ephesus*, ANGELO, *and* BALTHAZAR

    Ant. E.   Good Signior Angelo, you must excuse us all;
My wife is shrewish when I keep not hours.
Say, that I lingered with you at your shop
To see the making of her carcanet,
And that to-morrow you will bring it home.
But here's a villain that would face me down
He met me on the mart and that I beat him,
And charged him with a thousand marks in gold;
And that I did deny my wife and house.—
Thou drunkard, thou, what didst thou mean by this?
    Dro. E.   Say what you will, sir, but I know what I know.
That you beat me at the mart, I have your hand to show:
If the skin were parchment and the blows you gave were ink,
Your own handwriting would tell you what I think.
    Ant. E.   I think, thou art an ass.
    Dro. E.   Marry, so it doth appear,
By the wrongs I suffer and the blows I bear.
I should kick being kicked, and being at that pass,
You would keep from my heels and beware of an ass.
    Ant. E.   You are sad, Signior Balthazar: pray God, our cheer
May answer my good will, and your good welcome here.
    Bal.   I hold your dainties cheap, sir, and your welcome dear.
    Ant. E.   O Signior Balthazar, either at flesh or fish,
A table-full of welcome makes scarce one dainty dish.

Bal. Good meat, sir, is common; that every churl
 affords.
Ant. E. And welcome more common, for that's nothing
 but words.
Bal. Small cheer and great welcome makes a merry
 feast.
Ant. E. Ay, to a niggardly host and more sparing
 guest:
But though my cates be mean, take them in good part;
Better cheer may you have, but not with better heart.
But soft, my door is locked. Go bid them let us in.
Dro. E. Maud, Bridget, Marian, Cicely, Gillian, Jin!
Dro. S. [*Within*] Mome, malt-horse, capon, cox-comb,
 idiot, patch!
Either get thee from the door, or sit down at the hatch.
Dost thou conjure for wenches, that thou call'st for such
 store
When one is one too many? Go get thee from the door.
Dro. E. What patch is made our porter?—My master
 stays in the street.
Dro. S. [*Within*] Let him walk from whence he came,
 lest he catch cold on's feet.
Ant. E. Who talks within there? ho! open the door.
Dro. S. [*Within*] Right, sir: I'll tell you when and
 you'll tell me wherefore.
Ant. E. Wherefore? for my dinner: I have not dined
 to-day.
Dro. S. [*Within*] Nor to-day here you must not;
 come again when you may.
Ant. E. What art thou that keep'st me out from the
 house I owe?
Dro. S. [*Within*] The porter for this time, sir, and my
 name is Dromio.
Dro. E. O villain, thou hast stolen both mine office and
 my name:
The one ne'er got me credit, the other mickle blame.
If thou hadst been Dromio to-day in my place,
Thou wouldst have changed thy face for a name, or thy
 name for an ass.
Luce. [*Within*] What a coil is there! Dromio, who
 are those at the gate?
Dro. E. Let my master in, Luce.
Luce. [*Within*] Faith no; he comes too late;
And so tell your master.
Dro. E.   O Lord! I must laugh.—
Have at you with a proverb:—Shall I set in my staff?
Luce. [*Within*] Have at you with another: that's—
 When? can you tell?
Dro. S. [*Within*] If thy name be called Luce, Luce,
 thou hast answered him well.

Ant E. Do you hear, you minion? you'll let us in, I hope?

Luce. [*Within*] I thought to have asked you.

Dro. S. [*Within*]   And you said, no.

Dro. E. So; come, help: well struck! there was blow for blow.

Ant. E. Thou baggage, let me in.

Luce. [*Within*]   Can you tell for whose sake?

Dro. E. Master, knock the door hard.

Luce. [*Within*]   Let him knock till it ache.

Ant. E. You'll cry for this, minion, if I beat the door down.

Luce. [*Within*] What needs all that, and a pair of stocks in the town?

Adr. [*Within*] Who is that at the door, that keeps all this noise?

Dro. S. [*Within*] By my troth, your town is troubled with unruly boys.

Ant. E. Are you there, wife? you might have come before.

Adr. [*Within*] Your wife, sir knave? go get you from the door.

Dro. E. If you went in pain, master, this knave would go sore.

Ang. Here is neither cheer, sir, nor welcome: we would fain have either.

Bal. In debating which was best, we shall part with neither.

Dro. E. They stand at the door, master: bid them welcome hither.

Ant. E. There is something in the wind, that we cannot get in.

Dro. E. You would say so, master, if your garments were thin.

Your cake there is warm within; you stand here in the cold:

It would make a man mad as a buck to be so bought and sold.

Ant. E. Go fetch me something: I'll break ope the gate.

Dro. S. [*Within*] Break any breaking here, and I'll break your knave's pate.

Dro. E. A man may break a word with you, sir, and words are but wind;

Ay, and break it in your face, so he break it not behind.

Dro. S. [*Within*] It seems, thou wantest breaking. Out upon thee, hind!

Dro. E. Here's too much 'out upon thee'! I pray thee, let me in.

Dro. S. [*Within*] Ay, when fowls have no feathers and
    fish have no fin.
Ant. E. Well, I'll break in. Go borrow me a crow.
Dro. E. A crow without feather? master, mean you so?
For a fish without a fin there's a fowl without a feather.
If a crow help us in, sirrah, we'll pluck a crow together.
Ant. E. Go get thee gone: fetch me an iron crow.
Bal. Have patience, sir; O, let it not be so:
Herein you war against your reputation,
And draw within the compass of suspect
The unviolated honour of your wife.
Once this,—your long experience of her wisdom,
Her sober virtue, years, and modesty,
Plead on her part some cause to you unknown;
And doubt not, sir, but she will well excuse
Why at this time the doors are made against you.
Be ruled by me: depart in patience,
And let us to the Tiger all to dinner;
And about evening come yourself alone,
To know the reason of this strange restraint.
If by strong hand you offer to break in,
Now in the stirring passage of the day,
A vulgar comment will be made of it,
And that supposéd by the common rout
Against your yet ungalléd estimation,
That may with foul intrusion enter in
And dwell upon your grave when you are dead:
For slander lives upon succession;
For ever housed where it gets possessión.
Ant. E. You have prevailed. I will depart in quiet,
And, in despite of mirth, mean to be merry.
I know a wench of excellent discourse,—
Pretty and witty, wild and yet, too, gentle,—
There will we dine: this woman that I mean,
My wife—but, I protest, without desert—
Hath oftentimes upbraided me withal:
To her will we to dinner.—Get you home,
And fetch the chain; by this, I know, 't is made;
Bring it, I pray you, to the Porpentine;
For there's the house: that chain will I bestow—
Be it for nothing but to spite my wife—
Upon mine hostess there. Good sir, make haste.
Since mine own doors refuse to entertain me,
I'll knock elsewhere, to see if they'll disdain me.
Ang. I'll meet you at that place, some hour hence.
Ant. E. Do so. This jest shall cost me some expense.
                                              [*Exeunt*

SCENE II.—The Same

Enter LUCIANA *and* ANTIPHOLUS *of Syracuse*

   Luc. And may it be that you have quite forgot
A husband's office? Shall, Antipholus,
Even in the spring of love thy love-springs rot?
Shall love in building grow so ruinous?
If you did wed my sister for her wealth,
Then for her wealth's sake use her with more kindness:
Or if you like elsewhere, do it by stealth;
Muffle your false love with some show of blindness;
Let not my sister read it in your eye;
Be not thy tongue thy own shame's orator;
Look sweet, speak fair, become disloyalty;
Apparel vice like virtue's harbinger;
Bear a fair presence, though your heart be tainted;
Teach sin the carriage of a holy saint;
Be secret-false: what need she be acquainted?
What simple thief brags of his own attaint?
'T is double wrong, to truant with your bed
And let her read it in thy looks at board:
Shame hath a bastard fame, well managéd;
Ill deeds are doubled with an evil word.
Alas, poor women, make us but believe,
Being compact of credit, that you love us;
Though others have the arm, show us the sleeve;
We in your motion turn and you may move us.
Then, gentle brother, get you in again:
Comfort my sister, cheer her, call her wife.
'T is holy sport to be a little vain,
When the sweet breath of flattery conquers strife.
   Ant. S. Sweet mistress—what your name is else, I
            know not,
Nor by what wonder you do hit of mine—
Less in your knowledge and your grace you show not,
Than our earth's wonder, more than earth divine.
Teach me, dear creature, how to think and speak:
Lay open to my earthly-gross conceit,
Smothered in errors, feeble, shallow, weak,
The folded meaning of your words' deceit.
Against my soul's pure truth why labour you
To make it wander in an unknown field?
Are you a god? would you create me new?
Transform me then, and to your power I'll yield.
But if that I am I, then well I know
Your weeping sister is no wife of mine,
Nor to her bed no homage do I owe:
Far more, far more, to you do I decline.

O, train me not, sweet mermaid, with thy note,
To drown me in thy sister's flood of tears.
Sing, siren, for thyself, and I will dote:
Spread o'er the silver waves thy golden hairs,
And as a bed I'll take thee and there lie;
And, in that glorious supposition, think
He gains by death that hath such means to die:
Let Love, being light, be drownéd if she sink!

Luc.   What, are you mad, that you do reason so?

Ant. S.   Not mad, but mated; how, I do not know.

Luc.   It is a fault that springeth from your eye.

Ant. S.   For gazing on your beams, fair sun, being by.

Luc.   Gaze where you should, and that will clear your sight.

Ant. S.   As good to wink, sweet love, as look on night.

Luc.   Why call you me love? call my sister so.

Ant. S.   Thy sister's sister.

Luc.   That's my sister.

Ant. S.   No;
It is thyself, mine own self's better part;
Mine eye's clear eye, my dear heart's dearer heart,
My food, my fortune, and my sweet hope's aim,
My sole earth's heaven, and my heaven's claim.

Luc.   All this my sister is, or else should be.

Ant. S.   Call thyself sister, sweet, for I aim thee.
Thee will I love, and with thee lead my life:
Thou hast no husband yet, nor I no wife.
Give me thy hand.

Luc.   O, soft, sir, hold you still:
I'll fetch my sister, to get her good will.   [*Exit*

Enter from the House of ANTIPHOLUS *of Ephesus,*
DROMIO *of Syracuse, hastily*

Ant. S.   Why, how now, Dromio? where runn'st thou so fast?

Dro. S.   Do you know me, sir? am I Dromio? am I your man, am I myself?

Ant. S.   Thou art Dromio, thou art my man, thou art thyself.

Dro. S.   I am an ass, I am a woman's man, and besides myself.

Ant. S.   What woman's man? and how besides thyself?

Dro. S.   Marry, sir, besides myself, I am due to a woman; one that claims me, one that haunts me, one that will have me.

Ant. S.   What claim lays she to thee?

Dro. S.   Marry, sir, such claim as you would lay to your horse; and she would have me as a beast: not that, I being a beast, she would have me; but that she, being a very beastly creature, lays claim to me.

Ant. S. What is she?

Dro. S. A very reverend body; ay, such a one as a man may not speak of without he say, Sir-reverence. I have but lean luck in the match and yet she is a wondrous fat marriage.

Ant. S. How dost thou mean a fat marriage?

Dro. S. Marry, sir, she's the kitchen-wench, and all grease; and I know not what use to put her to but to make a lamp of her and run from her by her own light. I warrant, her rags and the tallow in them will burn a Poland winter: if she lives till doomsday, she'll burn a week longer than the whole world.

Ant. S. What complexion is she of?

Dro. S. Swart, like my shoe, but her face nothing like so clean kept: for why, she sweats: a man may go over shoes in the grime of it.

Ant. S. That's a fault that water will mend.

Dro. S. No, sir; 't is in grain: Noah's flood could not do it.

Ant. S. What's her name?

Dro. S. Nell, sir; but her name and three quarters, that is, an ell and three quarters, will not measure her from hip to hip.

Ant. S. Then she bears some breadth?

Dro. S. No longer from head to foot, than from hip to hip: she is spherical, like a globe; I could find out countries in her.

Ant. S. In what part of her body stands Ireland?

Dro. S. Marry, sir, in her buttocks: I found it out by the bogs.

Ant. S. Where Scotland?

Dro. S. I found it by the barrenness, hard in the palm of the hand.

Ant. S. Where France?

Dro. S. In her forehead; armed and reverted, making war against her heir.

Ant. S. Where England?

Dro. S. I looked for the chalky cliffs, but I could find no whiteness in them: but I guess, it stood in her chin, by the salt rheum that ran between France and it.

Ant. S. Where Spain?

Dro. S. Faith, I saw it not; but I felt it hot in her breath.

Ant. S. Where America, the Indies?

Dro. S. O, sir, upon her nose, all o'er embellished with rubies, carbuncles, sapphires, declining their rich aspect to the hot breath of Spain, who sent whole armadoes or caracks to be ballast at her nose.

Ant. S. Where stood Belgia, the Netherlands?

Dro. S. O, sir, I did not look so low. To conclude,

this drudge, or diviner, laid claim to me; called me Dromio,
swore I was assured to her; told me what privy marks I
had about me, as the mark on my shoulder, the mole in
my neck, the great wart on my left arm, that I, amazed,
ran from her as a witch.
And, I think, if my breast had not been made of faith, and
    my heart of steel,
She had transformed me to a curtail-dog, and made me
    turn i' the wheel.
    Ant. S.   Go hie thee presently post to the road;
And if the wind blow any way from shore
I will not harbour in this town to-night:—
If any bark put forth, come to the mart,
Where I will walk till thou return to me.
If every one knows us and we know none,
'T is time, I think, to trudge, pack, and be gone.
    Dro. S.   As from a bear a man would run for life,
So fly I from her that would be my wife.   *[Exit*
    Ant. S.   There's none but witches do inhabit here,
And therefore 't is high time that I were hence.
She that doth call me husband, even my soul
Doth for a wife abhor; but her fair sister,
Possessed with such a gentle sovereign grace,
Of such enchanting presence and discourse,
Hath almost made me traitor to myself:
But, lest myself be guilty to self-wrong,
I'll stop mine ears against the mermaid's song.

             Enter ANGELO

    Ang.   Master Antipholus?
    Ant. S.   Ay, that's my name.
    Ang.   I know it well, sir. Lo, here is the chain.
I thought to have ta'en you at the Porpentine;
The chain unfinished made me stay thus long.
    Ant. S.   What is your will that I shall do with this?
    Ang.   What please yourself, sir: I have made it for you.
    Ant. S.   Made it for me, sir? I bespoke it not.
    Ang.   Not once, nor twice, but twenty times you have.
Go home with it, and please your wife withal;
And soon at supper-time I'll visit you,
And then receive my money for the chain.
    Ant. S.   I pray you, sir, receive the money now,
For fear you ne'er see chain, nor money, more.
    Ang.   You are a merry man, sir. Fare you well. *[Exit;*
    Ant. S.   What I should think of this, I cannot tell;
But this I think, there's no man is so vain
That would refuse so fair an offered chain.
I see, a man here needs not live by shifts
When in the streets he meets such golden gifts.

I'll to the mart, and there for Dromio stay:
If any ship put out, then straight away.   *[Exit*

ACT FOUR

SCENE I.—A Public Place

Enter a Merchant, ANGELO, *and an Officer*

Mer. You know, since Pentecost the sum is due,
And since I have not much importuned you;
Nor now I had not, but that I am bound
To Persia, and want gilders for my voyage:
Therefore make present satisfaction,
Or I'll attach you by this officer.
    Ang. Even just the sum that I do owe to you
Is growing to me by Antipholus;
And, in the instant that I met with you,
He had of me a chain: at five o'clock
I shall receive the money for the same.
Pleaseth you walk with me down to his house,
I will discharge my bond, and thank you too.

Enter ANTIPHOLUS *of Ephesus and* DROMIO *of Ephesus*

    Off. That labour may you save: see where he comes.
    Ant. E. While I go to the goldsmith's house, go thou
And buy a rope's end, that will I bestow
Among my wife and her confederates
For locking me out of my doors by day.—
But soft, I see the goldsmith.—Get thee gone;
Buy thou a rope, and bring it home to me.
    Dro. E. I buy a thousand pound a year: I buy a rope!
                               [Exit
    Ant. E. A man is well holp up that trusts to you:
I promiséd your presence and the chain;
But neither chain nor goldsmith came to me.
Belike you thought our love would last too long
If it were chained together, and therefore came not.
    Ang. Saving your merry humour, here's the note
How much your chain weighs to the utmost carat,
The fineness of the gold, and chargeful fashion,
Which doth amount to three odd ducats more
Than I stand debted to this gentleman:
I pray you, see him presently discharged,
For he is bound to sea, and stays but for it.
    Ant. E. I am not furnished with the present money;
Besides, I have some business in the town

Good signior, take the stranger to my house,
And with you take the chain, and bid my wife
Disburse the sum on the receipt thereof:
Perchance, I will be there as soon as you.
 Ang. Then you will bring the chain to her yourself?
 Ant. E. No; bear it with you, lest I come not time
  enough.
 Ang. Well, sir, I will. Have you the chain about you?
 Ant. E. An if I have not, sir, I hope you have,
Or else you may return without your money.
 Ang. Nay, come, I pray you, sir, give me the chain:
Both wind and tide stay for this gentleman,
And I, to blame, have held him here too long.
 Ant. E. Good Lord, you use this dalliance, to excuse
Your breach of promise to the Porpentine.
I should have chid you for not bringing it,
But, like a shrew, you first begin to brawl.
 Mer. The hour steals on; I pray you, sir, despatch.
 Ang. You hear how he importunes me: the chain—
 Ant. E. Why, give it to my wife, and fetch your money.
 Ang. Come, come; you know, I gave it you even now.
Either send the chain, or send by me some token.
 Ant. E. Fie! now you run this humour out of breath.
Come, where's the chain? I pray you, let me see it.
 Mer. My business cannot brook this dalliance.
Good sir, say, whether you'll answer me or no:
If not, I'll leave him to the officer.
 Ant. E. I answer you! what should I answer you?
 Ang. The money that you owe me for the chain.
 Ant. E. I owe you none till I receive the chain.
 Ang. You know I gave it you half an hour since.
 Ant. E. You gave me none: you wrong me much to
  say so.
 Ang. You wrong me more, sir, in denying it:
Consider how it stands upon my credit.
 Mer. Well, officer, arrest him at my suit.
 Off. I do,
And charge you in the duke's name to obey me.
 Ang. This touches me in reputation.—
Either consent to pay this sum for me,
Or I attach you by this officer.
 Ant. E. Consent to pay thee that I never had?
Arrest me, foolish fellow, if thou dar'st.
 Ang. Here is thy fee: arrest him, officer.—
I would not spare my brother in this case,
If he should scorn me so apparently.
 Off. I do arrest you, sir. You hear the suit.
 Ant. E. I do obey thee, till I give thee bail.—
But, sirrah, you shall buy this sport as dear
As all the metal in your shop will answer.

Ang.   Sir, sir, I shall have law in Ephesus
To your notorious shame, I doubt it not.

Enter DROMIO *of Syracuse*

Dro. S.   Master, there is a bark of Epidamnum
That stays but till her owner come aboard,
And then, sir, she bears away.   Our fraughtage, sir,
I have conveyed aboard, and I have bought
The oil, the balsamum, and qua-vitæ.
The ship is in her trim; the merry wind
Blows fair from land; they stay for nought at all,
But for their owner, master, and yourself.
Ant. E.   How now? a madman!   Why, thou peevish
      sheep,
What ship of Epidamnum stays for me?
Dro. S.   A ship you sent me to, to hire waftage.
Ant. E.   Thou drunken slave, I sent thee for a rope.
And told thee to what purpose and what end.
Dro. S.   You sent me for a rope's end as soon.
You sent me to the bay, sir, for a bark.
Ant. E.   I will debate this matter at more leisure,
And teach your ears to list me with more heed.
To Adriana, villain, hie thee straight;
Give her this key, and tell her, in the desk
That's covered o'er with Turkish tapestry,
There is a purse of ducats: let her send it.
Tell her, I am arrested in the street,
And that shall bail me.   Hie thee, slave, be gone.
On, officer, to prison till it come.
            [*Exeunt Merchant, Angelo, Officer, and Ant. E.*
Dro. S.   To Adriana? that is where we dined,
Where Dowsabel did claim me for her husband:
She is too big, I hope, for me to compass.
Thither I must, although against my will,
For servants must their masters' minds fulfil.   [*Exit*

SCENE II.—The Same

Enter ADRIANA *and* LUCIANA

Adr.   Ah, Luciana, did he tempt thee so?
Mightst thou perceive austerely in his eye
That he did plead in earnest? yea or no?
Looked he or red or pale? or sad or merrily?
What observation mad'st thou, in this case,
Of his heart's meteors tilting in his face?
Luc.   First he denied you had in him no right.
Adr.   He meant, he did me none: the more my spite.

Luc.   Then swore he, that he was a stranger here.

Adr.   And true he swore, though yet forsworn he were.

Luc.   Then pleaded I for you.

Adr.   And what said he?

Luc.   That love I begged for you, he begged of me.

Adr.   With what persuasion did he tempt thy love?

Luc.   With words that in an honest suit might move.
First, he did praise my beauty; then, my speech.

Adr.   Didst speak him fair?

Luc.   Have patience, I beseech.

Adr.   I cannot, nor I will not hold me still:
My tongue, though not my heart, shall have his will.
He is deforméd, crooked, old, and sere,
Ill-faced, worse bodied, shapeless everywhere;
Vicious, ungentle, foolish, blunt, unkind,
Stigmatical in making, worse in mind.

Luc.   Who would be jealous then of such a one?
No evil lost is wailed when it is gone.

Adr.   Ah, but I think him better than I say,
And yet would herein others' eyes were worse.
Far from her nest the lapwing cries away:
My heart prays for him, though my tongue do curse.

Enter DROMIO *of Syracuse*

Dro. S.   Here, go: the desk! the purse! sweet now,
         make haste.

Luc.   How hast thou lost thy breath?

Dro. S.   By running fast.

Adr.   Where is thy master, Dromio? is he well?

Dro. S.   No, he's in Tartar limbo, worse than hell:
A devil in an everlasting garment hath him,
One whose hard heart is buttoned up with steel;
A fiend, a fairy, pittiless and rough;
A wolf, nay, worse, a fellow all in a buff;
A back friend, a shoulder-clapper, one that countermands
The passages of alleys, creeks and narrow lands:
A hound that runs counter, and yet draws dry-foot well;
One that, before the judgment, carries poor souls to hell.

Adr.   Why, man, what is the matter?

Dro. S.   I do not know the matter: he is 'rested on the
         case.

Adr.   What, is he arrested? tell me at whose suit.

Dro. S.   I know not at whose suit he is arrested well;
But he's in a suit of buff which 'rested him, that can I tell.
Will you send him, mistress, redemption, the money in his
         desk?

Adr.   Go fetch it, sister.   [*Exit Luciana*]—This I
         wonder at,
That he, unknown to me, should be in debt:—

Tell me, was he arrested on a band?
   Dro. S.   Not on a band, but on a stronger thing;
A chain, a chain.   Do you not hear it ring?
   Adr.   What, the chain?
   Dro. S.   No, no, the bell.   'T is time that I were gone:
It was two ere I left him, and now the clock strikes one.
   Adr.   The hours come back! that did I never hear.
   Dro. S.   O yes; if any hour meet a sergeant, a' turns
     back for very fear.
   Adr.   As if Time were in debt! how fondly dost thou
     reason!
   Dro. S.   Time is a very bankrout, and owes more than
     he's worth, to season.
Nay, he's a thief too: have you not heard men say,
That Time comes stealing on by night and day?
If Time be in debt and theft, and a sergeant in the way,
Hath he not reason to turn back an hour in a day?

Re-enter LUCIANA

   Adr.   Go Dromio: there's the money, bear it straight,
And bring thy master home immediately.—
Come, sister; I am pressed down with conceit;
Conceit, my comfort and my injury.   *[Exeunt*

SCENE III.—The Same

Enter ANTIPHOLUS *of Syracuse*

   Ant. S.   There's not a man I meet but doth salute me
As if I were their well-acquainted friend;
And every one doth call me by my name.
Some tender money to me, some invite me;
Some other give me thanks for kindnesses;
Some offer me commodities to buy:
Even now a tailor called me in his shop
And showed me silks that he had bought for me,
And, therewithal, took measure of my body.
Sure, these are but imaginary wiles,
And Lapland sorcerers inhabit here.

Enter DROMIO *of Syracuse*

   Dro. S.   Master, here's the gold you sent me for.—What
have you quit the picture of old Adam new-apparelled?
   Ant. S.   What gold is this?   What Adam dost thou
     mean?
   Dro S.   Not that Adam that kept the Paradise, but that
Adam that keeps the prison: he that goes in the calf's
skin that was killed for the Prodigal: he that came behind
you, sir, like an evil angel, and bid you forsake your liberty.

Ant. S.   I understand thee not.

Dro. S.   No? why, 't is a plain case: he that went, like a bass-viol, in a case of leather; the man, sir, that, when gentlemen are tired, gives them a fob and 'rests them; he, sir, that takes pity on decayed men, and gives them suits of durance; he that sets up his rest to do more exploits with his mace than a morris-pike.

Ant. S.   What, thou mean'st an officer?

Dro. S.   Ay, sir, the sergeant of the band; he that brings any man to answer it that breaks his band; one that thinks a man always going to bed, and says, "God give you good rest!"

Ant. S.   Well, sir, there rest in your foolery.   Is there any ship puts forth to-night? may we be gone?

Dro. S.   Why, sir, I brought you word an hour since that the bark *Expedition* put forth to-night; and then were you hindered by the sergeant to tarry for the hoy *Delay.*   Here are the angels that you sent for to deliver you.

Ant. S.   The fellow is distract, and so am I,
And here we wander in illusions.
Some blesséd power deliver us from hence!

Enter a Courtesan

Cour.   Well met, well met, Master Antipholus.
I see, sir, you have found the goldsmith now:
Is that the chain you promised me to-day?

Ant. S.   Satan, avoid!   I charge thee, tempt me not!

Dro. S.   Master, is this Mistress Satan?

Ant. S.   It is the devil.

Dro. S.   Nay, she is worse, she is the devil's dam, and here she comes in the habit of a light wench: and thereof comes that the wenches say, 'God damn me,' that's as much as to say, 'God make me a light wench.'   It is written, they appear to men like angels of light: light is an effect of fire, and fire will burn; *ergo*, light wenches will burn.   Come not near her.

Cour.   Your man and you are marvellous merry, sir. Will you go with me? we'll mend our dinner here.

Dro. S.   Master, if you do, expect spoonmeat, or be-speak a long spoon.

Ant. S.   Why, Dromio?

Dro. S.   Marry, he must have a long spoon that must eat with the devil.

Ant. S.   Avoid, thou fiend! what tell'st thou me of
                supping?
Thou art, as you are all, a sorceress:
I conjure thee to leave me, and be gone.

Cour.   Give me the ring of mine you had at dinner,

Or for my diamond the chain you promised,
And I'll be gone, sir, and not trouble you.
   Dro. S. Some devils ask but the parings of one's nail,
A rush, a hair, a drop of blood, a pin,
A nut, a cherry-stone;
But she, more covetous, would have a chain.
Master, be wise: an if you give it her
The devil will shake her chain, and fright us with it.
   Cour. I pray you, sir, my ring, or else the chain.
I hope you do not mean to cheat me so.
   Ant. S. Avaunt, thou witch! Come, Dromio, let us go.
   Dro. S. 'Fly pride,' says the peacock: mistress, that
     you know.
                   [Exeunt Ant. S. and Dro. S.
   Cour. Now, out of doubt, Antipholus is mad,
Else would he never so demean himself.
A ring he hath of mine worth forty ducats,
And for the same he promised me a chain:
Both one and other he dénies me now.
The reason that I gather he is mad,
Besides this present instance of his rage,
Is a mad tale he told to-day at dinner
Of his own doors being shut against his entrance.
Belike, his wife, acquainted with his fits,
On purpose shut the doors against his way.
My way is now, to hie home to his house
And tell his wife that, being lunatic,
He rushed into my house, and took perforce
My ring away.   This course I fittest choose,
For forty ducats is too much to lose.   *[Exit*

SCENE IV.—The Same

Enter ANTIPHOLUS *of Ephesus and the Officer*

   Ant. E. Fear me not, man; I will not break away:
I'll give thee, ere I leave thee, so much money
To warrant thee as I am 'rested for.
My wife is in a wayward mood to-day,
And will not lightly trust the messenger.
That I should be attached in Ephesus,
I tell you, 't will sound harshly in her ears.

Enter DROMIO *of Ephesus with a rope's end*

Here comes my man: I think he brings the money.—
How now, sir? have you that I sent you for?
   Dro. E. Here's that, I warrant you, will pay them all.
   Ant. E. But where's the money?

Dro. E.   Why, sir, I gave the money for the rope.

Ant. E.   Five hundred ducats, villain, for a rope?

Dro. E.   I'll serve you, sir, five hundred at the rate.

Ant. E.   To what end did I bid thee hie thee home?

Dro. E.   To a rope's end, sir; and to that end am I returned.

Ant. E.   And to that end, sir, I will welcome you.

                                                     [*Beating him*

Off.   Good sir, be patient.

Dro. E.   Nay, 't is for me to be patient; I am in adversity.

Off.   Good now, hold thy tongue.

Dro. E.   Nay, rather persuade him to hold his hands.

Ant. E.   Thou whoreson, senseless villain!

Dro. E.   I would I were senseless, sir, that I might not feel your blows.

Ant. E.   Thou art sensible in nothing but blows, and so is an ass.

Dro. E.   I am an ass, indeed; you may prove it by my long ears. I have served him from the hour of my nativity to this instant, and have nothing at his hands for my service but blows. When I am cold, he heats me with beating; when I am warm, he cools me with beating; I am waked with it, when I sleep; raised with it, when I sit; driven out of doors with it, when I go from home; welcomed home with it, when I return; nay, I bear it on my shoulders, as a beggar wont her brat, and, I think, when he hath lamed me, I shall beg with it from door to door.

Ant. E.   Come, go along; my wife is coming yonder.

Enter ADRIANA, LUCIANA, *the Courtesan, and* PINCH

Dro. E.   Mistress, *respice finem*, respect your end; or rather the prophecy, like the parrot, 'Beware the rope's end.'

Ant. E.   Wilt thou still talk?   [*Beats him*

Cour.   How say you now? is not your husband mad?

Adr.   His incivility confirms no less.—

Good Doctor Pinch, you are a conjurer;

Establish him in his true sense again,

And I will please you what you will demand.

Luc.   Alas, how fiery and how sharp he looks!

Cour.   Mark, how he trembles in his ecstasy!

Pinch.   Give me your hand, and let me feel your pulse.

Ant. E.   There is my hand, and let it feel your ear.

Pinch.   I charge thee, Satan, housed within this man,

To yield possession to my holy prayers,

And to thy state of darkness hie thee straight:

I conjure thee by all the saints in heaven.

Ant. E.   Peace, doting wizard, peace!   I am not mad.

Adr.   O, that thou wert not, poor distresséd soul!

Ant. E.   You minion, you, are these your customers?
Did this companion with the saffron face
Revel and feast it at my house to-day,
Whilst upon me the guilty doors were shut,
And I denied to enter in my house?

Adr.   O husband, God doth know, you dined at home;
Where would you had remained until this time,
Free from these slanders and this open shame;

Ant. E.   Dinéd at home!   Thou, villain, what say'st thou?

Dro. E.   Sir, sooth to say you did not dine at home.

Ant. E.   Were not my doors lock up, and I shut out?

Dro. E.   Perdy, your doors were locked, and you shut out.

Ant. E.   And did not she herself revile me there?

Dro. E.   Sans fable, she herself reviled you there.

Ant. E.   Did not her kitchen-maid rail, taunt, and scorn me?

Dro. E.   Certes, she did; the kitchen-vestal scorned you.

Ant. E.   And did not I in rage depart from thence?

Dro. E.   In verity, you did.—My bones bear witness,
That since have felt the vigour of his rage.

Adr.   Is't good to soothe him in these contraries?

Pinch.   It is no shame: the fellow finds his vein,
And, yielding to him, humours well his frenzy.

Ant. E.   Thou hast suborned the goldsmith to arrest me.

Adr.   Alas, I sent you money to redeem you,
By Dromio here, who came in haste for it.

Dro. E.   Money by me? heart and good will you might,
But, surely, master, not a rag of money

Ant. E.   Went'st not thou to her for a purse of ducats?

Adr.   He came to me, and I delivered it.

Luc.   And I am witness with her that she did.

Dro. E.   God and the rope-maker bear me witness,
That I was sent for nothing but a rope!

Pinch.   Mistress, both man and master is possessed:
I know it by their pale and deadly looks.
They must be bound, and laid in some dark room.

Ant. E.   Say, wherefore didst thou lock me forth to-day?
And why dost thou deny the bag of gold?

Adr.   I did not, gentle husband, lock thee forth.

Dro. E.   And, gentle master, I received no gold;
But I confess, sir, that we were locked out.

Adr.   Dissembling villain! thou speak'st false in both.

Ant. E.   Dissembling harlot! thou art false in all,
And art confederate with a damnéd pack,
To make a loathsome abject scorn of me;
But with these nails I'll pluck out these false eyes,

That would behold in me this shameful sport.

   Adr. O, bind him, bind him! let him not come near me.

   Pinch. More company!—the fiend is strong within him.

   Luc. Ah me! poor man, how pale and wan he looks!

Enter three or four, and bind ANTIPHOLUS *of Ephesus*

   Ant. E. What, will you murder me? Thou gaoler, thou,

I am thy prisoner: wilt thou suffer them

To make a rescue?

   Off.   Masters, let him go:

He is my prisoner, and you shall not have him.

   Pinch. Go bind this man, for he is frantic too.

                                    [They offer to bind Dro. E.

   Adr. What wilt thou do, thou peevish officer?

Hast thou delight to see a wretched man

Do outrage and displeasure to himself?

   Off. He is my prisoner; if I let him go,

The debt he owes will be required of me.

   Adr. I will discharge thee, ere I go from thee.

Bear me forthwith unto his creditor,

And, knowing how the debt grows, I will pay it.

Good master doctor, see him safe conveyed

Home to my house.—O most unhappy day!

   Ant. E. O most unhappy strumpet!

   Dro. E. Master, I am here entered in bond for you.

   Ant. E. Out on thee, villain! wherefore dost thou mad me?

   Dro. E. Will you be bound for nothing? be mad, good master;

Cry, the devil!

   Luc. God help, poor souls! how idly do they talk!

   Adr. Go bear him hence.—Sister, go you with me.—

                 [Exeunt Pinch and Assistants with Ant. E.

                                and Dro. E.

Say now, whose suit is he arrested at?

   Off. One Angelo, a goldsmith; do you know him?

   Adr. I know the man. What is the sum he owes?

   Off. Two hundred ducats.

   Adr. Say, how grows it due?

   Off. Due for a chain your husband had of him.

   Adr. He did bespeak a chain for me, but had it not.

   Cour. When as your husband, all in rage, to-day

Came to my house, and took away my ring

(The ring I saw upon his finger now),

Straight after did I meet him with a chain.

   Adr. It may be so, but I did never see it.—

Come, gaoler, bring me where the goldsmith is:

I long to know the truth hereof at large.

Enter ANTIPHOLUS *of Syracuse, with his rapier drawn,
and* DROMIO *of Syracuse*

Luc. God, for thy mercy! they are loose again.
Adr. And come with naked swords. Let's call more
        help.
To have them bound again.
        Off.   Away, they'll kill us!
                [*Exeunt Adriana, Luciana, Courtesan,
                                    and Officer*

Ant. S. I see, these witches are afraid of swords.
Dro. S. She that would be your wife now ran from you.
Ant. S. Come to the Centaur; fetch our stuff from
           thence:
I long that we were safe and sound aboard.
Dro. S. Faith, stay here this night; they will surely
do us no harm; you saw they speak us fair, give us gold.
Methinks they are such a gentle nation that, but for the
mountain of mad flesh that claims marriage of me, I could
find in my heart to stay here still and turn witch.
Ant. S. I will not stay to-night for all the town;
Therefore away, to get our stuff aboard.   [*Exeunt*

ACT FIVE

SCENE I.—Before an Abbey

Enter Merchant and ANGELO

Ang. I am sorry, sir, that I have hindered you;
But, I protest, he had the chain of me,
Though most dishonestly he doth deny it.
Mer. How is the man esteemed here in the city?
Ang. Of very reverend reputation, sir,
Of credit infinite, highly beloved,
Second to none that lives here in the city:
His word might bear my wealth at any time.
Mer. Speak softly: yonder, as I think, he walks.

Enter ANTIPHOLUS *of Syracuse and* DROMIO *of
Syracuse*

Ang. 'T is so; and that self chain about his neck,
Which he forswore most monstrously to have.
Good sir, draw near to me, I'll speak to him.—
Signior Antipholus, I wonder much
That you would put me to this shame and trouble,
And, not, without some scandal to yourself,

With circumstance and oaths so to deny
This chain, which now you wear so openly:
Beside the charge, the shame, imprisonment,
You have done wrong to this my honest friend
Who, but for staying on our controversy,
Had hoisted sail and put to sea to-day.
This chain you had of me: can you deny it?
   Ant. S.   I think I had: I never did deny it.
   Mer.   Yes, that you did, sir, and forswore it too.
   Ant. S.   Who heard me to deny it, or forswear it?
   Mer.   These ears of mine thou know'st did hear thee.
Fie on thee, wretch, 't is pity that thou liv'st
To walk where any honest men resort.
   Ant. S.   Thou art a villain to impeach me thus.
I'll prove mine honour and mine honesty
Against thee presently, if thou dar'st stand.
   Mer.   I dare, and do defy thee for a villain. [*They draw*

Enter ADRIANA, LUCIANA, *Courtesan, and others*

   Adr.   Hold! hurt him not, for God's sake! he is mad.—
Some get within him, take his sword away.
Bind Dromio too, and bear them to my house.
   Dro. S.   Run, master, run; for God's sake take a house!
This is some priory;—in, or we're spoiled.
               [*Exeunt Ant. S. and Dro. S. to the Abbey*

Enter the Abbess

   Abb.   Be quiet, people. Wherefore throng you hither?
   Adr.   To fetch my poor distracted husband hence.
Let us come in, that we may bind him fast
And bear him home for his recovery.
   Ang.   I knew he was not in his perfect wits.
   Mer.   I am sorry now that I did draw on him.
   Abb.   How long hath this possession held the man?
   Adr.   This week he hath been heavy, sour, sad,
And much different from the man he was;
But, till this afternoon, his passion
Ne'er brake into extremity of rage.
   Abb.   Hath he not lost much wealth by wrack of sea?
Buried some dear friend? Hath not else his eye
Strayed his affection in unlawful love,
A sin prevailing much in youthful men
Who give their eyes the liberty of gazing.
Which of these sorrows is he subjected to?
   Adr.   To none of these, except it be the last;
Namely, some love that drew him oft from home.
   Abb.   You should for that have reprehended him.
   Adr.   Why, so I did.
   Abb.   Ay, but not rough enough.

Adr. As roughly as my modesty would let me.
Abb. Haply, in private.
Adr.   And in assemblies too.
Abb. Ay, but not enough.
Adr. It was the copy of our conference:
In bed, he slept not for my urging it;
At board, he fed not for my urging it;
Alone, it was the subject of my theme;
In company, I often glanced it:
Still did I tell him it was vile and bad.
Abb. And therefore came it that the man was mad.
The venom clamours of a jealous woman
Poison more deadly than a mad dog's tooth.
It seems, his sleeps were hindered by thy railing,—
And therefore comes it that his head is light.
Thou say'st, his meat was sauced with thy upbraidings,—
Unquiet meals make ill digestions,
Thereof the raging fire of fever bred,
And what's a fever but a fit of madness?
Thou say'st, his sports were hindered by thy brawls,—
Sweet recreation barred, what doth ensue
But moody and dull-eyed melancholy,
Kinsman to grim and comfortless despair,
And at their heels a huge infectious troop
Of pale distemperatures and foes to life?
In food, in sport, and life-preserving rest
To be disturbed, would mad or man or beast.
The consequence is then, thy jealous fits
Have scared thy husband from the use of wits.
Luc. She never reprehended him but mildly,
When he demeaned himself rough, rude, and wildly.—
Why bear you these rebukes and answer not?
Adr. She did betray me to my own reproof.—
Good people, enter, and lay hold on him.
Abb. No; not a creature enters in my house.
Adr. Then let your servants bring my husband forth.
Abb. Neither: he took this place for sanctuary,
And it shall privilege him from your hands
Till I have brought him to his wits again,
Or lose my labour in assaying it.
Adr. I will attend my husband, be his nurse,
Diet his sickness, for it is my office,
And will have no attorney but myself,
And therefore let me have him home with me.
Abb. Be patient, for I will not let him stir
Till I have used the approvéd means I have,
With wholesome syrups, drugs, and holy prayers,
To make of him a formal man again.
It is a branch and parcel of mine oath,
A charitable duty of my order;

Therefore depart, and leave him here with me.
    Adr.   I will not hence and leave my husband here;
And ill it doth beseem your holiness
To separate the husband and the wife.
    Abb.   Be quiet, and depart: thou shalt not have him.
                                     [*Exit*
    Luc.   Complain unto the duke of this indignity.
    Adr.   Come, go: I will fall prostrate at his feet,
And never rise until my tears and prayers
Have won his grace to come in person hither,
And take perforce my husband from the abbess.
    Mer.   By this, I think, the dial points at five:
Anon, I'm sure, the duke himself in person
Comes this way to the melancholy vale,
The place of death and sorry execution
Behind the ditches of the abbey here.
    Ang.   Upon what cause?
    Mer.   To see a reverend Syracusan merchant,
Who put unluckily into this bay
Against the laws and statutes of this town,
Beheaded publicly for his offence.
    Ang.   See, where they come; we will behold his death.
    Luc.   Kneel to the duke before he pass the abbey.

Enter DUKE, *attended;* ÆGEON *bareheaded; with the
        Headsman and other Officers*

    Duke.   Yet once again proclaim it publicly,
If any friend will pay the sum for him,
He shall not die, so much we tender him.
    Adr.   Justice, most sacred duke, against the abbess!
    Duke.   She is a virtuous and a reverend lady:
It cannot be that she hath done thee wrong.
    Adr.   May it please your grace, Antipholus, my husband,—
Whom I made lord of me and all I had,
At your important letters,—this ill day
A most outrageous fit of madness took him,
That desperately he hurried through the street—
With him his bondman all as mad as he—
Doing displeasure to the citizens
By rushing in their houses, bearing thence
Rings, jewels, anything his rage did like.
Once did I get him bound, and sent him home.
Whilst to take order for the wrongs I went
That here and there his fury had committed.
Anon, I wot not by what strong escape,
He broke from those that had the guard of him,
And with his mad attendant and himself,
Each one with ireful passion, with drawn swords,
Met us again. and, madly bent on us,

Chased us away; till, raising of more aid,
We came again to bind them.   Then they fled
Into this abbey, whither we pursued them;
And here the abbess shuts the gates on us,
And will not suffer us to fetch him out,
Nor send him forth that we may bear him hence.
Therefore, most gracious duke, with thy command,
Let him be brought forth and borne hence for help.
    Duke.   Long since thy husband served me in my wars,
And I to thee engaged a prince's word,
When thou didst make him master of thy bed
To do him all the grace and good I could.—
Go, some of you, knock at the abbey-gate,
And bid the lady abbess come to me.
I will determine this, before I stir.

Enter a Servant

    Serv.   O mistress, mistress! shift and save yourself.
My master and his man are both broke loose,
Beaten the maids a-row, and bound the doctor,
Whose beard they have singed off with brands of fire;
And ever as it blazed they threw on him
Great pails of puddled mire to quench the hair.
My master preaches patience to him, the while
His man with scissors nicks him like a fool;
And, sure, unless you send some present help,
Between them they will kill the conjurer.
    Adr.   Peace, fool! thy master and his man are here,
And that is false thou dost report to us.
    Serv.   Mistress, upon my life, I tell you true;
I have not breathed almost, since I did see it.
He cries for you, and vows, if he can take you,
To scorch your face and to disfigure you.   [*Cry within*
Hark, hark, I hear him, mistress: fly, be gone.
    Duke.   Come, stand by me, fear nothing.   Guard with
        halberds!
    Adr.   Ah me, it is my husband!   Witness you,
That he is borne about invisible:
Even now we housed him in the abbey here,
And now he's there, past thought of human reason.

Enter ANTIPHOLUS *of Ephesus and* DROMIO *of Ephesus*

    Ant. E.   Justice, most gracious duke!   O, grant me
        justice,
Even for the service that long since I did thee,
When I bestrid thee in the wars, and took
Deep scars to save thy life; even for the blood
That then I lost for thee, now grant me justice.

262

Æge.　Unless the fear of death doth make me dote,
I see my son Antipholus, and Dromio!
　　Ant. E.　Justice, sweet prince, against that woman
　　　　　there!
She whom thou gav'st to me to be my wife,
That hath abuséd and dishonoured me
Even in the strength and height of injury.
Beyond imagination is the wrong
That she this day hath shameless thrown on me.
　　Duke.　Discover how, and thou shalt find me just.
　　Ant. E.　This day, great duke, she shut the doors upon
　　　　　me,
While she with harlots feasted in my house.
　　Duke.　A grievous fault.　Say, woman, didst thou so?
　　Adr.　No, my good lord: myself, he, and my sister,
To-day did dine together.　So befall my soul
As this is false he burdens me withal.
　　Luc.　Ne'er may I look on day, nor sleep on night,
But she tells to your Highness simple truth.
　　Ang.　O perjured woman!　They are both forsworn:
In this the madman justly chargeth them.
　　Ant. E.　My liege, I am adviséd what I say,
Neither disturbed with the effect of wine,
Nor heady-rash provoked with raging ire,
Albeit my wrongs might make one wiser mad.
This woman locked me out this day from dinner:
That goldsmith there, were he not packed with her,
Could witness it, for he was with me then;
Who parted with me to go fetch a chain,
Promising to bring it to the Porpentine,
Where Balthazar and I did dine together.
Our dinner done, and he not coming thither,
I went to seek him: in the street I met him,
And in his company that gentleman.
There did this perjured goldsmith swear me down,
That I this day of him received the chain,
Which, God he knows, I saw not; for the which
He did arrest me with an officer.
I did obey, and sent my peasant home
For certain ducats; he with none returned.
Then fairly I bespoke the officer
To go in person with me to my house.
By the way we met
My wife, her sister, and a rabble more
Of vile confederates; along with them
They brought one Pinch, a hungry lean-faced villain,
A mere anatomy, a mountebank,
A threadbare juggler and a fortune-teller,
A needy, hollow-eyed, sharp-looking wretch,
A living dead man.　This pernicious slave

Forsooth, took on him as a conjurer,
And gazing in mine eyes, feeling my pulse,
And with no face, as't were, outfacing me,
Cries out, I was possessed.   Then, altogether
They fell upon me, bound me, bore me thence,
And in a dark and dankish vault at home
There left me and my man, both bound together,
Till, gnawing with my teeth my bonds in sunder,
I gained my freedom, and immediately
Ran hither to your grace, whom I beseech
To give me ample satisfaction
For these deep shames, and great indignities.
    Ang.   My lord, in truth, thus far I witness with him,
That he dined not at home, but was locked out.
    Duke.   But had he such a chain of thee, or no?
    Ang.   He had, my lord; and when he ran in here,
These people saw the chain about his neck.
    Mer.   Besides, I will be sworn, these ears of mine
Heard you confess you had the chain of him,
After you first forswore it on the mart,
And, thereupon, I drew my sword on you;
And then you fled into this abbey here,
From whence, I think, you're come by miracle.
    Ant. E.   I never came within these abbey-walls,
Nor ever didst thou draw thy sword on me.
I never saw the chain.   So help me Heaven,
As this is false you burden me withal.
    Duke.   Why, what an intricate impeach is this!
I think, you all have drunk of Circe's cup.
If here you housed him, here he would have been;
If he were mad, he would not plead so coldly;—
You say, he dined at home; the goldsmith here
Denies that saying.—Sirrah, what say you?
    Dro. E.   Sir, he dined with her there, at the Porpentine.
    Cour.   He did, and from my finger snatched that ring.
    Ant. E.   'T is true, my liege; this ring I had of her.
    Duke.   Saw'st thou him enter at the abbey here?
    Cour.   As sure, my liege, as I do see your grace.
    Duke.   Why, this is strange —Go call the abbess hither.—
I think you all are mated, or stark mad.

                        [Exit an Attendant
    Æge.   Most mighty duke, vouchsafe me speak a word.
Haply, I see a friend will save my life
And pay the sum that may deliver me.
    Duke.   Speak freely, Syracusan, what thou wilt.
    Æge.   Is not your name, sir, called Antipholus,
And is not that your bondman Dromio?
    Dro. E.   Within this hour I was his bondman, sir;
But he, I thank him, gnawed in two my cords:
Now am I Dromio, and his man unbound.

Æge. I am sure you both of you remember me,
Dro. E. Ourselves we do remember, sir, by you;
For lately we were bound, as you are now
You are not Pinch's patient, are you, sir?
Æge. Why look you strange on me? you know me well.
Ant. E. I never saw you in my life, till now.
Æge. O, grief hath changed me, since you saw me last;
And careful hours, with Time's deforméd hand,
Have written strange defeatures in my face:
But tell me yet, dost thou not know my voice?
Ant. E. Neither.
Æge. Dromio, nor thou?
Dro. E.   No, trust me, sir, nor I.
Æge. I am sure thou dost.
Dro. E. Ay, sir, but I am sure I do not; and whatsoever
a man denies, you are now bound to believe him.
Æge. Not know my voice! O, time's extremity,
Hast thou so cracked and splitted my poor tongue
In seven short years, that here my only son
Knows not my feeble key of untuned cares?
Though now this grainéd face of mine be hid
In sap-consuming winter's drizzled snow,
And all the conduits of my blood froze up,
Yet hath my night of life some memory,
My wasting lamps some fading glimmer left,
My dull deaf ears a little use to hear:
All these old witnesses—I cannot err—
Tell me thou art my son Antipholus.
Ant. E. I never saw my father in my life.
Æge. But seven years since, in Syracusa, boy,
Thou know'st we parted. But, perhaps, my son,
Thou sham'st to acknowledge me in misery.
Ant. E. The duke, and all that know me in the city,
Can witness with me that it is not so.
I ne'er saw Syracusa in my life.
Duke. I tell thee, Syracusan, twenty years
Have I been patron to Antipholus,
During which time he ne'er saw Syracusa.
I see, thy age and dangers make thee dote.

Enter Abbess, with ANTIPHOLUS *of Syracuse and* DROMIO
of Syracuse

Abb. Most mighty duke, behold a man much wronged.
                              [*All gather to see them*
Adr. I see two husbands, or mine eyes deceive me!
Duke. One of these men is Genius to the other;—
And so of these! Which is the natural man,
And which the spirit? who deciphers them?
Dro. S. I, sir, am Dromio: command him away.

Dro. E.   I, sir, am Dromio: pray, let me stay.
Ant. S.   Ægeon art thou not? or else his ghost?
Dro. S.   O, my old master!   Who hath bound him here?
Abb.   Whoever bound him, I will loose his bonds,
And gain a husband by his liberty—
Speak, old Ægeon, if thou be'st the man
That hadst a wife once called Æmilia,
That bore thee at a burden two fair sons.
O, if thou be'st the same Ægeon, speak,
And speak unto the same Æmilia!
Ege.   If I dream not, thou art Æmilia.
If thou art she,—tell me, where is that son
That floated with thee on the fatal raft?
Abb.   By men of Epidamnum, he, and I,
And the twin Dromio, all were taken up:
But, by-and-by, rude fishermen of Corinth
By force took Dromio and my son from them
And me they left with those of Epidamnum.
What then became of them, I cannot tell:
I to this fortune, that you see me in.
Duke.   Why, here begins his morning story right:
These two Antipholuses, these two so like,
And these two Dromios, one in semblance,—
Besides her urging of her wreck at sea;—
These are the parents to these children,
Which accidentally are met together.
Antipholus, thou cam'st from Corinth first?
Ant. S.   No, sir, not I: I came from Syracuse.
Duke.   Stay, stand apart: I know not which is which.
Ant. E.   I came from Corinth, my most gracious lord.
Dro. E.   And I with him.
Ant. E.   Brought to this town by that most famous
          warrior,
Duke Menaphon, your most renownéd uncle.
Adr.   Which of you two did dine with me to-day?
Ant. S.   I, gentle mistress.
Adr.   And are not you my husband?
Ant. E.   No; I say nay to that.
Ant. S.   And so do I; yet did she call me so;
And this fair gentlewoman, her sister here,
Did call me brother.—What I told you then,
I hope I shall have leisure to make good,
If this be not a dream I see and hear.
Ang.   That is the chain, sir, which you had of me.
Ant. S.   I think it be, sir: I deny it not.
Ant. E.   And you, sir, for this chain arrested me.
Ang.   I think I did, sir: I deny it not.
Adr.   I sent you money, sir, to be your bail,
By Dromio; but I think, he brought it not.
Dro. E.   No, none by me.

Ant. S.   This purse of ducats I received from you,
And Dromio, my man, did bring them me.
I see, we still did meet each other's man,
And I was ta'en for him and he for me,
And thereupon these Errors are arose.
   Ant. E.   These ducas pawn I for my father here.
   Duke.   It shall not need. Thy father hath his life.
   Cour.   Sir, I must have that diamond from you.
   Ant. E.   There, take it; and much thanks for my good
            cheer.
   Abb.   Renownéd duke, vouchsafe to take the pains
To go with us into the abbey here,
And hear at large discourséd all our fortunes;
And all that are assembled in this place,
That by this sympathizéd one day's Error
Have suffered wrong, go keep us company,
And we shall make full satisfaction.
Thirty-three years have I but gone in travail
Of you, my sons; and till this present hour
My heavy burden ne'er deliveréd.—
The duke, my husband, and my children both,
And you the calendars of their nativity,
Go to a gossips' feast and joy with me:
After so long grief such festivity!
   Duke.   With all my heart: I'll gossip at this feast.
                    [*Exeunt Duke, Abbess, Ægeon, Courtesan,
                         Merchant, Angelo, and Attendants*
   Dro. S.   Master, shall I fetch your stuff from shipboard?
   Ant. E.   Dromio, what stuff of mine hast thou
            embarked?
   Dro. S.   Your goods, that lay at host, sir, in the Centaur.
   Ant. E.   He speaks to me.—I am your master, Dromio:
Come, go with us; we'll look to that anon.
Embrace thy brother there; rejoice with him.
                    [*Exeunt Ant. S., Ant. E., Adr., and Luc.*
   Dro. S.   There is a fat friend at your master's house,
That kitchened me for you to-day at dinner:
She now shall be my sister, not my wife.
   Dro. E.   Methinks, you are my glass, and not my
            brother:
I see by you I am a sweet-faced youth.
Will you walk in to see their gossiping?
   Dro. S.   Not I, sir; you are my elder.
   Dro. E.   That's a question: how shall we try it?
   Dro. S.   We'll draw cuts for the senior: till then, lead
thou first.
   Dro. E.   Nay, then thus:
We came into the world like brother and brother;
And now let's go hand in hand, not one before another.
                                        [*Exeunt*

THE PEEBLES CLASSIC LIBRARY